Everybody
Who Was Anybody

Everybody Who Was Anybody

A Biography of Gertrude Stein

JANET HOBHOUSE

G. P. Putnam's Sons
New York

For Nicholas

FIRST AMERICAN EDITION 1975

SBN: 399-116-05-2

Library of Congress Catalog Card Number: 75-10844

Printed in England

Contents

Principal Works of Gertrude Stein

The author has used the following editions of Gertrude Stein's works:

Alphabets and Birthdays, Intro. by Donald Gallup, Yale University Press, New Haven, Conn., 1957.

As Fine As Melanctha, Foreword by Nathalie Barney, Yale University Press, New Haven, Conn., 1954.

Autobiography of Alice B. Toklas, The, in *Selected Writings of Gertrude Stein*, ed. by Carl Van Vechten, with Essay by F. W. Dupee, Vintage Books, Random House, New York, 1972.

Bee Time Vine and Other Pieces, Prefaced by Virgil Thomson, Yale University Press, New Haven, Conn., 1953.

Before the Flowers of Friendship Faded Friendship Faded, Plain Edition, Paris, 1931.

Brewsie and Willie, Random House, New York, 1946.

'Composition As Explanation' in *Selected Writings of Gertrude Stein*.

Everybody's Autobiography, William Heinemann, London, 1938

Fernhurst, Q.E.D., and Other Early Writings by Gertrude Stein, ed. with Intro. by Leon Katz, Peter Owen, London, 1972.

Four Im America, Intro. by Thornton Wilder, Yale University Press, New Haven, Conn., 1947.

'Four Saints in Three Acts' in *Selected Writings of Gertrude Stein*.

Geographical History of America Or the Relation of Human Nature to the Human Mind, The, Intro. by William Gass, Vintage Books, Random House, New York, 1973.

Geography and Plays, Four Seas Company, Boston, 1922.

How To Write, Plain Edition, Paris, 1931.

Ida A Novel, Random House, New York, 1941.

Last Operas and Plays, ed. with Intro. by Carl Van Vechten, Rinehart, New York, 1949.

Lectures in America, Random House, New York, 1935.

Look at Me Now and Here I Am: Writings and Lectures 1909–45, ed. by Patricia Meyerowitz with Intro. by Elizabeth Sprigge, Penguin Books, Harmondsworth, 1971. Includes 'Composition As Explanation', most of the American lectures, 'What Are Masterpieces and Why Are There So Few of Them', *Tender Buttons*, various Portraits, *Before the Flowers of Friendship Faded Friendship Faded*, the Money Pieces written for the *Saturday Evening Post*, and most of *Ida A Novel* and *Brewsie and Willie*.

Lucy Church Amiably, Something Else Press, New York, 1969.

Principal Works of Gertrude Stein

Making of Americans, The, Preface by Bernard Faÿ, Harcourt, Brace & World, 1962.

Matisse Picasso and Gertrude Stein with Two Shorter Stories, Plain Edition, Paris, 1933.

Mrs. Reynolds and Five Earlier Novelettes, Foreword by Lloyd Frankenberg, Yale University Press, New Haven, Conn., 1952.

Narration: Four Lectures by Gertrude Stein, Intro. by Thornton Wilder, University of Chicago Press, Chicago, 1935.

Novel of Thank You, A, Intro. by Carl Van Vechten, Yale University Press, New Haven, Conn., 1958.

Painted Lace and Other Pieces, Intro. by Daniel-Henry Kahnweiler, Yale University Press, New Haven, Conn., 1955.

Paris France, Batsford, London, 1940.

Picasso, Batsford, London, 1938.

Portrait of Mabel Dodge at the Villa Curonia, in *Selected Writings of Gertrude Stein*.

Portrait of Matisse in *Selected Writings of Gertrude Stein*.

Portrait of Picasso in *Selected Writings of Gertrude Stein*.

Portraits and Prayers, Random House, New York, 1934.

Q.E.D. see *Fernhurst, Q.E.D., and Other Early Writings*.

Selected Writings of Gertrude Stein, ed. by Carl Van Vechten, with Essay by F. W. Dupee, Vintage Books, Random House, New York, 1972. Includes *The Autobiography of Alice B. Toklas*, excerpts from *The Making of Americans*, Portraits of Cézanne, Matisse, Picasso, 'Melanctha', *Tender Buttons*, 'Composition As Explanation', *Portrait of Mabel Dodge at the Villa Curonia*, 'Susie Asado', 'Preciosilla', 'Ladies Voices', 'Miss Furr and Miss Skeene', 'Four Saints in Three Acts', 'The Winner Loses: A Picture of Occupied France', and an excerpt from *Wars I Have Seen*.

'Sitwell Edith Sitwell' in *What Are Masterpieces*, ed. with Foreword by Robert B. Haas, Pitman Publishing Corp., New York, 1970.

Stanzas in Meditation and Other Poems, Preface by Donald Sutherland, Yale University Press, New Haven, Conn., 1956.

Tender Buttons, in *Selected Writings of Gertrude Stein*.

Three Lives, Vintage Books, Random House, New York.

Two: Gertrude Stein and Her Brother and Other Early Portraits, Foreword by Janet Flanner, Yale University Press, New Haven, Conn., 1951.

Useful Knowledge, Bodley Head, London, 1929.

Wars I Have Seen, Batsford, London, 1945.

What Are Masterpieces, ed. and Foreword by Robert B. Haas, Pitman Publishing Corp., New York, 1970. Includes Gertrude's 1936 lecture 'What Are Masterpieces and Why Are There So Few of Them', various short pieces such as 'Sitwell Edith Sitwell', 'Susie Asado', 'Preciosilla', and the interview given to Robert B. Haas in January 1946.

'Winner Loses: A Picture of Occupied France, The', in *Selected Writings of Gertrude Stein*.

Illustrations

Illustrations

Ephraim Keyser (Collection of American Literature, The Beinecke Rare Book and Manuscript Library, Yale University)

Bernard Berenson (Collection of American Literature, The Beinecke Rare Book and Manuscript Library, Yale University)

Gertrude c. 1906 (Collection of American Literature, The Beinecke Rare Book and Manuscript Library, Yale University)

Ambroise Vollard by Picasso (Metropolitan Museum of Art, Elisha Whittelsey Collection, 1947)

The Chat Noir (Collection Robert Giraud, from *Montmartre Vivant*, J.P. Crespelle)

The Bateau Lavoir (Roger-Viollet)

Picasso in 1904 (Collection of René Jacques, from *Montmartre Vivant*, J.P. Crespelle)

Marie Laurencin (Collection of American Literature, The Beinecke Rare Book and Manuscript Library, Yale University)

Fernande Olivier (Collection of American Literature, The Beinecke Rare Book and Manuscript Library, Yale University)

Guillaume Apollinaire (George Sirot)

Fernande Olivier by Marie Laurencin (A.D.A.G.P. Paris)

Marie Laurencin by Fernande Olivier (*Picasso et ses Amis*, Fernande Olivier)

Dr Claribel Cone (Collection of American Literature, The Beinecke Rare Book and Manuscript Library, Yale University)

Leo Stein by Picasso (Baltimore Museum of Art, Cone Collection)

The Steins c. 1907 (Collection of American Literature, The Beinecke Rare Book and Manuscript Library, Yale University)

BETWEEN PAGES 52 AND 69

The Collector

Matisse, *La Femme au chapeau* (Mrs Walter Haas Collection, San Francisco)

Gertrude with her portrait by Picasso (The Bettmann Archive)

27 rue de Fleurus in 1906 and 1913 (Collection of American Literature, The Beinecke Rare Book and Manuscript Library, Yale University)

Cézanne, *Grandes Baigneuses* (Collection of American Literature, The Beinecke Rare Book and Manuscript Library, Yale University)

Picasso, *Study for Nude with Drapery* (owned by Mr and Mrs John Hay Whitney, photograph from Collection of American Literature, The Beinecke Rare Book and Manuscript Library, Yale University)

Picasso, *La Maison sur la colline, Horta de Ebro* (Collection of American Literature, The Beinecke Rare Book and Manuscript Library, Yale University)

Matisse, *The Blue Nude* (Baltimore Museum of Art, Cone Collection)

Picasso, *The Reservoir, Horta de Ebro* (owned by Mr and Mrs David Rockefeller, photograph from Collection of American Literature, The Beinecke Rare Book and Manuscript Library, Yale University)

Picasso, *The Architect's table* (owned by Mr and Mrs William S. Paley, photograph from Collection of American Literature, The Beinecke Rare Book and Manuscript Library, Yale University)

Picasso, *Daniel-Henry Kahnweiler* (Courtesy of the Art Institute of Chicago)

Picasso, *Portrait of Gertrude Stein* (Metropolitan Museum of Art, New York, Bequest of Gertrude Stein, 1946)

27 rue de Fleurus (The Bettmann Archive)

Douanier Rousseau, *La Muse inspirant le Poète* (Kunstmuseum, Basle)

27 rue de Fleurus (Collection of American Literature, The Beinecke Rare Book and Manuscript Library, Yale University)

Gris, *Still-life* (Collection of American Literature, The Beinecke Rare Book and Manuscript Library, Yale University)

Illustrations

ACKNOWLEDGMENTS

The author wishes to express her grateful thanks to the various companies, agencies and individuals who gave permission to quote from the following works:

Random House, the Estate of Gertrude Stein and Mr Calman A. Levin for Gertrude Stein: *The Autobiography of Alice B. Toklas, Everybody's Autobiography, Wars I Have Seen* and *Lectures in America.*

Liveright and Co. for Gertrude Stein: *Fernhurst, Q.E.D.,* and *Other Early Writings by Gertrude Stein.*

Crown Publishers Inc. for Leo Stein: *Journey Into the Self: Being the Letters, Papers and Journals of Leo Stein,* and *Appreciation: Painting, Poetry and Prose.*

Harcourt, Brace, and Curtis Brown for Mabel Dodge Luhan: *Intimate Memories* (Vols 2 and 3).

Alfred A. Knopf Inc. for Donald C. Gallup (ed.): *The Flowers of Friendship: Letters Written to Gertrude Stein* (copyright 1963 by Donald C. Gallup).

McIntosh and Otis Inc. for William Rogers: *When This You See Remember Me: Gertrude Stein in Person.*

The author also expresses her thanks to the Beinecke Rare Book and Manuscript Library, Yale University, for the illustrations they provided.

I

Being The Youngest

'THERE IS SOMETHING in this native land business', Gertrude Stein wrote in the last of her autobiographies. 'After all, anybody is as their land and air is. Anybody is as the sky is low or high. Anybody is as there is wind or no wind there. That is what makes a people, makes their kind of looks, their kind of thinking, their subtlety and their stupidity, and their eating and their drinking and their language.'

That she was born an American had a life-long significance for Gertrude Stein. To it she credited her sense of time and space and rhythm, her belief in the possibilities of change, her indifference to conventions of dress or manner, and her belief in her fundamental right to take what she had been given – in this case, the English language – use it as she liked, and leave it richer and more interesting than she found it.

As an American born in 1874, Gertrude Stein shared the heritage of the Civil War heroes, the frontiersmen, cowboys and indians, travelling salesmen, mammoth industrialists, quack inventors and soap-box democrats that characterised the not-yet one-hundred-year-old nation. In the years that Gertrude grew up, America was still an adventure and a dream, a place in which to believe that anything was possible. Yet for Gertrude, America was no mere frontier-land – it was also the most advanced country in the world. As she later wrote: '. . . America was the oldest country in the world and the reason why was that she was the first country to enter into the twentieth century. She had her birthday of the twentieth century when all other countries were still all either in the nineteenth century or still farther back in other centuries. . . . America began to live in the twentieth century in the eighties with the Ford car and all other series manufacturing.' Having been born into a dying nineteenth century, Gertrude Stein was destined to bring the future to Europe, where, as she wrote, she was to play a large role in killing the old century, 'killing it dead, quite like a gangster with a mitraillette'.

Although Gertrude Stein's inclination to legendise her past was always great – indeed she believed the truth of legend to be superior to that of mere fact – her claims that her roots were in pioneer America were real enough. In 1841 Meyer Stein was one of several thousands of young Germans immigrating to America with the hope of making their fortunes. Unlike most of these, however, within a few months of his arrival in Baltimore, Maryland, Meyer was enough convinced of his chances of success to bring over the rest of his family: his mother and father and their four other sons, among them the eight-year-old Daniel, future father of Gertrude Stein.

Twenty-one years later, in 1862, the second year of the Civil War, Daniel and his younger brother Solomon moved to Pittsburgh to set up the Stein Bros. clothing store, rival to the business of their extremely successful brother Meyer in Baltimore. Having moved into adjoining houses in Allegheny, a suburb of the coal-mining city of Pittsburgh, Daniel and Solomon began the intense quarrelling which was to characterise their partnership until its dissolution in 1875.

In 1864 Daniel married Amelia Keyser, the twenty-one-year-old daughter of German immigrants from his own native town of Baltimore. Quiet, often distant, Amelia Stein also had a quick temper which promoted the state of discord existing between the contentious and dogmatic Daniel and his younger, gentler brother. Early in 1875, after years of running battles with her sister-in-law Pauline, Amelia left Pennsylvania with her children to follow her husband to his new place of business in Vienna.

By 1874 the Stein family was complete. Their son Michael had been born in 1865, Simon, two years later, and Bertha, born in 1870. After the deaths at birth of two further children, there was room in the calculated five-child family for both Leo, born in May 1872 and Gertrude, born on 3 February 1874. The sheer chance of their existence was a fact which both bound and haunted Gertrude and Leo throughout their lives. It was a near miss 'we never talked about . . . once we had heard it . . . it made us feel funny'.

In Vienna, accompanied by Amelia's unmarried sister Rachel, the Stein family lived the comfortable, correct life of the prosperous middle-classes of the 1870s. There were servants, a Hungarian governess and a Czech tutor for the children, riding and dancing lessons, numerous treats and excursions, and frequent long and heavy meals, regulated occasionally by the dietary whims of Daniel Stein.

Of her early years in Vienna, Gertrude could remember walks in the laid-out public gardens of the city, which delighted her because 'in a kind of way a formal garden pleases a child's fancy more than a natural garden. It is more like a garden that you would make yourself'. There were outdoor concerts where she heard the Austrian national anthem, and where the old emperor Franz Joseph was once pointed out to her – 'a natural figure to have in a formal garden'. On her third birthday Gertrude remembered her first taste of beer, and her first contact with books – 'picture books, but books all the same since pictures in picture books are narrative'. Occasionally Amelia and Daniel Stein would leave the children in the care of Rachel and take trips to other parts of Europe: to Switzerland, where Daniel Stein - increasingly preoccupied by his health and digestion (an obsession that he seems to have passed on in later years to Leo) – took the cure; and to Italy where Amelia's younger brother Ephraim was then studying art with the financial support of his brother-in-law. When Daniel returned to America in pursuit of a continuously elusive business success, Ephraim was asked to replace Rachel as a companion to Amelia and the children. More often he was left alone to watch over the infant Gertrude. 'He was young then,' Gertrude wrote later, 'but I was so much younger that he did not like it.'

Rachel's letters to Daniel in America describe a fairly orthodox domestic existence. They solemnly recount the children's adventures and illnesses, and record their progress. One passage in particular has since been seized upon by biographers as prophetic of the manner of the future writer: 'Our little Gertie is a little Schnatterer. She talks all day long and so plainly. *She outdoes them all.* She's such a round little pudding, toddles around the whole day & repeats everything that is said or done.'

Gertrude Stein seems to have had a decidedly happy babyhood. As the youngest member of a reasonably well-to-do family she sensed her special position and used it to the full. '. . . You are privileged, nobody can do anything but take care of you, that is the way I was and that is the way I still am, and any one who is like that necessarily liked it. I did and I do.'

In those years before Gertrude was thrown out into the world to meet children of her own age, she was a figure in the family without peer. Everyone doted on her, coddled her, fondled her, entertained her, while she sat and simply was. It was an existence she not only revelled in but was to prolong into adult life. As she was the centre of attention during her first years so she managed to remain throughout her life, egocentric, self-fascinated, secure, passive and child-like in her relationships with her friends, her lover, her work. The extraordinary result of this, however, was to be both a literary achievement of enormous importance, and a place in legend as one of the great personalities of the modern age.

'One should always be the youngest member of the family,' she wrote later. 'It saves you a lot of bother, everybody takes care of you.' And so they did: first Leo, then Alice B. Toklas, then unfailingly devoted friends. During the Second World War, an enemy alien as well as a Jew in Nazi-occupied France, Gertrude held her ground, expecting from other people, and finding, the protection she had known all her life.

It was part of her enormous charm that she should expect life to be constantly, naturally pleasing. People did, naturally, love Gertrude Stein as people are meant naturally to love puppies and kittens and babies – and with a fervour which is not always easy to understand in the light of her often baby-like attacks of pique and bad temper, the tantrums in which she would dismiss guests at the rue de Fleurus salon with a regal 'we are not amused'. For her friends, as for Alice, who was 'Pussy' and later 'Mama Woojums', she remained 'Darling Baby', 'Lovey', 'Baby Woojums'. For her admirers, like Sylvia Beach, she was 'an infant prodigy'; for her detractors, such as Wyndham Lewis, 'a huge, lowering, dogmatic Child'.

Lewis's essay, 'The Prose-Song of Gertrude Stein', remains among the sharpest criticisms of her work. He names accurately, though with evident disgust and lifted skirts, certain of the fundamental characteristics of her method of writing: 'This child (often an idiot-child as it happens, but none the less sweet to itself for that) throws big, heavy

3

words up and catches them; or letting them slip through its fingers they break in pieces; and down it squats with a grunt, and begins sticking them together again.' Two things are important in his account of Gertrude's 'infantile' method of writing and thinking. One is that by the clumsy, slow, totally empirical manner of experimenting and learning, she did in the end come to know more than most writers what words were. Secondly, that she did *play* with words, as she played with ideas. For her whole life words entertained and fascinated her, they were her companions. Knowing how to play, she was one of the few outsiders ready to enter into the spirit of modernism which dominated Paris in the first fifteen or so years of this century. Play or an 'aggressive liveliness', as she called it, was the essential element in the artistic revolution in which she was to participate. Gertrude, together with Picasso, was the great child of the twentieth century.

Play was also the way by which she prolonged the wisdom and the curiosity of a child. As she wrote in her, mostly unread, masterpiece, *The Making of Americans*, certain people are gifted with this childishness: '. . . these always have it in them to be very lively so as to keep adolescence from giving sorrow to them, they are lively and they try all their living to keep up dancing so that adolescence will be scared away from them. . . .' Hers was not a false naïveté (as Wyndham Lewis claimed), for '. . . these have not in them sentimental feeling, they have aggressive liveliness in them.' Putting off the future – the adolescence – and keeping up the dance were also ways of remaining, as a child does, in consciousness of only the present. It is not difficult to see that it was the child nature in Gertrude Stein that led to the creation of what is perhaps her best-known literary form: the use of constant repetition and the present participle to prolong in words the sense of the existing moment: Gertrude Stein's famous 'continuous present'.

The importance of Gertrude's security and happiness in these early years cannot be overestimated in an account of the development of the later writer. During these first few years away from America in the total safety of her family, she begins to be what she became. By the age of four and a half she was in a certain, more than the obvious, sense, made.

When she was four and a half Gertrude and her family left Vienna. Impatient with Daniel's absences from home, tired of middle-class Austrian living, homesick, and bored with Vienna, in November 1878 Amelia Stein suddenly dismissed the servants, the governess, the tutor, and took herself and her children to join Daniel in Paris. In Passy, where the family took a house, Gertrude and Bertha were sent to a little boarding school, where they improved their French and began to make contact with children outside the family. But the pleasures of life in Paris were not to last. Once more left alone while Daniel pursued the shadows of business ventures, Amelia Stein tried in vain to occupy herself with riding lessons and shopping expeditions, until – as Gertrude described it – '. . . my mother had enough even in Paris of being away from America and all her family in Baltimore and my father going back to do business. . . .' In 1879, after one legendary shopping expedition in which the Steins '. . . bought everything that pleased their fancy, seal skin coats and caps and muffs for the whole family from the mother to the small sister Gertrude Stein, gloves dozens of gloves, wonderful hats, riding costumes, and

4

finally ending up with a microscope and a whole set of famous french history of zoology . . .', they sailed home for America by way of London.

On their arrival in New York, Daniel and Amelia Stein were once more persuaded to effect a reconciliation with Solomon Stein, now a successful banker in the city, and with his wife Pauline. This time, however, Amelia Stein proved stubborn and not long after their arrival in America the Stein family moved back to Baltimore, to the home of Amelia's parents, the Keysers. Here, in a big house inhabited 'by those cheerful pleasant little people', Gertrude Stein's aunts, Gertrude Stein began her American living.

In the story of her early life which Gertrude Stein later reconstructed, partly from self-prompted legend, partly from memory, her arrival in Baltimore had great significance. It was here that 'emotions began to feel themselves in English'. She had been born in America, and that was extremely important to her because it made her an American, but her formative years had been spent in Europe. 'Of course I had been born in America,' she wrote in *Wars I Have Seen*: '. . . of course we were all of us born in America but all the same when I was eight months old we were not there.' Her first and most crucial years were spent with the sounds of 'Austrians German and French French, and now American English'. The fact that her first words were spoken in foreign languages is recorded in her mother's letters and diaries of the period, documents which also reveal the difficulty with which Amelia – the daughter of recent immigrants from Germany – herself used English. Neither was Daniel's command of the language perfect. According to his son Leo, he was a man '. . . with no book learning whatever (I never knew him to read a book) and with [only] three winters of schooling in early boyhood.' For both Gertrude's parents English was a second language, and it is highly likely that not until she was able to read her first books in America and to live with other Americans can Gertrude have known the look and sound of 'proper English'. Although she later read English with a passion and cited an enormous list of childhood reading in the classics, her early essays at Harvard in the 1890s show that as late as age twenty-one (her critics would claim even later), Gertrude Stein was writing simple English sentences with great difficulty, failing in her command of basic grammatical constructions and simple spelling. On this and on the later stylistic practices of the accomplished writer – if only in terms of the fascination with simple words which that writing conveys – Gertrude's early years without English must have had some bearing.

Life with the Keyser grandparents in Baltimore was a great pleasure for all the Stein family – with the exception of Daniel. Becoming increasingly restless with his unsuccessful attempts to find satisfying work, he soon left the family once again – this time heading West to the thirty-year-old state of California, where after trying life in Los Angeles and San José, he eventually settled in Oakland, taking up work in one of the new street railway companies. In 1880 he returned to Baltimore, bid good-bye to his in-laws, and took his family with him on the long trip by railway from Maryland to California. Of this early adventure across the American continent, the six-year-old Gertrude retained few memories: 'I naturally did remember, not all, but at least really some landscape as well as eating and moving. I do not remember that we saw Indians

E.A.—2

but I was told afterwards that we had. . . .' She was also told later that when her sister's feathered hat flew out of the window, her father had, with autocratic cool, pulled the emergency cord, jolting the train to a halt while he stepped out to retrieve it.

After their arrival in East Oakland, the Steins spent the first year at the comfortable Tubb's Hotel. Then, following another brief move, they rented for $50 a month a small farm of ten acres, the 'Old Stratton House' on the outskirts of the city. Here in this rambling house with its fenced-in orchard, the family bought a cow and a piano, and Gertrude's 'half-city half-country living' began.

The Stratton House was located in a part of Oakland where there were poorer families of various nationalities and religions, some of them happily bohemian like their neighbours the Duncans, whose children, Isadora and Raymond, when they later met the Steins in Paris, confessed to having frequently stolen apples from the Stratton House orchard. California was a haven for such people, with its warm and healthy climate, its low cost of living, its indifference to Eastern city conventions, and its democratic heritage. Here, where as she later wrote, 'no one was conscious of a grandfather and not held responsible for a father', Gertrude enjoyed the socially mixed and cosmopolitan companionship of the neighbourhood, and of the school (the public Swett School) attended by children of German, French, Spanish, Chinese, and Japanese parents.

Occasionally, Gertrude would be embarrassed to bring her friends back to a house with 'servants seamstresses governesses', but the social difference that existed between herself and her schoolmates did not yet make itself felt. Later, adolescence would divide her from her contemporaries as they began to earn their living. But her greatest friend, and in a few years' time almost her exclusive friend, was her brother Leo. Together, they roamed at will in the surrounding countryside of California, bathing in the swimming hole near a mine where the 'coolies' worked, walking miles in pursuit of birds and rabbits on hunting expeditions, helping the neighbourhood farmers at harvest-time. All these sweet and sensual memories of her early life in California Gertrude later described in her novel *The Making of Americans*:

> There was, just around the house, a pleasant garden, in front were green lawns not very carefully attended and with large trees in the center whose roots always sucked up for themselves almost all the moisture, water in this dry western country could not be used just to keep things green and pretty and so, often, the grass was very dry in summer, but it was very pleasant then lying there watching the birds, black in the bright sunlight and sailing, and the firm white summer clouds breaking away from the horizon and slowly moving. It was very wonderful there in the summer with the dry heat, and the sun burning, and the hot earth for sleeping; and then in the winter with the rain, and the north wind blowing that would bend the trees and often break them, and the owls in the wall scaring you with their tumbling. . . .

> In the summer it was good for generous sweating to help the men to make the hay into bales for its preserving and it was well for ones growing to eat radishes pulled with

the black earth sticking to them and to chew the mustard and find roots with all kinds of funny flavors in them, and to fill one's hat with fruit and sit on the dry ploughed ground and eat and think and sleep and read and dream and never hear them when they would all be calling; and then when the quail came it was fun to go shooting, and then when the wind and the rain and the ground were ready to help seeds in their growing, it was good fun to help plant them, and the wind would be so strong it would blow the leaves and branches of the trees down around them and you could shout and work and get wet and be all soaking and run out full into the strong wind and let it dry you, in between the gusts of rain that left you soaking. It was fun all the things that happened all the year there then.

The languorous, passive enjoyment of life which Gertrude felt at this time was to characterise the way she took her pleasure throughout her life, but her intense enjoyments were not limited to life outdoors. It was at home, in her early years, that she discovered passions she was to have for the rest of her life: '. . . Most of all there were books and food, food and books, both excellent things.' Food she enjoyed during these years and in adolescence in private 'orgies of eating'. But books could be both private and shared. Sharing, for Gertrude, always meant sharing with Leo, closest to her of her family, in both age and cleverness, and, like her, unable to form strong attachments with his contemporaries. Together, and at an early age, they began to read everything they could find – Mark Twain, Jules Verne, nineteenth-century English novels, science handbooks, encyclopaedias and, above all, history plays, historical novels, and everything of Shakespeare. There is a story that she and Leo set out to write an Elizabethan play under the influence of this early enthusiasm. According to Gertrude, she was eight years old at the time, though Leo claims she was fourteen. Leo wrote a masterly pastiche of Marlowe, and Gertrude of a Shakespeare history play, getting as far as the list of characters, and the stage directions: 'the courtiers make witty remarks'. However, as she was unable 'to think of any witty remarks', the writing was abandoned.

In school, Gertrude was a clever and precocious student, though she remained sublimely uninterested in the acquisition of certain skills. Her handwriting, for example, was, and remained, atrocious. When one of her compositions was chosen for special mention and public display, it was another student who had finally to copy it out. Even twenty-five years before her association with Alice B. Toklas, Gertrude was willing to distinguish between the roles of creator and handmaiden. In drawing, too, Gertrude was delinquent. Once in a school drawing competition, Gertrude, with an early but characteristic indifference to working according to other people's rules, and having failed several times in her attempt to draw a simple still-life, got one of her older brothers to do it for her. As a result she won the leather trophy that was meant to pass from week to week to each winner. With her remarkable casualness she seems to have lost it on her way home from school, thus bringing the competition forever to an end.

Gertrude's increasing indifference to her childhood contemporaries was to a large extent fostered by her closeness to Leo. Accepting the comradeship of her brother was easier and more pleasant for Gertrude than making and retaining friends of her own. Clever and resourceful, it was Leo who provided amusements and adventures; and always preferring a passive to an active role in life, Gertrude accepted Leo's leadership without question. As she later wrote in *Everybody's Autobiography*: 'It is better if you are the youngest girl in a family to have a brother two years older, because that makes everything a pleasure to you, you go everywhere and do everything while he does it all for you and with you which is a pleasant way to have everything happen to you. . . .'

But the bond was also something that Leo encouraged and needed. Two years older than Gertrude, Leo suffered from what he later called his 'pariah complex', a feeling of unlovableness he attributed to his being the only Jewish boy at school. (For Gertrude, on the other hand, being Jewish never made any difference.) Although his attendance at synagogue was irregular and tended to depend – as a lot of things did – on the whims of his father, Leo claimed to have suffered because of it from an acute shyness with his contemporaries, multi-national and multi-racial though they were. Inside the family, relationships were little better. For both Gertrude and Leo the society of their other brothers and sister was unwelcome. Michael, whom they did both admire, was far too old to be a companion for the youngest Steins. Simon, fat and slow-witted, they regarded as simply 'funny' and their sister Bertha simply annoying. As Gertrude later wrote, 'My sister four years older simply existed for me because I had to sleep in the same room with her.' Besides, 'It is natural not to care about a sister, certainly not when she is four years older and grinds her teeth at night.'

Leo and Gertrude were superior creatures who ignored as best they could the existence of other members of their family, and the pressures of what discipline there was. Outside their home too, they apparently chose what was and what was not worth their participation. So they failed weekly in the 'Lend a Hand Society' at school, not once being able to report that they had ever 'lent a hand' to anyone. The bond that grew between Leo and Gertrude set them apart from both their family and their contemporaries, but it was also, as later friends saw, to affect their relationships with the outside world for the rest of their lives.

Discipline inside the Stein family was haphazard in the extreme, and there is little doubt that as a child Gertrude was allowed the run of the house. 'I was a very happy child,' she wrote in *Wars I Have Seen*, '. . . and continuing being the youngest in the family continued being very well taken care of by everybody, also as being the youngest I had cajoling ways, one has when one continues to be the youngest.' Left in the charge of their mother while their father was busy at work in his now prospering and increasingly demanding job as Vice-President of the Omnibus Cable Company, the Stein children soon discovered that although she could have 'a fierce little temper', Amelia Stein was an indulgent mother. She is described in the part of *The Making of Americans* that deals with Gertrude's family, as small and gentle, 'very loving in her feeling to all of her children, but they had been always . . . after they stopped being very little children, too big for her ever to control them. She could not lead them nor could she know what they needed inside them. She could not help them, she could only be hurt not angry when any bad thing happened to them.' More brutally, Gertrude wrote, 'The little mother was not very important to them. They were good enough children in their daily living but they were never very loving to her inside them. They had it too strongly in them to win their own freedom.' If the children liked her, it was because she was elegantly dressed, wore rich furs, 'and pleasant stuffs for children to rub against', was romantic and indulgent. But she never commanded their respect.

In 1885 Amelia Stein began to make regular visits to the doctor, and when she became so weak that the family had to move to a smaller house in Oakland which would be easier for her to manage, the children knew that she was ailing. Then, wrote Gertrude, '. . . the little stubborn temper in her broke into weakness and helplessness inside her and they had in a way to be good to her'. Three years later, when Gertrude was fourteen, Amelia Stein finally died of cancer. Few of the children were shaken by her death. As Gertrude wrote later in *Everybody's Autobiography*, '. . . we had all already had the habit of doing without her.'

If the loss of their mother made no real difference to the inner lives of her children, it did result in one important change. Daniel Stein assumed the governing of the household, and his children, who had never really liked him because of his domineering ways and his habit of laying down arbitrary and conflicting rules on the subject of diet or education (at one time they were to speak nothing but French or German in the house, soon afterwards, only English), began to find him 'more of a bother than he had been'. 'Naturally,' wrote Gertrude, 'my father was never satisfied with anything. . . . Naturally our father was often irritated.' Leo remembers him as 'a stocky, positive, dominant, aggressive [and illiterate] person'. Such a man was hardly likely to appeal to two such intellectual and head-strong children as Gertrude and Leo, and clashes between them became frequent. Early on in the motherless household Gertrude was given a role in the housekeeping, a job she performed with such lack of skill and such ill grace that her father was forced to resort to the help of the equally unwilling but less stubborn Bertha. Sometimes Gertrude's father would encourage her to visit and be like the feminine and domesticated daughters of families in the neighbourhood. At other times he would forbid her to keep company with such children, finding the association demeaning for one of his daughter's social standing.

When, in his rare and excessive moods of good nature, he would take his children into the city, they were often embarrassed by his company. He behaved oddly with strangers. Gertrude remembered that he would frequently offer the children fruit he had picked from the grocer's stall, insisting that they enjoy what neither they nor the fruitseller was certain he would pay for. At other times, there were injustices committed which neither Leo nor Gertrude could forgive. Some sixty years after the event, Leo could still recall one such incident: 'My father was as insistent as he was positive, and at home he was often making rules which were never observed after the first few days. One of these rules, when we were still in Vienna, was that the children should eat everything that was put before them. It was an unfortunate fact that boiled turnips and carrots nauseated me, and generally I didn't eat them, but one Sunday we had visitors for dinner, and so my

9

father was showing off his discipline and made me eat them anyway, and I was sick all the rest of the day.'

During these years, their father's society was one which both Gertrude and Leo preferred to avoid. In Gertrude's case, this dislike of her father became a life-long aversion to all authorities and father-figures. 'Fathers are depressing,' she later wrote, 'mothers may not be cheering but they are not as depressing as fathers.' It was a feeling which was later to form the core of her political opinions in the 1930s, a time of dictatorships in which 'there [was] too much fathering going on'.

The death of Gertrude's mother and the reign of Daniel Stein over the household coincided with a period in Gertrude's life which she was later to call 'the agony of adolescence'. In *Wars I Have Seen*, the autobiography which she wrote in 1943–4, Gertrude described the different stages of growing up in terms of world history. Childhood to her was like the nineteenth century. There was order and progress and the security of evolution. Adolescence, however, was 'mediæval': 'Mediæval means that life and place and the crops you plant and your wife and children, all are uncertain. They can be driven away or taken away, or burned away, or left behind. . . . Fifteen is really mediæval and pioneer and nothing is clear and nothing is sure, and nothing is safe and nothing is come and nothing is gone. But it all might be.'

Above all, there was the realisation of death, or 'not so much of death as of dissolution'. As she wrote in *Everybody's Autobiography*: 'It was frightening when the first comet I saw made it real that the stars were worlds and the earth only one of them, it is like the Old Testament, there is a God but there is no eternity.' The realisation of death was a profound jolt to her sense of herself. So was the beginning awareness of sex and of the value the outside world places on beauty; both made her suddenly self-conscious. 'Funny things happen, you milk a goat for the first time, you see a girl taller than yourself for the first time and you are not sure whether she is beautiful or not, you spend all day intending to go somewhere and nothing happens and you wonder if you will ever be revenged.' Adolescence was not only an intimidating period of life, it also consisted of long stretches of nothingness, emptiness and waiting: 'Fifteen the times does not pass slowly but a great deal of time there is nothing to do except stand around, in games and in the evening and in the day, stand around, not even get up and sit down but just stand around.'

Even the pleasure of reading, was coloured by the emotions of adolescence, for 'nothing is so intense as being alone with a book'. Yet the medieval insecurities of 'the dark and dreadful days of adolescence' intruded even here. In *The Autobiography of Alice B. Toklas*, Alice is made to say of Gertrude: 'She once told me that when she was young she had read so much; read from the Elizabethans to the moderns, that she was terribly uneasy lest some day she would be without anything to read.' These were worries that she could not divulge to an intolerant father, nor to her old brothers and sisters. Nor had she any close friends other than Leo. But, as Leo recalled later in his memoir *Journey Into the Self*, '. . . Gertrude and I despite constant companionship throughout our childhood and early youth, in which we talked endlessly about books and people and things, never said a word to each other about our inner life.' Adolescence was an 'agony' that Gertrude had to suffer alone.

In 1891, however, there occurred an event in Gertrude's life which was to alleviate much of the misery of her adolescent years. It is described in two sentences of characteristic unsentimentality when she recalled it in *Everybody's Autobiography*: 'Then one morning we could not wake up our father. Leo climbed in by the window and called out to us that he was dead in his bed and he was.' 'Then,' she adds, 'our life without a father began a very pleasant one.'

It soon fell to the eldest of them, Michael Stein, now twenty-six, to take care of the family. As an assistant superintendent of his father's cable car company, Michael worked across the bay from Oakland, in San Francisco; and it was here, on Turk Street, that he now set up house with his new charges: Simon, aged twenty-three, Bertha, twenty, Leo, nineteen, and Gertrude, aged seventeen. It soon fell to him, too, to clear the unexpected and, for Gertrude, 'frightening debts which his father had amassed during his last few years in business.'. . . Then I found out that profit and loss is always loss . . . but Mike expalined that this always happened in a business and it was discouraging because we always had a habit in the family never to owe anybody any monek.' But for Michael, although, as Gertrude said, business 'made him nervous', the discouragement soon proved a challenge, and he set about to clear the debts and win for his family some freedom from the pressures of earning a living. As Gertrude wrote, '. . . Mike's own statement was that he knew if it was not done he had us all on his hands because none of us could earn anything not even Simon enough to live on and something had to be done. . . .'

With extraordinary application, Michael soon rose within his business, selling their father's fairly worthless holdings at a profit to the head of the Central Pacific Railway, and soon becoming a branch manager of that company. He also found a job for Simon as a cable car gripman (though, as Gertrude wrote, 'most of the time only on Sunday or when they were too busy'). But though the job was offered to Simon largely out of charity, it was one which '. . . really suited him, he liked everyone, that is almost everyone, and he liked giving the children candy and the men cigars. . . .' Simon was the only member of the family to remain in San Francisco, a gripman all his life, until 'finally he was too heavy to stand so long and then he stopped'. He died in San Francisco, 'still fat and fishing', according to Gertrude.

Life with Michael soon proved to be delightful for the younger Steins. Gertrude and Lel had always liked and admired him. Some years earlier, when Michael had been a student at Johns Hopkins University in Baltimore, they had come across a love poem he had written. Given though they were to general sniggering at this time, it was something which touched and impressed them both: '. . . It was then that Mike wrote the poem that Leo and I found and it said that he always had looked at a plot of grass and it had been a plot of grass to him and then he met the one he loved and then when he looked at the plot of grass there were birds and butterflies on the plot of grass and before that there never had been. That was what love was.'

Besides that, 'He used to make nice little jokes too that pleased us and Leo and I always liked giving him a book to read, he never read any book except one that we gave him and that he always read from the beginning to the ending. He always had those pleasant little ways he still has them.' Although never an intellectual like Gertrude and Leo, Michael respected their views and tried to show a polite interest in their enthusiasms. Once when Gertrude and Leo returned from an important exhibition with a photograph of Millet's *Man with a Hoe*, he was eager to agree. 'It is a hell of a hoe,' he told them.

But there was also the matter of discipline. Leo and Gertrude would often overspend their small allowances of those days, chiefly by buying books. Then they would have to call on Michael at his office and explain. 'Mike would always sigh,' wrote Gertrude, 'but he liked to have us with him and so he would take us out to dinner but before that we would sit and watch him disciplining.' Gertrude's remarks about her elder brother are not without a characteristic condescension, but they also always show a deep affection and a gratitude for the way he saved the family after the death of Daniel Stein. When in 1892 the family split up, Leo moving from the University of California to attend Harvard, and Bertha and Gertrude going to stay with their mother's married sister Fanny Bachrach in Baltimore, Gertrude was fully aware of what Michael was doing for them. 'When we left San Francisco for Baltimore,' she wrote in *Everybody's Autobiography*, 'we left Mike all alone Simon did not count and Mike was alone, later he married but at that time he was alone and he had to save everything for all of us and he did it but he never knew quite how he did it.'

2

Knowledge Is
What You Know

WHEN, AT THE AGE OF EIGHTEEN, Gertrude moved once more to her mother's family in Baltimore, she exchanged '. . . the rather desperate inner life that she had been living for the last few years to the cheerful life of all her aunts and uncles'. Baltimore itself she found delightfully romantic. 'Baltimore, sunny Baltimore,' she was to write in a college essay, 'where no one is in a hurry and the voices of the negroes singing as their carts go lazily by, lull you into drowsy reveries.' But the company of her sister Bertha, who 'naturally did not like anything' began to irritate her. It was a poor substitute for the companionship of Leo, now at the University of Harvard in Cambridge, Massachusetts. In the early winter of 1893, Gertrude visited him there, listened to his enthusiastic accounts of his philosophy studies and soon had made up her mind to join him in his new pursuit. By that autumn she had enrolled as a student of philosophy at the Harvard Annex, the ladies' branch of the University, which in 1894 would be renamed Radcliffe.

Harvard in the 1890s was a lively centre of American intellectual life. Among the teachers of philosophy at the time Gertrude began her studies were Josiah Royce, George Santayana, and William James, Professor of the new branch of philosophy known as psychology, and whose great book *Principles of Psychology* had recently been published, establishing him as the most important American philosopher of his day. There was also Hugo Münsterberg, lately arrived from Berlin, whose course on experimental psychology dealt with the most recent findings of its authorities in Germany.

A spirit of experiment and adventure characterised the atmosphere of the university in these years, a sense that the nineteenth-century boundaries of thought were about to be pushed forward by the discoveries of the twentieth. New ideas were welcomed and new contributors to those ideas, among them the recently admitted female students to the university, who had joined in 1879, and who were now, though in certain areas of study grudgingly, in general, magnanimously offered equality of opportunity with the academic elite of the nation.

The sudden intellectual freedom which Gertrude was to encounter at Harvard was

13

not, for her, matched in spirit by the New England surroundings. A 'Westerner' from what she thought of as the wide-open, democratic state of California, whose family and most recent living had been in the 'dreamy' South, Gertrude Stein found little warmth in the stiff and puritanical world of Massachusetts. Instead of the bohemian and ragged playmates of her California youth, the 'laughing Negroes' of 'sunny' Baltimore, she began to encounter the tight-lipped coolness of the New Englander. In the boarding-house where she lived during her first year as a student, Gertrude was impressed both by the meanness of comfort and the ironic wit to which it gave voice: 'The landlord at the boarding-house was funny,' she wrote, 'he sat at the end of the table and did not like low lights, he said if they had another light like that he would be in total darkness. . . . Everybody was New England there.'

Whatever warmth was lacking among the townspeople of Cambridge and Boston was more than matched by the zeal of the Harvard undergraduates and teachers, among them William James, whom Gertrude quickly idolised. In an early composition for her English course, Gertrude was to write with mannered though unguarded enthusiasm: 'Is life worth living? Yes, a thousand times yes when the world still holds such spirits as Prof. James.'

Already at the age of seventeen, Gertrude Stein had 'decided that all knowledge was not my province', and backed by the example of her brother Leo, also a devoted pupil of William James, Gertrude joined the classes of the great teacher. Since she was not interested in taking a degree at Harvard (with only one year of high school in Oakland, and no Latin, she had not fulfilled all the entrance requirements) she was allowed to sit in on courses intended for older students. In these she soon proved an exceptional participant, and two anecdotes of the period indicate the regard with which she was held by her teacher. One concerns a report by a student on the workings of the subconsciou: and its automatic responses. When giving the results of his experiment the student explained that one subject had shown positively no response, thereby considerably lowering the average result and upsetting the desired conclusion. Since this case was unique in his tests, he requested permission to ignore it in his report. 'Whose record is it? said James. Miss Stein's said the student. Ah, said James, if Miss Stein gave no response I should say it was as normal not to give a response as to give one and decidedly the result must not be cut out.' The other, more famous, anecdote describes an examination which Gertrude did not wish to take – it being 'a lovely spring day'. Therefore, according to *The Autobiography of Alice B. Toklas*, she wrote on the top of the paper: 'I am so sorry but really I do not feel a bit like an examination to-day. . . .' Then she left the room. The following day, according to the story, she received a post-card from William James: 'Dear Miss Stein, I understand perfectly how you feel I often feel like that myself.' Furthermore, he 'gave her work the highest mark in his course'.

The likely truth of such anecdotes has been less a matter of dispute for Gertrude Stein's critics than the question of James's own influence on the later development of the writer. There is no doubt that the character and integrity of the man made a deep impression on her, as they seem to have made on most of his students. As late as 1946,

14

the year of her death, she was able to pay tribute to his teaching, in a conversation with Robert Haas on the subject of her life's work:

> I like a thing simple but it must be simple through complication. Everything must come into your scheme, otherwise you cannot achieve real simplicity. A great deal of this I owe to a great teacher William James. He said, 'Never reject anything. Nothing has been proved. If you reject anything, that is the beginning of the end as an intellectual.' He was my big influence when I was at college. He was a man who always said 'complicate your life as much as you please, it has got to simplify'.

James's insistence that no possible truth or method be discounted, his willingness to accept what was not readily understandable (James was also a founding member of the Society for Psychical Research), were attitudes Gertrude was to adopt not only with regard to her own experimental writing but – like Leo, and under his guidance – in her approach to the artistic experiments that she would come upon in Paris in the first years of the twentieth century. But unlike Leo, her accessibility to the new was to last throughout her lifetime. 'If not why not' became a catchphrase which described the element of Jamesian curiosity and agnosticism in her work.

James's description of how the human mind works (including what was discovered during the much-disputed experiments with automatic writing), his concept of, in his phrase, the 'stream of consciousness', and his discussion of the psychological apprehension of time and the present moment, were all accepted principles that lay at the base of much of Gertrude's writing. But her great stylistic inventions, which conveyed and imitated these processes, her use of repetition, circling, and re-tracing in the 'continuous present', were attributable to his influence only in so far as he inspired her with the courage to make of these discoveries a literary application.

Gertrude's studies in psychology and philosophy at Harvard are of great significance for her later writing in terms of what she learned of methods of observation and analysis. But there was also a subject of apparently more direct relevance to her later career – English composition, a course taught at the time by the young and talented poet, William Vaughn Moody. Under his direction, Gertrude struggled weekly to give her prose compositions a sturdiness which they had always lacked. Moody was a gentle and patient teacher, but his remarks on her compositions indicate that Gertrude was showing early a worrying indifference to conventional forms of written expression. 'I wish', Moody writes prophetically at one point, 'you might overcome your disdain for the more necessary marks of punctuation.' Gertrude's themes were also awkwardly expressed. Romantic, often melodramatic, many of them deal with subjects inspired by Victorian writing, particularly by such authors as Edgar Allan Poe and George Eliot. But the subject of the themes was usually Gertrude Stein. Deeply personal, and intensely and unsuccessfully expressed, they reveal in often ludicrous form her adolescent longings and frustrations. 'Books, books,' she writes in one example, 'is there no end to it. Nothing but myself to feed my own eager nature.'

Both the new intellectual adventures and the emotional experiences of the recent past –

the loss of her parents and the division and moves of the family – together with her own responses to fellow students welled up inside her and exploded in her weekly compositions. The results were often a cleansing of the spirit, a painful appeal for affection, vulnerably expressed in a style which buckles under the weight of the feeling. It was a manner of writing not to be abandoned in her work until her third attempt at serious writing, in *Three Lives*.

English composition and psychology were not the only courses Gertrude pursued at Harvard. As an undergraduate she took the general subjects required for the Bachelor's degree, among them economics, German, French, history and mathematics. But both English and psychology were crucial subjects to Gertrude Stein at a time when, as she later described it, '. . . I was tremendously occupied with finding out what was inside myself to make me what I was. . . . I became more and more interested in my own mental and physical processes and less in that of others.' Her study of psychology, in particular the experiments she undertook with her fellow pupil Leon Solomons in which she was the chief subject under investigation, encouraged her in this interest, and her exercises in English helped her express her findings. During the first years of her studies at Harvard, Gertrude Stein's introspection flourished.

Gertrude had, of course, outside interests. She joined the amateur dramatics society called the Idler Club, and for two years was Secretary to the Philosophy Club. With Leo at the University she was never friendless, and together they participated in the normal run of student activities – visits to the theatre, galleries, the opera, picnics and bicycle trips, and long and heated general discussions of art and morality. With her women friends, Gertrude remained independently uninterested in the questions of female suffrage and sexual equality. ('I am for having women learn what they can but not to mistake learning for action nor to believe that a man's work is suited to them because they have mastered a boy's education,' she was to write in *Fernhurst* a few years later.) Nor was she noticeably interested in fashion or her appearance, and her large, squat and uncorsetted figure was the subject of frequent though affectionate mockery. She was, as a contemporary described her, 'jolly, natural and simple. She wasn't easy to know, but once you knew her you found her charming'. Simple and direct, sometimes aggressive in debate, she had a sense of humour and an intelligence that made her society welcome.

But for the first two years at Harvard, Gertrude remained for most of her acquaintances 'Leo's little sister'. She followed him in her choice of friends, as she had in her choice of studies. When in 1895 Leo graduated from Harvard and left America to join his cousin Fred Stein on a trip around the world, Gertrude's work at university began to take direction. In the following year she published, together with her colleague and friend Leon Solomons, the results of their work in experimental psychology. With the appearance of the paper on 'Normal Motor Automatism' in *Psychological Review*, her professors, always admiring (the previous year the visiting Professor of experimental psychology, Hugo Münsterburg, had called her his 'ideal student'), now began to take her seriously. She was invited by James to attend the graduate seminar on psychology, a rare honour indeed, and was asked by him about her plans for future work. James suggested either philosophy or psychology as suitable for further study. But philosophy demanded a satisfactory grounding in logic, a subject for which Gertrude showed little inclination. The practice of psychology required a degree in medicine, and this she decided to get. Accordingly, Gertrude began to attend classes in zoology, botany, physics and chemistry, faring well in all but the last of these. Further study also meant that she must have a BA degree from Harvard. The final exams for the degree would, she was told, be no problem, and she was assured of passing *magnum cum laude*, but since she had never passed the Radcliffe entrance exams, she would need to study Latin. To this end she began in 1896 to take lessons with a private tutor.

Despite James's urgings to concentrate for the sake of her assuredly brilliant future in medicine, Gertrude took her Latin studies with disheartening levity. When, at the end of the university year in 1896, she was faced with the choice of a summer studying Caesar and Latin grammar or one spent in the company of Leo in Holland, she unhesitatingly chose to join Leo, with the result that in the spring of 1897 she failed to pass her exam and was not awarded her Bachelor's degree. Nevertheless, her Harvard professors continued to back her and, following once again in the footsteps of her elder brother – now back in Baltimore studying biology at Johns Hopkins University – Gertrude Stein was admitted to the Johns Hopkins School of Medicine in the autumn of 1897. The following spring she was awarded her BA from Harvard.

Together in Baltimore, Leo and Gertrude now set up house – presided over by the motherly housekeeper who was to figure in Gertrude's short story 'The Good Anna' – and the two Steins resumed their close intellectual and emotional relationship. Having returned from his trip around the world full of new enthusiams for art and science, Leo held forth in their salon on a variety of subjects, while once again Gertrude listened, content to remain in the shadow of her brilliant and dogmatic brother. In her work, too, Gertrude accepted a passive role. At first her medical studies went well. She got good marks in all her classes, and despite her inability to draw, enjoyed making models of brain tracts, which according to Leo she found 'purely mechanical work and rather restful'. She was not willing to fight for her rights as one of a new group of female medical students, and did not mind being given the more prosaic laboratory duties by which the male students maintained their superior status. Leo recalls that a visiting German anatomist commented on the making of these brain tracts that 'it was an excellent occupation for women and Chinamen, and Gertrude quite agreed'.

During the next two years at Johns Hopkins, Gertrude's marks began to decline. She herself was rapidly losing interest. When a fellow student urged her to greater diligence: 'Gertrude Gertrude remember the cause of women,' Gertrude answered, 'you don't know what it is to be bored.' According to Gertrude's later explanation in *The Autobiography of Alice B. Toklas*, 'the practice and theory of medicine did not interest her at all'. There was too much study of disease, for one thing. 'She always says she dislikes the abnormal it is so obvious. She says the normal is so much more simply complicated and interesting.'

In 1900, when Leo himself had left Baltimore and the university to study art and poetry in Florence, Gertrude began seriously to drag her feet. Without the promptings of the beloved William James and without constant pushing of her brother (although a letter from Leo in Italy urged: 'It would be too bad if the first person in the family who had gone so far as to get the adequate preparation for anything should go back on it. . . . If you had my superior talents for loafing it might do but you haven't, so it won't.'), Gertrude Stein's desire to graduate from Medical School quickly waned. In 1901, having failed her exams, Gertrude left Baltimore to join Leo once again in Europe.

Besides, there were other reasons for wishing to leave America. In her last year at Johns Hopkins Medical School, Gertrude had fallen in with a 'fast' crowd. The debates on morality which she had enjoyed with Leo during her early years at Baltimore were not the only ones taking place at the time, and there were many women at the university who gave vent to attacks on middle-class morality, and some who practised what they avowed. 'Decadence' was in the air. The nineties poets in England and the French Symbolists had their followers in America, and American versions of the *Yellow Book* (*The Chapbook*, founded in 1894; *The Bibelot* and *Mlle New-York*, both of 1895) were commonly displayed on university salon tables, just as Beardsley prints and *japonaiserie* decorated the Aesthetic drawing-rooms of the day. In *Fernhurst*, a short story which Gertrude wrote in 1904–5, based on a three-cornered affair which had scandalised Bryn Mawr college in the last years of the century, she describes with superior hindsight a typical common room scene, in which academics 'moved about drinking tea, making epigrams, talking of college matters, and analysing Swinburne, Oscar Wilde and Henry James . . .'.

The fashion of Decadence also encouraged a new tolerance for, and in some cases the advocation of, homosexuality among students. The martyrdom of Oscar Wilde and his trial in 1895–7 were fresh in memory. Indeed, years later Gertrude was to remember how upset she had been by the event. But it was not just the aesthetic of Decadence which flourished at the universities at the time. Together with the common pretences of dark pasts and sinister capabilities which became an academic fashion in the last years of the century must also be reckoned the combined forces of the philosophy of Pragmatism and the new spirit of women's equality – both powerful ideas in the circles in which Gertrude began to move. The philosophy of Pragmatism, whose most famous exponent in America was William James, rejected the idea of morality for its own sake, and the doctrine of woman's equality demanded an end to the fine, simpering sensibilities of the hitherto fashionable woman. In her story about the Dean of Fernhurst college and her hold over a young female professor, Gertrude described the Dean as typical of her time and background, one who believed in 'the essential sameness of sex', taught her students to 'proclaim this doctrine of equality with a mental reservation in favour of female superiority', and was 'hard-headed, practical, unmoral [Pragmatic] in the sense that all values give place to expediency'. During the last years of her stay at the University, the combined force of the ideas of women's equality, Pragmatism, and Decadence was to create an atmosphere in which female homosexuality flourished. For

Gertrude it was to provide the answer for her sexually ignorant and deeply lonely existence. With all the eagerness of a new convert, she embraced its doctrines and fell in love.

The object of Gertrude's passion was a lively and intelligent girl called May Bookstaver. According to Leon Katz, who has uncovered the connection, *Q.E.D.* (*Quad Erat Demonstrandum*), later published as *Things As They Are*, was written about this first and traumatic affair. In the novel, which Gertrude wrote in 1903, May is described as 'the American version of the English handsome girl', a courageous and unconventional beauty, who was in some way also involved amorously with one Mabel Haynes, a more worldly undergraduate whose wealth brought certain pressures to bear against May's relation with Gertrude. In *Q.E.D.* Mabel is the corrupt 'decadent' (a word which Gertrude uses frequently in the book). Her character and her hold on May Bookstaver revolted Gertrude, as did her appearance: 'heavy about the mouth, not with the weight of flesh but with the drag of unidealised passion, continually sated and continually craving. The long formless chin accentuated the lack of moral significance.' In *Q.E.D.* the character of the author is a bumptious innocent, pulled by both desire and a sense of adventure into areas of feeling over which she has no control. At one point the character of May is made to tell her: 'That is what makes it possible for a face as thoughtful and strongly built as yours to be almost annoyingly unlived and youthful and to be almost foolishly happy and content.' To which Adele – the character of Gertrude – replies: 'I could undertake to be an efficient pupil if it were possible to find an efficient teacher.'

It is clear from the novel that Gertrude had both the desire to love and a cowardice which restrained her from indulgence in the kind of behaviour which repelled her. For this she is taunted: ' "I am afraid . . . that after all you haven't a nature much above passionettes. You are so afraid of losing your moral sense that you are not willing to take it through anything more dangerous than a mud-puddle." ' Such a charge accurately described Gertrude's state at the beginning of this fairly dangerous liaison. Another is the portrait which she gives in *Fernhurst* of the young woman professor before her affair with the hero Philip Redfern:

> . . . her deepest interest was in the varieties of human experience [an echo of William James's famous title] and her constant desire was to partake of all human relations but by some quality of her nature she never succeeded in really touching any human creature she knew. Her transfigured innocence too was not an ignorance of the facts of life nor a puritan's instinct indeed her desire was to experience the extreme forms of sensuous life and to make even immoral experience her own. . . . A passionate desire for worldly experience filled her entirely and she was still waiting for the hand that could tear down the walls that enclosed her and let her escape into a world of humans.

The waiting that she describes here, and had described in her Radcliffe themes, and which had for so long been the un-'revenged' feature of her adolescence, was suddenly to come to an end. Gertrude was hardly prepared for it.

How far the affair with May Bookstaver led Gertrude away from 'middle-class morality', which Gertrude upheld, it is hard to determine. (At one point in *Q.E.D.*, Adele says, 'You have a foolish notion that to be middle-class is to be vulgar, that to cherish the ideals of respectability and decency is to be commonplace and that to be the mother of children is to be low.') In the novel which describes their relationship, a [Henry] Jamesian obscurity clothes the actions of the participants. Lesbianism was a difficult, if not a dangerous subject for literature in 1903 and Gertrude never attempted to have the book published – partly in deference to Alice Toklas's feelings. Though the novel describes secret meetings, passionate love-letters, infidelities and recriminations, the sexual encounter is confined to a kiss which 'seemed to scale the very walls of chastity' and which provoked a 'fierce tide of disgust'. On the other hand, Gertrude's friend Mabel Weeks can remember Gertrude in tears in 1901, giving the affair 'Oscar Wildean justifications'. Whatever the actions involved, it is clear that Gertrude's emotions were totally invested in a sophisticated and triangular affair that took its course over the years between 1900 and 1903, and which was to keep her moving between Europe and America in alternating bouts of optimism and depression.

What Leo thought of Gertrude's affair with May Bookstaver is not known. It is quite possible he was told little or nothing about it for, as he said, they never discussed their private feelings. But even had he known, it is more than likely that his characteristic preoccupation with his own state of mind would have spared him undue worry about his sister.

For Gertrude, on the other hand, the summer visits with Leo in Europe provided a much-needed release from a situation which she was too inexperienced to handle. In *Q.E.D.* Leo makes his appearance as a cousin with whom the heroine 'enjoyed to the full the sense of family friendship'. She was content to enter with him into the old routine of 'agreeing and disagreeing in endless discussion with an intensity of interest that long familiarity had in no way diminished, varied by indulgence in elaborate foolishness and reminiscent jokes'. But Europe itself was an escape into innocence. Her recent experiences 'belonged to another less pleasant and more incomplete emotional world'. Years later she could still remember the other-worldly peace and magic of those summer visits in Europe. In 1943 in *Wars I Have Seen*, she wrote about an outing in Italy of 1900:

> . . . We spent one summer some weeks in Perugia at a pension and there were lots of us there and one day some of us went off to see Lake Trasimena because there was supposed to be a whole army at the bottom well an army of ancient days naturally with gold chariots, and we thought we would like a swim in the lake, and the young men took the boatmen with them at one end of a little island in the middle of the lake and we girls went to the other end to swim, and we swam without clothes in the sunset in Lake Trasimena. . . .

Europe was for Gertrude, as for most Americans of her age and station, an exotic and extravagant adventure, but it was also, as it was not for most Americans of her age

Childhood

N. STOCKMANN HOF-FOT.   WiEN.

Gertrude Stein, aged about four.

ABOVE Gertrude Stein, aged about three,
c. 1877.
RIGHT Gertrude's parents, Amelia and
Daniel Stein.
BELOW The Stein children in Vienna, with
their Hungarian governess and Czech tutor.

OPPOSITE:
ABOVE San Francisco, where the Stein children
moved after their father's death in 1891.
BELOW The Stein family in Oakland, California.
From left to right : Simon, Daniel, Gertrude
at his feet, Michael, Amelia, Leo and Bertha.

University Days

OPPOSITE
Gertrude Stein *c*. 1895.

RIGHT Henry and
William James.
BELOW A Harvard outing,
31 July 1897.

RIGHT Gertrude and Leo Stein at Harvard in the 1890s.
BELOW Gertrude Stein in a play with other members of the Idler Club, the Harvard amateur dramatics society.

OPPOSITE:
LEFT Gertrude Stein at Johns Hopkins University, Baltimore, c. 1897.
RIGHT Gertrude in California with her young nephew Allan, son of Michael and Sally Stein.
BELOW With friends at Johns Hopkins.

In 1900.

and station, an experience with which she had been familiar in her first five years of life. There is something in her descriptions of these summers in Europe which conveys a sense of a rediscovered peace and innocence in a non-American world she had known as a child, and which suggests how great a contrast it made to the very sophisticated, and for Gertrude, often frightening, world she had left in America. Europe was both an exotic luxury and a familiar haven, and in 1902 she decided to make it her home.

It was also, now, the permanent home of her brother Leo. In 1900 Leo had written from Florence that he intended not to finish his studies at Johns Hopkins but to stay in Europe where he would devote himself to his intellectual life. Extraordinarily changeable in his pursuits, he gave himself with total devotion successively to biology, history, philosophy, aesthetics, painting, poetry and in his later life psychology. An exceptionally gifted man, Leo expended his not inconsiderable energies in talk and analysis. He had a passion for debate and a curiosity for knowledge which had been fostered both by his teacher, William James, and by the atmosphere of intellectual excitement which he found at university. But like his father, Daniel Stein, Leo's enthusiasm and pontifications never held for very long, and he spent his life in pursuit of the ultimate philosophy he longed to espouse. Pompous, passionate, and able to outspeak most people on most subjects, he was a tiresome and demanding partner in debate. But to Leo Gertrude owed an important and intense contact with a large range of ideas, offered at a period when she might have stifled intellectually but for the playfulness and brilliance of her brother's thinking. To him, too, she owed the acquaintance with many whose society she, as a single woman, and certainly a highly unconventional one, might otherwise not have had. There is no doubt that in their early years together in Europe, Leo was Gertrude's guide and teacher, and the provider of the entrée into the distinguished company in which they soon found themselves.

Foremost among this company was Bernard Berenson, a Harvard alumnus of thirty-five living in Florence when Leo met him in 1900. Before his arrival in Florence, Leo had been to Paris to look at the museums. As he wrote to Gertrude in Baltimore in October 1900, 'I knew the Beaux Arts pretty well before I got through and decided definitely that there was extraordinarily little in it.' Contact with Berenson, however, gradually tempered Leo's disdain: 'His house is filled with beautiful old Italian furniture and hangings and he has a really magnificent art library,' he wrote. And then, 'I saw Berenson again Wednesday evening. He's certainly very conversable and in the main very sensible. There's simply that tremendous excess of the I.' Two months after this letter, Leo wrote to Gertrude of his decision to stay on in Florence and devote himself to art and aesthetics. The influence of Berenson on this decision is evident, and for both Gertrude and Leo it had profound consequences.

Leo's friendship with Berenson blossomed between 1900 and 1902, the year that Gertrude joined them, first in Italy and then that summer in England, where she and Leo first spent weekends at the Berenson home near Haslemere, in Surrey, and then in September rented a cottage nearby. The Berensons and their circle must have found the Stein pair unusual company. Leo and BB, as he was called, had already established a

E.A.—4

29

routine of meeting over dinner to take on in heated discussion whatever ideas might be thrown to them by family or visitors, and into this procedure Gertrude crashed with the full weight of enthusiasm untempered by feminine reserve or conventional manners. As her friend Mabel Weeks later recalled, Gertrude was early convinced of her right to comment, and of her position among company, however distinguished. 'As early as 1900, Gertrude was most outspoken about wanting glory from life. I remember her telling me about it on the Grand Canal, on the way to the Academy. She repeated it again and again "la gloire".' Berenson, to be sure, was not alone in noting a certain intractability in his young guests. 'By the way,' Leo wrote in a letter to Mabel Weeks that summer, 'what do you think of the susceptibility of the American mind to fresh political ideas? Gertrude was the other day trying to hold up the American end of a general discussion against Russell, Berenson and a young journalist, Dill. I was home with my busted leg and didn't hear it, but one of Russell's contentions was that as compared with the cultivated Englishman the cultivated American is thus unsusceptible.' Nor was the cultivated American above ordering her host about. As Leo further reported, 'Gertrude has put Berenson on eggs and milk, under which he is flourishing like a Green Bay Tree.'

Gertrude and Leo entered unselfconsciously into the delicate sensibilities of the English intellectual elite. There was no New World inferiority on the part of the Steins in Europe. Rather, they were accustomed, as Leo wrote, to 'blow the American trumpet as though it were the whole of Sousa's band'. Among certain of the Bloomsbury crowd, the Steins' extraordinary confidence was to make a lasting impression.

Both Gertrude and Leo thoroughly enjoyed their stay in the English countryside. Leo found the area around Haslemere '. . . so absolutely lovely, so rich and brilliant in its deep sun-washed color and so beautiful in its contours and composition'. The cottage which they had taken for some weeks he described as '. . . set among some fine oaks on a little hill soft with the springy English turf on which some nice red cows, lamby sheep, white ducks, lordly roosters and clucky hens wander in pastoral freedom. . . . If the English climate hadn't so much juice in it and if, notwithstanding, English landscape could remain as juicy as now it is I should certainly want to stay right here for some time.' As it was, however, the Steins decided to settle for some months in London, and in the autumn of 1902 they were housed in comfortable rooms at number 20 Bloomsbury Square.

The juice of the English autumn soon began to turn into the icy swamp of the English winter. Although Leo found London 'a great place for buying books', by 24 December he was making his way back to Paris. Gertrude, left alone in London, continued the reading she had begun at the British Museum, working gradually through English literature, becoming, as she later wrote, '. . . absorbed in Elizabethan prose and particularly in the prose of Greene. She had little note-books full of phrases that pleased her as they had pleased her when she was a child.' Some time between the shouting parties at the Berensons and the listening to Leo she must have decided that her path to 'la gloire' lay in writing, and the reading she was engaged on was a preparation for this career. But her emotions were still caught in the spikes of the Bookstaver affair. Without the company of Leo or the rural shelter with its 'lamby sheep and white ducks', she fell prey to the terrors of the London winter. As she wrote later in *The Autobiography of Alice B. Toklas*, '. . . she wandered about the London streets and found them infinitely depressing and dismal'. London looked 'just like Dickens and Dickens had always frightened her. . . . The dismalness of London and the drunken women and children and the gloom and the lonesomeness brought back all the melancholy of her adolescence and one day she said she was leaving for America and she left.' What she suffered in London was powerfully described in *Q.E.D.*, the book she began to write on her return to New York in February 1903:

> There is no passion more dominant and instinctive in the human spirit than the need of the country to which one belongs. . . .

An American in the winter fogs of London can realise this passionate need, this desperate longing in all its completeness. The dead weight of that fog and smoke-laden air, the sky that never suggests for a moment the clean blue distance that has been the accustomed daily comrade, the dreary sun, moon and stars that look like painted imitations on the ceiling of a smoke-filled room, the soggy, damp, miserable streets, and women with bedraggled, frayed-out skirts, their faces swollen and pimply with sordid dirt ground into them until it has become a natural part of their ugly surface all become day after day a more dreary weight of hopeless oppression.

A hopeful spirit resists. It feels that it must be better soon, it cannot last so forever; this afternoon, to-morrow this dead weight must lift, one must soon again realise a breath of clean air, but day after day the whole weight of fog, smoke and low brutal humanity rests a weary load on the head and back and one loses the power of straightening the body to actively bear the burden, it becomes simply a despairing endurance.

Obsessional and over-written though it is, Gertrude's description of her last months in London powerfully conveys the weight of her unhappiness during the last phase of her entanglement with the absent May Bookstaver. In New York, in the apartment on Riverside Drive which she shared with friends from university, Gertrude began to write the novel that was to purge all the poisoning traces of the painful affair. The writing out of the story of the relationship not only acted as a purification for her, but the story itself describes a purification. In the novel the heroine is seen to pass through an experience which transforms initial ignorance ('crude virginity') and cowardice ('I hate to risk hurting myself or anybody else,' the heroine says. 'All I want to do is meditate endlessly and think and talk,') into a bitter wisdom.

In *Fernhurst*, the short story written the following year (1904–5) about a similar situation of complicated and illicit passion, Gertrude makes a hearty renunciation of the style of living she had encountered with May and her friends. In this passage she attacks the Dean (in real life the powerful and faintly sinister Helen Carey Thomas of Bryn Mawr) and the spirit of her college:

31

Honorable and manly as are the ostensible ideals that govern the place the unmoral methods of the dean the doctrine of the superiority of woman and a sensitive and mystic appreciation of the more decadent forms of art are the more vital influences and many a graduate spends sorrowful years in learning in after-life that her quality is not more fine nor her power greater than that of many of her more simple fellows and that established virtues and methods are at once more honourable and more efficient.

Such was Gertrude's extraordinary recantation of her avowed desire for experience, of all that she had wanted for herself when she first encountered May and her group at Medical School in 1900. It is an extraordinary piece of writing from a woman who in later years was to seem to the unknowing public the very symbol of decadence in art, as the 'Sybil of Montparnasse'. But Gertrude's position was made clear even in 1903, and in *Q.E.D.* her heroine declares:

> I never claimed to be middle-class in my intellect and in truth, I probably have the experience of all apostles. I am rejected by the class whose cause I preach but that has nothing to do with the case. I simply contend that the middle-class ideal which demands that people be affectionate, respectable, honest and content, that they avoid excitements and cultivate serenity is the ideal that appeals to me. . . .

As she wrote out the story of this traumatic affair, Gertrude began to feel the rightness of simple, uncomplicated living. In 1903, even the look of the city of New York seemed to convey a message about purity and to correspond to her new, cleansed state of mind: 'I simply rejoiced in the New York streets, in the long spindling legs of the elevated, in the straight high undecorated houses, in the empty upper air and in the white surface of the snow. It was such a joy to realise that the whole thing was without mystery and without complexity, that it was clean and straight and meagre and hard and white and high.' Apart from what is revealed by such symbolism, it is clear that the experience of writing *Q.E.D.* in America fulfilled a deep psychological rather than aesthetic need.

Gertrude was capable of forgetting what she wished not to know (twenty years after her separation from Leo in Paris she actually told someone who had just seen him that she had only one brother, and that one called Michael). When, many years later, Gertrude was looking through a pile of manuscripts, she came across this first novel and was troubled by it. By that stage, however, her belief in her own genius was strong enough for her to overcome much of the shame surrounding the book and the affair on which it was based. As she recalls in *The Autobiography of Alice B. Toklas* of 1932:

> The funny thing about this short novel is that she completely forgot about it for many years. She remembered herself beginning a little later the Three Lives but this first piece of writing was completely forgotten, she had never mentioned it to me, even when I first knew her. *She must have forgotten about it almost immediately.* [My own italics.] This spring just two days before our leaving the country she was looking for some manuscript of *The Making of Americans* that she wanted to show

Bernard Faÿ and she came across these two carefully written volumes of this completely forgotten first novel. She was very bashful and hesitant about it, did not really want to read it. Louis Bromfield was at the house that evening and she handed him the manuscript and said to him, you read it.

The novel remained among her unpublished works when she died; and the decision whether to publish it was left to the discretion of Alice B. Toklas.

With this monument to disappointed passion out of the way, Gertrude Stein set out in the summer of 1903 to join Leo once more in Europe. By the autumn she had settled with him in Paris, in the flat that was to become famous in the course of the next few years as 27 rue de Fleurus.

3
What Are Masterpieces?

W HEN, IN THE AUTUMN OF 1903, Gertrude Stein moved into Leo's flat in the rue de Fleurus, she did not intend to become a permanent exile. It was a condition of her stay in Paris that she would return to America every year, and indeed, in the winter of 1903–4 she did go back to New York, perhaps in pursuit of the last wisps of the May Bookstaver romance, perhaps merely in response to the routine already established. She had begun a first draft of her long novel, *The Making of Americans*, earlier that year in New York, and now she began to write out the story of *Fernhurst* in which she resolved for herself the conflict between the attractions of passionate love and the safety of 'established virtues'. She had also, apparently, come to some decision about her own future. By the time she returned to Paris in June 1904 at the age of thirty, Gertrude had made up her mind to settle down to life with Leo and to devote herself to writing. To her it felt like a real beginning:

It happens often in the twenty-ninth year of a life that all the forces that have been engaged through the years of childhood, adolescence and youth in confused and ferocious combat range themselves in ordered ranks – one is uncertain of one's aims, meaning and power during these years of tumultuous growth when aspiration has no relation to fulfillment and one plunges here and there with energy and misdirection during the storm and stress of the making of a personality until at last we reach the twenty-ninth year the straight and narrow gate-way of maturity and life which was all uproar and confusion narrows down to form and purpose and we exchange a great dim possibility for a small hard reality.

Also in our American life where there is no coercion in custom and it is our right to change our vocation so often as we have desire and opportunity, it is a common experience that our youth extends through the whole first twenty-nine years of our life and it is not until we reach thirty that we find at last that vocation for which we feel ourselves fit and to which we willingly devote continued labor.

Gertrude Stein's decision about her future coincided with and was spurred on by the characteristically tortured vocational seeking of her brother Leo. That she emerged after her first few years with him in Paris, not only with a certainty of her own abilities and a direction for her talents, but also with a position at the centre of a world which was to become legendary in the history of art, was due largely to his influence and early activities.

Leo, as we have seen, had decided in 1900 to devote his significant intellectual abilities to the study of art, and with the companionship of Bernard Berenson over the next two years he 'became really intimate with quattrocento Italian art'. He abandoned his plan to write a book on Mantegna when he discovered there were two such studies in the making, and for the next few years he devoted himself to general speculation on art and aesthetics. In 1902–3, however, two things happened which were to influence the course of his and his sister's lives. In London, that autumn, Leo bought his first modern painting, a picture by Wilson Steer. Although Leo and Gertrude had previously bought prints and objets d'art on their frequent 'junking' expeditions in Baltimore and Europe, this was their first real purchase. As Leo remembers, it made him feel '. . . a bit like a desperado. Oil paintings were for the rich: that was part of the American credo'. With the acquisition of the Steer (not long thereafter replaced) came the realisation that 'one could actually own paintings even if one were not a millionaire'.

The second event occurred in the early weeks of 1903, while Leo was in Paris, in flight from that dismal London winter and en route to America, where he intended to settle: 'One night when Pablo Casals and I were dining together, as we did once a week, I said to him that I felt myself growing into an artist. The leaven of pictorial vision was working. When I got back to the hotel, I made a rousing fire, took off my clothes, and began to draw from the nude.' Such was the dramatic beginning of Leo's career as a painter. It was followed by 'a week drawing from statues in the Louvre', and it was important because 'it decided me to stay in Paris'.

In the studio which Leo found with the help of his sculptor uncle, Ephraim Keyser, then in Paris, Leo set himself to conquer painting, as he had previously set himself to conquer biology, philosophy and aesthetics – and would later set himself to conquer psychology. In April 1903 Leo wrote to his friend Mabel Weeks in America about the battle between his rather average artistic talents and his fiercely high ambitions. '. . . . Art is having its revenge on me,' he wrote, 'I don't mind it very seriously, though the plaguy brute often hits below the belt and sometimes seems to land what is next door to a knockout blow. However, I keep a stiff upper lip and slug away like a good 'un and hope to get the upper hand in time.'

When Gertrude arrived in Paris in the autumn of 1903, Leo was in the thick of this struggle. As with all of Leo's pursuits, painting became an obsession which began to express itself in words rather than action, and Gertrude soon found herself submitted to a barrage of talk about painting. As she wrote in *Everybody's Autobiography*: '. . . my brother needed to be talking and he was painting but he needed to talk about painting in order to be painting, he needed to understand painting in order to be painting.'

The outlet for Leo's mania was not work but talk, and it was in these early months

Early Days in Paris

Gertrude Stein in Paris about a year after her arrival.

OPPOSITE:
LEFT The Steins' uncle,
Ephraim Keyser, in his
Paris studio.
RIGHT Bernard Berenson,
whom Leo Stein had met
in Florence in 1900.
BELOW Gertrude Stein at
27 rue de Fleurus,
c. 1906.

RIGHT Ambroise
Vollard by Picasso.
BELOW An 'artistic'
evening at the
Chat Noir, in
Montmartre, *c.* 1906.

UNE SOIREE AU CHAT NOIR
Cabaret Artistique
68, Boulevard de Clichy - PARIS-MONTMARTRE

The Bateau Lavoir, at 13 rue de Ravignan, where Picasso, his mistress Fernande Olivier and Max Jacob lived.

A mes chers amis Suzanne et Henri Picasso 1904

ABOVE Picasso in 1904.

OPPOSITE ABOVE:
LEFT The painter Marie Laurencin.
RIGHT Fernande Olivier,
Picasso's mistress.

OPPOSITE BELOW:
LEFT Guillaume Apollinaire.
CENTRE Portrait drawing of
Fernande Olivier by Marie Laurencin, 1910.
RIGHT Pencil drawing of
Marie Laurencin by Fernande Olivier.

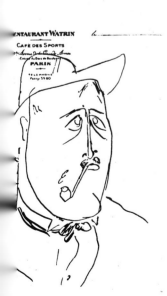

ABOVE Dr Claribel Cone.
RIGHT Portrait of Leo Stein
by Picasso, 1906.
BELOW The Steins in Paris, *c.* 1907.

of artistic effort that he began to create what he was later to call 'the atmosphere of propaganda', the phrase he used to describe the situation at the rue de Fleurus salon in those early days in Paris. In 1903, however, Leo was a propagandist without a cause. He had seen no modern paintings in Paris, his only purchase of that year being a Du Gardier picture of a Whistleresque woman in white with a white dog. It was not until the following year when he saw Berenson and complained of the 'dearth of art' that the heralding of the modern art messiah became possible. In one of the most important exchanges in the history of art collecting, Berenson, as Leo described it, said ' "Do you know Cézanne?" I said that I did not. Where did one see him? He said, "At Vollard's"; so I went to Vollard's, and was launched.'

At Vollard's tiny gallery on the rue Laffite Leo was able to look at his leisure at paintings which were to alter his taste as they were eventually to revolutionise the aesthetic vision of the rest of the world. That year he spent many hours in what was commonly mistaken for a junk shop, looking through the canvasses which were piled under layers of dust. According to Leo, Vollard 'didn't mind my turning things upside down, since they were already in that state, and so we got on nicely'. Leo did buy one Cézanne landscape from Vollard that year, but since most of Vollard's paintings were in an unfinished state, and since the organisation of the shop was such that Vollard was actually able to lose, on more than one occasion, paintings which had already been sold to clients, it was not here that Leo sated his new-found appetite for modern art. Instead, and again thanks to Berenson, Leo was able to see the prominent collection of Cézannes owned by Charles Loeser, another Harvard alumnus living in Florence, and heir to the fortune of Macy's Brooklyn department store. That summer of 1904 Leo spent looking at the Cézannes which Loeser kept in the bedroom and dressing room of his sumptuous villa in Italy. Leo describes that summer as his 'Cézanne debauch', an absorbing of the principles of modern art which was to enable him in the next few years to buy with certainty the first scorned and terrific products of the modern sensibility. As Leo recalls, by the opening of the Autumn Salon in 1904, he had assimilated the lessons of Cézanne (as a critic, if not as a painter) and 'was ready to look further'.

The *vernissages* of the two chief events of the Paris art calendar – the Salon d'Automne and the Salon des Indépendants, held each year in the autumn and spring respectively – were major social occasions. The great Paris crowds arrived, sporting new hats or new lovers, sometimes to look at the pictures. Leo recalled those early scenes in his memoir *Appreciation*: '. . . one saw there everybody who was anybody. Willy with his flat-brimmed top hat, his wife Colette, and Polaire, who had the slimmest waist in France, were a trio one can't forget. The old salon was full of pictures big enough to cover a wall, sprawling with pink nudes and landscapes painted with a kind of leaden colour.' Among these canvasses Leo was able to see works by artists such as Bonnard, Vuillard, Maurice Denis, Marquet, Vallotton, Rouault, Van Gogh, and Seurat. He was already familiar with the work of Renoir and Gauguin, and by now owned some of their paintings, but at the Autumn Salon of 1904 he saw nothing which could satisfy the craving for modern art which the summer's study of Cézanne had aroused. However, he kept his enthusiasm well stoked – as always, by the fuel of talk. In a letter to Mabel Weeks, he refers to 'the obligation that I have been under ever since the Autumn Salon, of expounding L'Art Moderne (you will observe that this is not the same thing as L'Art Nouveau). . . . The Big Four are Manet, Renoir, Degas and Cézanne.'

Among the people to whom Leo expounded 'L'Art Moderne' were not only his recently arrived sister Gertrude, but also their older brother Michael and his wife Sally, who with their son Allan had recently moved to Paris, to a flat in rue Madame. In 1902 a strike of cable-car workers in California had made it clear to Michael that there was no place for him 'in management'. After a year or so extricating himself from his thriving business, Michael sold his belongings and moved to Paris. There they could not only be with Leo and Gertrude, but Sally – a former art student – could continue her studies; their son Allan was old enough to go to school, and, providing they all 'lived quietly', the entire family could continue to exist off what Michael's business skills had provided. Now, in the company of their intellectual brother Leo, Sally and Michael Stein also began to look at pictures.

None of them lived extravagantly. According to Leo, in those early days, he and Gertrude had about $150 a month to spend on books or pictures or travel, an income which kept the more expensive painters out of their reach. But as Leo wrote, 'Life was then cheap in Paris, rents were low, food was not dear, we had no doctor's bills. . . . We despised luxury except when someone else paid for it, and got what we most wanted. That made a satisfactory living.' Occasionally there would be a windfall, as when one day Michael told Leo and Gertrude that there was an extra 8000 francs to be spent. 'As this was regarded as a criminal waste, we went at once to Vollard's.' On that occasion they bought two Gauguins, two Cézanne figure compositions, two Renoirs, and, 'for good measure Vollard threw in a Maurice Denis'.

Although in later years the Stein family were regarded as eccentric American millionaires who merely affected bohemian dress and style, in those very early days no one thought them rich. According to Leo, 'Vollard liked to sell us pictures because, as he told me, we were the only customers who bought pictures, not because they were rich, but despite the fact that they weren't'.

In the spring of 1905, the Stein family followed Leo to the Salon des Indépendants. Something new had appeared in the work of an artist called Manguin, a style which Leo later recognised as the beginnings of what was soon to be called Fauvism. As Leo said, had he been able to see a Fauve by Matisse at that time, he would not have bought the Manguin; but Matisse as far as Leo knew from his work at the previous Salon d'Automne was still under the influence of Signac, and painting in the pointilliste style. That spring Leo bought two pictures, a nude by Manguin and another by Vallotton, 'a Manet for the impecunious', as Gertrude later called him. The following autumn the Stein family again trooped off to the *vernissage*. This time, as Leo remembers, there was 'something decisive'. 'Matisse came out from pointillism with the *Femme au chapeau*. It was a tremendous effort on his part, a thing brilliant and powerful, but the nastiest smear of paint I had ever seen. It was what I was unknowingly waiting for, and

I would have snatched it at once if I had not needed a few days to get over the unpleasantness of the putting on of the paint.'

Leo was not alone in finding the Matisse horrific. The public and the critics were scandalised. Matisse, together with a group of painters, including Derain, Manguin, Vlaminck, and two Russians working in France, Kandinsky and Jawlensky, had exhibited pictures whose jarring, broad slabs of colour seemed to violate every assumption of what painting ought to be. This challenge to a deeply-held conception of beauty now provoked an anger not known since the days of the first Impressionist exhibitions. 'A paint pot has been flung in the face of the public,' said one critic. 'Poor Donatello,' said another, referring to a sculpture in the centre of the group's exhibition, 'surrounded by wild animals.' Most savage among these wild animals, or *fauves*, were the paintings by Matisse, and he and his work soon became the chief objects of the public fury. Crowds gathered in front of his work, not merely jeering, but some poking their canes at the paintings, trying, as Gertrude later wrote, 'to scratch off the paint'. Matisse himself, severely shaken by the reaction, ventured into the Salon only once – his wife, the model for the picture, not at all.

Such a reaction must have convinced Leo that the *Femme au chapeau* was an important work, and he set about to persuade his family they must own it. According to Gertrude in *The Autobiography of Alice B. Toklas*, it was her decision to buy the painting, while Leo wasn't sure. According to Michael and Sally Stein, it was they who wanted to own it. Their friend Therese Jelenko remembers their reaction. 'I still can see Frenchmen doubled up with laughter before it, and Sarah saying "it's superb" and Mike couldn't tear himself away.'

Such a purchase is bound to be glorified in retrospect. In any event, the decision to buy the painting was made, and Leo carried it out. The Salon committee advised him not to pay the stated price for the work, but to offer twenty per cent less – a customary negotiating manoeuvre which in this case they were sure could not fail. The Matisses, however, poor as they were, reacted to the battering by the press and the public by holding out for the full 500 francs. To this sum Leo finally agreed, and in the days that followed the purchase, he set out, by means of his acquaintance with Vallotton and Manguin, to meet the painter whose work had rocked the Paris art world.

The Stein family's friendship with the Matisses greatly altered the fortunes of the painter and his wife. They now not only had loyal patrons (later especially in Michael and Sally Stein), but an intelligent and responsive audience for work which few others were then willing to support. In the immediate period that followed their meeting, Leo was to buy each year the most important works of the artist (*La Femme au chapeau* of 1905, *Le Bonheur de vivre* of 1906, *Blue Nude* of 1907), and to sustain Matisse's belief in his own work. They were also to provide the artist with new patrons and with the society of painters (chief among these Picasso) whose works he might otherwise not have known. For the Stein family, on the other hand, the Matisses provided both the charm of their own company and the pleasures of patronage. They added to the Stein acquaintances in Paris a circle of artists that had begun with Vallotton and Manguin, and was soon to include friends like the Van Dongens, Derain, and Braque. For Leo, moreover, the society of Matisse had other rewards. He found him 'really intelligent [an unusual and high tribute from Leo]. He was also witty and capable of saying exactly what he meant when talking about art'. He had 'great maturity, and the temper of the eternal pupil: he was willing to learn anyhow, anywhere, and from anyone'. Such a man would have had enormous attraction for Leo, then at the high-point of what Gertrude called his period of 'explaining'. Sally Stein, on the other hand, found Matisse an extraordinarily inspiring teacher. In 1908 she started, together with Hans Purrmann, the famous, though short-lived, Matisse atelier, where he began to teach the principles of his painting. She also continued to buy his work long after Leo and Gertrude had gone on to fresh enthusiasms.

But in 1905 both Leo and Gertrude were delighted with their new friendship with the Matisses, and they were soon inviting them and their fellow artists back to dinner at the rue de Fleurus. Within a few months of their meeting the Steins began to be known as collectors of strange works of modern art, and people asked to see the Cézannes and Matisses that were gradually filling the walls of their flat and adjoining studio. According to Gertrude, it was because of the irregular times of these different visits that she and Leo decided to institute their Saturday evenings. Michael and Sally soon followed their example. They chose to hold their 'salons' at an earlier hour on Saturday, so that visitors could go from one house to the other to view the latest bizarre acquisitions of the eccentric American family.

The early salons of Gertrude and Leo were dominated by Leo's propagandising efforts on behalf of modern art. Various of the artists and writers that Leo had met would assemble with their friends some time after nine in the evening to take tea and engage in the verbal pyrotechnics which the Stein household encouraged. Leo predominated, unashamedly lecturing the artists on the significance of their own work, while Gertrude, quietly and comfortably seated in a large armchair, would sit and listen. 'I expounded and explained, . . .' Leo wrote later. 'People came, and so I explained, because it was my nature to explain.' Of course many people came to mock both Leo and the paintings, but this merely spurred him on to greater efforts. As their friend Mabel Dodge [later Luhan] wrote in her autobiography: 'In those early days when everyone laughed, and went to the Steins, for the fun of it, and half angrily, half jestingly giggled and scoffed after they left (not knowing that all the same they were changed by seeing those pictures), Leo stood patiently night after night wrestling with the inertia of his guests, expounding, teaching, interpreting. . . .' According to Mabel Dodge, 'Buying those distorted compositions and hanging them in his apartment, [Leo] felt the need for making others see what he found in them, and this turned him eloquent.'

There were some who were convinced: 'One man who came to my place in Paris,' Leo wrote in *Appreciation* 'told me that the only Cézannes he cared for were those he saw there. Certainly they were not the best Cézannes, but the place was charged with the atmosphere of propaganda and he succumbed.' Leo's energy created the Steins' reputation in those early days, as much as their irregular behaviour and dress: their cigar smoking and loud laughter in public places (they were barred from the Café Royal); the brown corduroy suits which they wore with sandals (even in winter) made by Isadora and Raymond Duncan, recent neighbours in rue de Fleurus and early participants in the Saturday evenings. Some of the Stein acquaintances found Leo's posturings obnoxious, but others were openly charmed. Mabel Weeks described him as 'very playful, very personal, something of a flirt. Both men and women liked him and he was pleasant company'. But, she admits, 'He was not particularly gentle – indeed sometimes almost cruel in showing up people whose arguments he disliked. He felt that a very important element in affection and comradeship was tenderness, yet he understood tenderness only in a limited way, and admitted a lack of it in himself.' Both Leo and Mabel Weeks agreed that Leo's roughness with others was due to a sense of inferiority, a shyness: 'Although he wanted to talk – he was tremendously interested in ideas – and wanted a response, with people he didn't know he often assumed an *ex-cathedra* lecturing manner. With people whose intellectual capacities were not stimulating, he was impatient.' Although Leo could be pompous and unpleasant, he could also be entertaining. He sang, he was a clever mimic, and he did an extraordinary imitation of Isadora Duncan, which one lady told him was 'too beautiful to be burlesque'. Whatever he did, Leo was always impressive. In those early days at the rue de Fleurus, before his own defeats had weakened him, he was a vital part of the energising forces taking place in pre-war Paris. He successfully conveyed his sense of the importance of these times. In November 1905 he came across a painter whose work was to reinforce Leo's conviction that he was right.

Leo had at that time the habit of visiting, among other places of the fringe art-world of Paris, the café run by a former clown named Clovis Sagot. Sagot, a theatrical little man with a goatee, miserly and devilish, according to his painter acquaintances, took a fervent interest in two things: painting and a brand of licorice called Zan. Leo described their meetings in which 'He would interrupt the talk on modern art to put a bit of Zan between his teeth and commend its virtues; then we were back again on the latest show, the latest artistic scandal, the prospects for the future'. He was also particularly fond of a group of young Spanish painters and had persuaded Leo to buy one of their works, apparently against Leo's better judgment. One day Clovis told him of a new discovery, the twenty-four-year-old Pablo Picasso. 'Is he like the other Spaniard?' Leo asked. Sagot assured him he was not. 'This,' he said 'is the real thing.' Then, according to *Appreciation*, Leo went to Sagot's haphazard exhibition of the artist's works and discovered that this 'in fact was the real thing'. Leo bought a painting – a *saltimbanque* with wife, child and an ape – and was soon seeking an introduction to the painter himself.

He found the means of meeting Picasso in his friend Henri-Pierre Roché, according to Leo, '. . . a born liaison officer, who knew everybody and wanted everybody to know everybody else'. Roché had already introduced Leo to the society of writers who gathered on Tuesdays at the Cloiserie des Lilas in Montparnasse, among them Paul Fort, Paul Moréas, Alfred Jarry (author of the scabrous *Ubu Roi*), Stuart Merrill, and other famous and soon-to-be famous poets and critics of the time. It was no problem now to find Picasso, already known among a small group as a talented, newly arrived painter from Spain, whose Lautrec-influenced 'Blue' style was just beginning to give way to the manner that was later known as the Harlequin or 'Rose period'.

Leo was immediately struck by the power and vitality of Picasso and – as everyone always was – by 'his extraordinary seeing eyes. I used to say that when Picasso had looked at a drawing or a print, I was surprised that anything was left on the paper, so absorbing was his gaze. He spoke little and seemed neither remote nor intimate – just quite completely there.'

A few days after their introduction, Leo decided to buy another painting, this time a pale blue picture of a girl with a basket of red flowers. He took Gertrude along with him to Sagot's to hear her opinion. As Gertrude remembers, the picture frightened her; she found the depiction of the legs and feet especially ugly. Clovis Sagot, eager as ever to clinch a deal, offered to cut off the bottom half of the painting and sell them the rest. But Leo was determined, and some days later came back and bought it. When he returned with the picture to rue de Fleurus, Gertrude who was eating put down her fork and told him, 'Now you've spoiled my appetite. I hated that picture with feet like a monkey's.'

The painter that soon followed his work into the rue de Fleurus flat proved, unlike his painting, to hold an immediate charm for Gertrude. She found his brilliant black eyes, his handsome, compact appearance – like, she said, 'a good-looking bootblack' – his rough manner, all engaging. For Leo, Picasso seemed the essence of the artist. Unlike the older Matisse who was quiet, professorial and gently dignified, Picasso conveyed a brilliant violence very near the surface. As Leo described him, 'He felt himself a man apart – what the story books call a man of genius, though not pretentiously so. But in those days he was not sure. He was not aggressive, but felt the right to be aggressive.' Once after they had been waiting together in a bus queue, Picasso became angry as the places on the bus were taken by those first in line. 'This is not the way it ought to be,' he said. 'The strong should go ahead and take what they want.'

Gertrude also liked Picasso's brutish qualities. One Saturday evening when she and Leo were giving dinner to a select few who were invited for the pre-salon meal, she and Leo engaged in a customary quarrel while Picasso, sitting next to Gertrude, kept his usual silence. Absent-mindedly, Gertrude picked up a piece of bread lying on the table between them. 'This,' said Picasso, snatching it back with violence, 'this piece of bread is mine.' Then, according to Gertrude, 'She laughed and he looked sheepish. That was the beginning of their intimacy.'

There is no doubt that in those early days artists were something of an amusement for Gertrude, a form of entertainment which delighted the tourist in her. Matisse noticed this: '. . . The world is a theatre for you,' he is said to have told her, 'but there are theatres and theatres, and when you listen so carefully to me and so attentively and do not hear a word I say then I do say you are very wicked.' Before one lunch party to which Gertrude invited her artist friends she hung their pictures in such a way that each would be seated opposite his own work. This, she correctly predicted, would make them happy all evening. Matisse was the only one who noticed her trickery.

That Picasso was also detached from the goings-on at the rue de Fleurus, often sullen and churlish, rarely forthcoming in speech, except for, as Leo wrote, 'an occasional sparkle', must have proven an early attraction for Gertrude. When, in 1906, he asked to paint her portrait (he had not used a model in eight years) she was delighted. Over the months that Gertrude came to pose for him at his studio – some ninety sittings in all – their friendship was formed.

Picasso's appearance at the rue de Fleurus salon changed the style of the soirées radically. He brought with him an extraordinary group of people, many of them neighbours of his at 13 rue de Ravignan, the establishment of studios in which he lived and worked, and which was known as the Bateau Lavoir because of its arresting similarity to the laundry barges of the Seine. In this peculiar building lived not only Picasso's young and clever mistress, 'la belle Fernande' Olivier, but his closest friend, the poet Max Jacob, who, according to Fernande, had 'sustained, encouraged and helped [Picasso] when he was very young and going through a period of great unhappiness'. Max could tell fortunes, and long, bizarre and witty stories. 'He was a singer, a singing-teacher, a pianist, a comedian if called upon to be,' and, according to Fernande, 'the life-and-soul of all our parties.' At the Stein evenings he would dance bare-footed, or improvise plays 'in which he was always the main actor'. There were also critics and would-be art patrons like Maurice Raynal and André Salmon, and the troop of Picasso's artist friends from Barcelona, who followed him everywhere and provided him with small gifts of food they could hardly afford. Another member of Picasso's 'gang', as Fernande called them, was Apollinaire, a young poet of obscure, reputedly scandalous Italo-Polish origin. He would read out his latest poems: 'Oh how badly he spoke his own verse, and how he loved to recite it!' Fernande wrote. 'He certainly rendered his poems with staggering inadequacy, though he managed to move us nonetheless.' Perhaps it was Apollinaire who was the most loved, despite his notorious meanness and frequent silliness: 'He would deliberately purse his lips to minimise an already diminutive mouth, as if to give bite to what he was saying. He possessed a mixture of nobility and a kind of vulgarity, which came out in his crude childish laugh.'

Marie Laurencin was Apollinaire's mistress. She was the only woman artist among them, and often had to try hard, some thought too hard, to keep up. There were certainly tensions between her and Fernande, as Fernande's description reveals:

She had the face of a goat, with eyelids drawn back and short-sighted eyes set too close to a pointed, burrowing nose, always a bit red at the tip. She took a great deal of trouble to appear to be just as simply naïve as she actually was. . . . She was quite tall, and her dresses always hugged her slim, somewhat angular figure very tightly. Her hands were long and red, as young girls' hands often are, and dry and bony. She looked like a rather vicious little girl, or a little girl who wants people to think she's vicious.

51

In any case, she and other members of Picasso's gang were all made welcome at the Stein evenings. They joined a growing number of 'regulars' who came now to see the people as well as the pictures in the Stein collection.

What Picasso and his friends thought of the Stein salon is another matter. They couldn't have failed to be impressed by the pictures they saw there. Fernande remembers that in 1905, when they first began going to the rue de Fleurus,

> Their collection of pictures was already superb. They had Gauguins and Cézannes: amongst others, that beautiful portrait of the painter's wife, wearing a blue dress and sitting in a garnet-coloured arm-chair; and many Cézanne water-colours; women bathing against a background of country landscape. There was a little Manet, not an important one, but wonderfully sensitive; an El Greco; Renoirs – amongst them, *La Baigneuse de dos*, which is so amazingly luminous; some beautiful Matisse works; a Vallotton, as precise and cold as usual, and paintings by Manguin and Puy. There were dozens more, and now they were joined by some of Picasso's.

The people, on the other hand, were often baffling, even to the uneasily surprised Picasso. The American ladies he met, like the Cones of Baltimore, the mouselike Etta, and her overpowering sister Dr Claribel (whom Picasso called 'The Empress') and the group of homosexual ladies, two of whom Gertrude described and evocatively re-named in her story 'Miss Furr and Miss Skeene', were clearly alarming. '*Ils sont pas des hommes,*' he is said to have remarked, '*ils sont pas de femmes. Ils sont des Américains.*' In any case, Picasso's entry into the strange and sexually ambiguous world of the Stein salon was soon to prove financially rewarding. The Cone sisters, for example, often came to visit Gertrude while she posed for her portrait at the artist's studio. Then they were prevailed upon to buy in batches the discarded sketches for paintings that littered the studio floor. At a price of about two dollars a drawing, Picasso and Gertrude must have believed they were taking the Americans for something of a ride. But after several trips to Paris, and under the direction of Gertrude, the Cones were able to amass in this way the collection of Picassos that would form part of the nucleus of the Baltimore Museum of Art.

Picasso and his artist friends were quickly taken up by Sally and Michael Stein as well, though they never allowed their loyalty to Matisse to weaken under the combined influence of Gertrude and the brilliant Spaniard. Undeniably, Picasso was in those early days of their friendship both morally and financially supported by the Stein family – to such an extent that his later remark to Berenson shows not only gross ingratitude but a ludicrous irony: 'Ah those Steins,' he complained to the art historian, 'how they did exploit me!'

Between 1905 and 1906 Gertrude and Picasso became close friends. They were similar in many ways. Both were direct, a little rough with company, greedy, childish in their enthusiasms and petulant in their dislikes. Both of them had a quick and strong sense of humour – in Gertrude's case expressed by a full laugh, 'like a beefsteak', as Mabel Dodge described it; in Picasso's, what Gertrude called his 'high Spanish winnying'. And both, at that time, were beginning to be convinced they were geniuses. 'What is a genius?'

Henri Matisse, *La Femme au chapeau*, bought by Leo Stein in 1905.

The Collector

OPPOSITE Gertrude Stein at 27 rue de Fleurus
beneath her portrait by Picasso.

27 rue de Fleurus in 1906 (above) and
in about 1913 (below).

ABOVE Paul Cézanne
Grandes Baigneuses, c. 1895.
LEFT Pablo Picasso
Study for Nude with Drapery, 1907.
RIGHT Pablo Picasso, *La Maison
sur la colline, Horta de Ebro,* 1909.

OPPOSITE:
ABOVE Henri Matisse, *The Blue Nude,* 1907.
LEFT Pablo Picasso, *The Reservoir, Horta de Ebro,* 1909.
RIGHT Pablo Picasso, *The Architect's table,* 1912.

ABOVE Pablo Picasso,
Daniel-Henry Kahnweiler, 1910.

OPPOSITE Pablo Picasso,
Portrait of Gertrude Stein, 1906.

27 rue de Fleurus.

OPPOSITE Douanier Rousseau, *La Muse inspirant le Poète*, a portrait of Apollinaire and Marie Laurencin.

ABOVE AND BELOW
At 27 rue de Fleurus.

OPPOSITE:
ABOVE LEFT Juan Gris, *Still-life*, 1914.
ABOVE RIGHT Juan Gris, *Painting*, 1914.
BELOW Armchairs upholstered in *petit point*
by Alice B. Toklas after a design
by Picasso.
ABOVE Gertrude Stein at 27 rue
de Fleurus *c.* 1914.

ABOVE Caricature of the Armory Show, New York, 1913.
OPPOSITE Two views of the Armory Show.

Pablo Picasso,
Jeune fille aux fleurs.

What Are Masterpieces?

Gertrude wrote in *Everybody's Autobiography*. 'Picasso and I used to talk about that a lot.' And she says, 'Picasso and I used to dream of the pleasure of if a burglar came to steal something he would steal his painting or my writing in place of silver or money. They might now they certainly would not have then. . . .' In later years, Picasso was true to his conviction of his own worth. While Matisse as he became successful invested in paintings by Renoir, Cézanne, and Degas, Picasso used his fortune to buy back his own work.

Something else which Picasso and Gertrude had in common was French as a new language. As expatriates they were hardly unique in a city which drew foreigners from most of the world. Nor did their awkward French prejudice them in conversation with the various exiles, poets, self-made originals that made up the bizarre 'avant-garde' society of pre-war Paris. It even enhanced the childlike enthusiasms and outbursts in which they communicated. But most important, it allowed them – when they ceased to strain to understand the language around them – means of withdrawal from the general society in which they worked, Picasso as a painter, Gertrude as a writer. It brought them both a kind of solitude and privacy in which to carry on the formal experiments in which they were both engaged.

Any language is loaded with assumptions, moral and social, with a manner of thinking that is the basis of the culture to which it belongs. For Picasso, living in Paris meant, among other things, not being shaped or controlled by a daily exposure to the Spanish language and the inherent assumptions of Spanish society. For Gertrude, it meant both this independence from American thinking and, more precious to her as a writer, a point from which to look at the English language itself – removed from its function as a form of daily, living communication. In the isolation of Paris the English language became for her almost a dead thing, not a force which shaped thought, but as an artist's medium, lifeless until shaped. Years later Gertrude recognised the gift which not living in America had, by sheer confidence, conferred:

> One of the things I have liked all these years is to be surrounded by people who know no english. It has left me more intensely alone with my eyes and my english. I do not know if it would have been possible to have english be so all in all to me otherwise. And they none of them could read a word I wrote, most of them did not even know that I did write. No, I like living with so very many people and being all, alone with english and myself.

For most of Gertrude's life, 'not the half that made me but the half in which I made what I made', she was left alone with her English in this way, barricaded by a wall of foreign speech conveying foreign thought against influence by ordinary users of her language. The effect of this on her work was of course profound. But unlike most expatriate writers of English, Gertrude was able to use the given privacy with her language to create sentences that would cease to function as normally living form and become, as in her later and most difficult writing, a series of new and vital associational objects. However, at the time when Gertrude and Picasso became friends, Gertrude's

English was merely beginning its process of recession from something which does to something which is. In 1905 she began, as any foreigner might have, a project to improve her understanding of French. She began to translate the collection of short stories by Flaubert called *Trois contes*.

Gertrude's earlier work had been in the style of the psychological novel as developed by Henry James, with long and convoluted sentences conveying oblique hints about character and motivation. In this style, rather unsuccessfully sustained and somewhat melodramatic, she had exorcised the ghosts of her affair with May Bookstaver in *Q.E.D.* and had written a moral tale against corruption and decadence in the women's universities in *Fernhurst*. She had also begun in 1903 the first draft of her long novel *The Making of Americans*, which she would take up again between 1906 and 1911. In this work she developed her theory of human nature, drawing upon her observations of human 'types' during her experiments in psychology at Harvard. There, testing the various subjects for their automatic responses in a series of simple trials of concentration, she grew bored with the ostensible object of the experiments and began to analyse the subjects themselves according to their basic type or 'bottom nature' as she called it.

In *Everybody's Autobiography* she described how these observations led to the writing of her long book:

> I was much interested because I gradually found out what was what in The Making of Americans I called the bottom nature of each and every one of them and I was very much interested in the way they had their nature in them and sitting there while their arm was in the planchette and hardly vaguely talking it was interesting to me to see how I came to feel that I could come sometime to describe every kind there is of men and women and the bottom nature of them and the way it was mixed up with the other natures in them, I kept notes of each one of them and watched the difference between being active and being tired, the way it made some go faster and some go slower and I finally felt and which in The Making of Americans I began to do that one could make diagrams and describe every individual man and woman who ever was or is or will be living.

Such was her intention in 1903 when she began to write for the book. Now in Paris she continued to observe – at the Saturday evenings she was ideally placed to so do – and to record and classify in little notebooks the characteristics of speech and reaction of her new friends. It was during these observations that Gertrude developed her interest in things being 'the same but different', an interest which is constant in her work, and which was her ability to see in individuals not only those characteristics which make them individual, but those which make them part of a class. She would show that individuals have a pattern of behaviour and thought which is similar to those patterns in various other individuals. By their repeated reactions to different pressures or stimuli in life they could be shown to behave in one of a very few different ways. That made it possible to classify individuals according to their type or 'bottom nature', and repetition was the key to this classification. *The Making of Americans* was in Gertrude's mind to some extent a scientific work. It was to set forth a theory of behaviour, and for this purpose the style that she had developed in *Q.E.D.* and *Fernhurst* was useless. The language which describes ambiguity of situation to make *suggestion* of character, as in the late style of Henry James (and in her interest in character and the manner of its revelation as well as in the use of monotone and nuance Gertrude Stein is a descendant of Henry James) was not suited to an exposition of the psychological theories inspired by his brother. For this exposition she would have to find a more direct method of expression, than that she had contentedly developed from the tradition of James (she never claimed to have been influenced by him). In this discovery, the translation of the Flaubert stories was an important beginning.

The exercise of translating Flaubert had yielded for Gertrude new insights into language, and into the narrative form and the relation of story-teller to his characters. In 1905 she abandoned the project and began, instead, to write her own stories, though one at least was directly inspired by his. 'The Good Anna' was close in subject to Flaubert's 'Un Coeur Simple', about a simple-minded and devout woman who believes her parrot to be God. 'The Gentle Lena' was also a character study in this vein, though neither story had the acid humour of Flaubert's original. But the most important of Gertrude's *Three Lives*, as the collection of tales was eventually called, was 'Melanctha', a story about a young black woman and her lover, Jeff. Gertrude drew upon her knowledge of the black population of Baltimore, whose quarters she had often visited when delivering babies as part of her medical training. But she also, as she said later, had composed the tale while sitting for her Picasso portrait, and during the long daily walks from his studio in Montmarte to her Montparnasse flat. In the character of Melanctha, passionate and impetuous, and of Jeff, rational, steady and even-tempered, Gertrude shows the same interest in character types and conflicts as she had in *Q.E.D.* and *Fernhurst*. But what was new and remarkable in the story was its use of dialogue, extraordinary in a work of that time for its closeness to actual speech. Although it appeared to its critics as successful imitation of black speech, it was not intended as dialect. Significantly it was ordinary human speech, repetitive and ungainly, unstructured by the demands of literary form:

Don't you ever think I can be jealous of anybody ever Melanctha, you hear me. It's just, you certainly don't ever understand me. It's just this way with me always now Melanctha. You love me, and I don't care anything what you do or what you ever been to anybody. You don't love me, then I don't care any more about what you ever do or what you ever be to anybody. But I never want you to be being good Melanctha to me, when it ain't your loving makes you need it. I certainly don't ever want to be having any of your kind of kindness to me. If you don't love me, I can stand it. All I never want to have is your being good to me from kindness. If you don't love me, then you and I certainly do quit right here Melanctha, all strong feeling, to be always living to each other. It certainly never is anybody I ever am thinking about when I am thinking with you Melanctha darling. That's the true way I am telling you Melanctha, always. . . .

71

For several years before the writing of 'Melanctha' Gertrude had sat passively listening to Leo hold forth in company. Mabel Dodge described her at the Saturday evenings: 'Gertrude used to sit silently in the background and listen like the others. Sometimes she had a little puzzled look in her eyes.' And, she adds, 'I believe by puzzlement and wishfulness she finally arrived at a way of doing something new too.' The puzzlement was an expression of the same interest which Matisse had noticed and resented. Gertrude was passively and consciously observing, or more to the point, listening. 'The essence of being a genius,' she wrote in 'What Are Masterpieces' in 1936, 'is to be able to talk and listen to listen while talking and talk while listening.' She was, quite simply, analysing the way people used and expressed their nature in language. The results of her analysis are the extraordinary dialogues of Melanctha, in which words and phrases are repeated, insisted on, discontinued, restarted, forming blocks of thought which directly define the character of the speaker. Repetition of action was the way in which, according to her psychological theory, people revealed their 'bottom nature'. Repetition in speech was the way in which it was expressed.

The discovery of the revelatory nature of repetition in speech led in Gertrude's work to an understanding of the value of repetition itself, in exposition. In her discovery of the constant truth about human nature, which repetition of word and action reveal, she discovered not only the element of truth, but the element of constancy as well. The insight led to the development of the 'continuous present', a prolonging of the present moment or thought by the device of circling and retracing which repeating is. In the narrative passages of 'Melanctha', and in the descriptions in *The Making of Americans*, which she took up again after the stories, Gertrude developed repetition as a conscious literary form to express this 'continuous present'. Like the formal analyses of Cézanne, beneath whose painting she later said she had composed *Three Lives*, and the experiments of Picasso, which were soon to lead to the first Cubist pictures, the 'continuous present' was a means of holding the object or the statement out of time for the purpose of discovering its 'reality'. In their pictures, Cézanne and Picasso would come back to the object again and again in the same work to analyse its form and mass. Gertrude was to hold the same piece of description and by repetition with slight alteration build up an instant of action or thought or emotion into a mass – a larger-than-life statement of its reality. Here is such a passage from 'Melanctha':

> Jeff never, even now, knew what it was that moved him. He never, even now, was ever sure, he really knew what Melanctha was, when she was real herself, and honest. He thought he knew, and then there came to him some moment, just like one, when she really woke him up to be strong in him. Then he really knew he could know nothing. He knew then, he never could know what it was she really wanted with him. He knew then he never could know what it was he felt inside him. It was all so mixed up inside him.

All the elements of Jeff's knowing and not knowing are spread out and analysed in this passage, as mass is analysed in Cézanne. According to Gertrude it was the painter's work

72

that had taught her 'that in composition one thing is as important as another thing. Each part is as important as the whole'. In 'Melanctha' for the first time all the parts of the statement appear, so that the description comes closer to the reality described (in this case, Jeff's emotion) than was previously possible.

Of course, the differences between what Cézanne and the Cubists attempted and what Gertrude attempted in the 'continuous present' are vital. While the painters strove to make a non-narrative form convey a sense of movement in time, the 'continuous present' was an attempt to suspend the passage of time inside a narrative form. (A sentence will not hold still; it, at least, has a beginning, a middle, and an end.)

Gertrude's use of the 'continuous present' preceded the invention of Cubism in Picasso's work, but after 1907 (the date of *Les Demoiselles d'Avignon*) it progressed in complexity along similar lines to those of Cubist painting. Here is a late, and a typically short, passage from *The Making of Americans*, which Gertrude wrote between 1906 and 1911:

> He was convincing to any one in being one understanding something, he was convincing to almost any one in being one understanding any one's understanding that thing. He was understanding something, he was understanding any one's understanding that thing.

As an expatriate and as a natural listener, Gertrude had learned to analyse and reify language. She held back and analysed description as the painters Cézanne and Picasso held back and analysed objects. In both cases the whole was composed of various views of itself.

In its way, the 'continuous present' was an invention as momentous as Cubism. Both deriving from the analysis of form and mass in Cézanne, and from an interest in aspects of 'primitive' culture (in the case of the Cubists from African sculpture and artifacts, in Gertrude's case from black and immigrant speech, as in *Three Lives*), they were to challenge the common view of perception of reality and of time. Cubism challenged the held theory of perception by demonstrating that an object was everything we knew about it, that it could be seen at one time as a whole, all 360 degrees of it. It challenged the theory of time by making vision synchronic. That is, a man sees a face and, at the same time, both remembers the back of the head which he has seen previously and projects a view which he may see (the view of both eyes in a profile is a case of this in Picasso's work), thus unifying past and future in the present view. Like Gertrude's famous 'a rose is a rose is a rose is a rose', which was painted on the circumference of a plate in the rue de Fleurus, the 'continuous present' is also a view of reality from 360 degrees. It also denies, in its way, a concept of time, what Gertrude called the 'nineteenth-century idea' of a beginning, a middle, and an end. By constant returns to a point of beginning, the 'continuous present' suspends the inevitability of arriving at this end. To someone who, since adolescence, had a fear of 'death, not so much of death as of dissolution', the discovery would obviously have deep psychological appeal. Having made its discovery in 'Melanctha', and developing it in *The Making of Americans*, Gertrude began to respond to the act of writing in a profoundly spiritual way. It became for her a form of meditation that enabled her to remove herself from the real world, with its real and cruel passage of time. The spiritual quality in her work, the urgency of her pursuit of thought out of time is the vital and exciting element in her writing, and it began to develop in 1906, after 'Melanctha', which she rightly called 'the first definite step away from the nineteenth century and into the twentieth century in literature'.

In the early spring of 1906 Gertrude finished *Three Lives* and gave the almost illegible manuscript to her new handmaiden, Etta Cone, for typing out – Etta refusing to read the words coming out on paper until Gertrude gave her permission to do so. In the meantime, while Gertrude continued her sittings for the Picasso portrait, Michael and Sally Stein received the news of the devastating fire which had followed the San Francisco earthquake of 18 April, and decided to return to California to inspect the condition of their various properties in the city. With them they took some of their Matisses, among them the *Femme à la raie verte*, one of the paintings which had scandalised Paris in the previous Salon d'Automne. These were the first Matisses to be seen in America, and their impact was enormous. On 8 October that year, Sally wrote to Gertrude about her delight in leading the avant-garde:

> . . . You see, Mikey sprang the Matisses on one just for fun, & since the startling news that there was such stuff in town has been communicated, I have been a very popular lady. . . .
>
>   Oh, Albert Bender has been our most faithful & devoted – as always . . . but his devotion hardly stood the test of the 'femme au nez vert'. . . . Upon his demand, I assured him that perhaps he'd better spare himself this test, as I knew his belief in my infallibility was something very dear to him. 'No' he said, 'I shall *never, never, never* say, as others have, that you are crazy.' Well – he saw it – for two minutes he was speechless – then he meekly inquired – 'But don't *you* think you're crazy?' . . .

Sally enjoyed every minute of it, and, she added, 'I do love to show my clothes; they always create such a sensation.'

   That autumn in Paris, Picasso and Gertrude met again after the summer recess which was a routine of Paris living in those years. Before Picasso had left with Fernande for his summer of painting in Gosol, Spain – a summer during which he was to work in a style which forecast the first Cubist painting, *Les Demoiselles d'Avignon* of the following winter – he had told Gertrude that her portrait was not going well. 'I can't see you any more when I look,' he had said, and then proceeded to paint out the features of the face he'd been working on for so long. Now, on his return from Gosol, he finished the portrait without Gertrude, and invited the sitter and her friends to view the result. Gertrude's friends and her brother were a little horrified by the monolithic simplicity of the portrait, but Gertrude saw in it both the same principles of abstraction of essentials which she had been developing in her renewed efforts that summer with *The Making of*

Americans, and a profound likeness to herself. '. . . I was and I still am satisfied with my portrait,' she later wrote, 'for me it is I, and it is the only reproduction of me which is always I, for me.'

Soon after Picasso's return to Paris he noticed a large and imposing new painting in the Stein flat, Matisse's *Le Bonheur de vivre*, which had been bought the previous spring at the Salon des Indépendants. It was the painting that Gertrude later said 'had created the new school of colour which was soon to leave its mark on everything'. Not long thereafter Picasso and Matisse finally met. It was the start of an artistic alliance of importance to the work of both men, and of a notorious rivalry. In *The Autobiography of Alice B. Toklas* Gertrude tells a story which, if it is not true, is as good as true:

> [Picasso and Matisse] exchanged pictures as was the habit in those days. Each painter chose the one of the other one that presumably interested him most. Matisse and Picasso chose each one of the other one the picture that was undoubtedly the least interesting either of them had done. Later each one used it as an example, the picture he had chosen, of the weaknesses of the other one. Very evidently in the two pictures chosen the strong qualities of each painter were not much in evidence.

The meeting with Matisse brought to Picasso a new circle of friends and admirers, among them the painters Derain, Vlaminck and Braque, all working in the Fauve style and soon to contribute new ideas and impetus to the painting of the young Spaniard. Derain and Vlaminck, for example, had recently discovered a strange form of sculpture from Africa, and had begun to amass an inexpensive collection of primitive masks and figures, with which Picasso soon grew familiar. He too began collecting these and adapting their formal laws to his own work. By 1907 their influence could be seen in the large *Les Demoiselles d'Avignon*, on which he had worked continuously during the winter of 1906–7. Now celebrated as the beginning of Cubism, at the time the painting was a source of profound distress to his greatest admirers. Neither Derain, Vlaminck, nor as yet even Braque could understand what Picasso was doing, or recognise the application of African abstraction in the painting. Apollinaire, the loyalest defender of all things Picasso, kept a nervous silence, as did his dealers, recently beginning to anticipate from the artist's work a future prosperity. Even the Russian Shchukine, who rivalled Leo as the most important collector of the period, and whose pre-war purchases were to form the basis of the fabled collection of the Moscow Museum of Art, could not follow. 'What a loss for French art,' he whimpered when he saw the canvas. As for Leo, this new work by a considered protégé was horrendous. In *Appreciation*, he speaks of the origins of the work with characteristic and sublime condescension:

> Picasso was pleasantly childlike at times. I had some pictures relined, and Picasso decided that he would have one of his pictures too treated like a classic, though in reverse order – he would have the canvas lined first and paint on it afterwards. This he did on a large scale, and painted a composition of nudes of the pink period, and then he repainted it again and again and finally left it as the horrible mess which was called, for reasons I never heard, the *Demoiselles d'Avignon*.

For Leo the painting, like the portrait of his sister, was an unconfessed botch, 'as a whole incoherent', a new style grafted on to the old, not a deliberate, integrated attempt to work out a particular problem. But for Gertrude, the picture's ugliness was irrelevant; so she wrote in *Picasso* in 1938: 'In the effort to create the intensity and the struggle to create this intensity, the result always produces a certain ugliness, those who follow can make of this thing a beautiful thing because they know what they are doing, the thing having already been invented, but the inventor because he does not know what he is going to invent inevitably the thing he makes must have its ugliness.'

The revolution in art that succeeded the appearance of the *Demoiselles* sadly left Leo behind. As Professor Alfred Barr has written, 'For two brief years, between 1905 and 1907, he was possibly the most discerning connoisseur and collector of twentieth-century painting in the world.' Because, as Leo said, 'I was the only person anywhere, so far as I know, who in those early days recognised Picasso *and* Matisse. Picasso had some admirers, and Matisse had some, but I was alone in recognising these two as the two important men.' But the advent of Cubism marked the end of Leo's career as a crusader for the avant-garde in painting. The era of propaganda in the salons gave way as Leo lost interest, confining his comment more and more to snide remarks at the expense of the new works. In his memoir of 1947 he described his change of heart: '. . . in the six years from the time I bought that first Cézanne, I had had enough of intensive concern with so-called modern art. I had come to find it only very occasionally good enough.'

For all the acidity which was Leo's reaction to a development he could not understand, his description of Picasso in his early Cubist days has a certain exaggerated plausibility. Picasso had, as even his devoutest friends would admit, a power of enthusiasm which led him into occasionally foolish postures. His belief in his own worth was often unaccompanied by a sense of humour about himself and his pursuits. Leo describes the effects of his meeting with one Maurice Princet, who introduced Picasso and his friends (now his followers, Braque, André Salmon, Guillaume Apollinaire, and Derain) to some of the new century's discoveries in physics and mathematics:

There was a friend of the Montmartre crowd, interested in mathematics, who talked about infinities and fourth dimensions. Picasso began to have opinions on what was and what was not real, though as he understood nothing of these matters the opinions were childishly silly. He would stand before a Cézanne or a Renoir picture and say contemptuously, 'Is that a nose? No, this is a nose', and then he would draw a pyramidal diagram. 'Is this a glass?' he would say, drawing a perspective view of a glass. 'No this is a glass', and he would draw a diagram with two circles connected by crossed lines. I would explain to him that what Plato and other philosophers meant by 'real thing' were not diagrams, that diagrams were abstract simplifications and not a whit more real than things with all their complexities, that Platonic ideas were worlds away from abstractions and couldn't be pictured, but he was bent now on doing something important – reality was important whatever else it might be, and so Picasso was off.

Since, for Leo, Cubism had such ludicrous origins, he could never take its results seriously. '. . . When analysis is only a kind of funny business,' he wrote, 'the synthesis will be only another kind of funny business.'

Leo's reaction against Picasso's experiments in the style that was soon to be called Cubism, led to a general disinterest in modern painting. Even Matisse was to lose Leo's patronage when, early in 1908, Leo bought his last painting from the artist. Although in his later life Leo was to praise Matisse as 'a fortunate man, who has accomplished his destiny', he ceased to take a serious interest in his work. As he later wrote, 'It was the rhythm in Matisse that I found insufficient.'

Fortunately for the Matisses, although by now they were beginning to be better off financially, not all the Steins shared Leo's view. Sally and Michael continued to buy regularly and to get their friends to buy from the painter. Furthermore, in the winter of 1907–8, while Picasso was making his Cubist diagrams and horrifying Leo, Sally instituted the short-lived Matisse classes. In an atelier hired for the occasion, Matisse taught a small band of faithful (including two later-known artists, Hans Purrmann and the American, Max Weber) the principles of his art. It was around this time that Gertrude began to refer to Matisse as *cher maître* – a piece of sarcasm which indicated a new and total allegiance to the work of his rival, Picasso.

In 1918, in a letter to Alfred Stieglitz in New York, Gertrude defended her refusal to follow Matisse after the development of Cubism. His work and the work of his followers (with whom she classed Delaunay, for example) was 'a disguised but poverty stricken realism; the realism of form having been taken away from them [by the discoveries of Cubism] they have solaced themselves with the realism of light'. Gertrude's acceptance of Picasso's work at a time when many of his previous supporters felt lost must not be taken too seriously as an act of aesthetic daring. She did not, now, for example, buy the much-mocked *Les Demoiselles d'Avignon*, which remained in the artist's studio until 1937, when it was bought by the Museum of Modern Art in New York. According to Leo, it was not until '1911 or 1912 [that] Gertrude bought a cubist Picasso, the first picture for which she was responsible to come into 27 rue de Fleurus.'

Unlike Leo, Gertrude was not a connoisseur, although that is now her reputation. She treated all pictures fairly casually. 'Once an oil painting is painted, painted on a flat surface, painted by anybody who likes or is hired or is interested to paint it, or who has or has not been taught to paint it, I can always look at it and it always holds my attention. The painting may be good it may be bad, medium bad or very bad or very good but anyway I like to look at it.'

Cubism did not present more difficulties than any other kind of painting. From her earliest experiences with art '. . . to the cubism of Picasso nothing was a bother to me. Yes of course in a way it was a bother to me but not the bother of a refusal. That would not have been possible being that I had become familiar with oil paintings, and the essence of familiarity being that you can look at any of it.'

Gertrude was able to accept Picasso's work precisely because, unlike Leo, she didn't really *care* about principles of art. It was Leo's caring that now hampered him; but

77

Gertrude's taste was totally personal and arbitrary. As Mabel Dodge later wrote, she was '. . . daring in a snobbish period of art. I remember she adored ridiculous miniature alabaster fountains, with two tiny white doves poised on the brink, that tourists bought at the shops on the Lung'Arno, and she had a penchant for forget-me-not mosaic brooches, and all kinds of odds and ends that she liked as much as a child likes things. She didn't care whether they were "good" or not.'

In her later years, when Leo was no longer there to direct her aesthetic views she began to collect odd, sometimes kitsch works by painters such as Berman and Tchelitchew, and Sir Francis Rose, painters who flattered her, or in whose lives she took a personal interest, or, most importantly, as was now the case with Picasso, whose work she thought proceeded along lines similar to her own. The great Stein collection was in reality Leo's making. When he no longer showed an interest in collecting, she took up the work of Picasso and his Cubist allies – but for reasons of her own.

Whether Picasso ever understood that Gertrude considered herself in artistic alliance with him is not clear. In *Appreciation*, Leo reported a meeting with the artist in 1929 in which Picasso told him: ' "By the way, I saw Gertrude recently. She said to me 'There are two geniuses in art today, you in painting and I in literature'." Picasso shrugged his shoulders "What do I know about it? I can't read English. What does she write?" ' Leo told him that Gertrude was using words 'cubistically' and that most people could not understand what she wrote; Picasso, according to Leo, said: ' "That sounds rather silly to me. With lines and colours one can make patterns, but if one doesn't use words according to their meaning they aren't words at all." '

On the other hand, it is probable that, whether or not he listened, Picasso would have heard from Gertrude what it was they had in common. In any case, it soon became important to her to think that they did. If, as people said, Picasso was a genius, although his paintings to many seemed ugly and inept, then perhaps she, too, was a genius, although her writing might seem, by ordinary standards, equally clumsy and grotesque. It was an important alliance for one who was just beginning to know that her writing would be radically different from that of other users of English.

Gertrude embraced Cubism, in part, precisely *because* it was an obstacle for her brother. For years she had sat patiently taking a secondary role in the goings-on at the rue de Fleurus. Now she began to tire of his leadership. 'He continued to believe in what he was saying when he was arguing,' she wrote later, 'and I began not to find it interesting.' Cubism was a game she could play without her brother.

4

Grammar Is As Disappointed

THE COLLECTION OF PAINTINGS at the Stein flat continued to attract visitors, both those who wanted to see the Picassos and Matisses (there was still no gallery showing their work) and tourists eager to mock. Sally Stein's triumphant trip to San Francisco had spread the fame of the Stein collection to the West Coast, and visitors from America were frequent at both Stein ménages.

One afternoon in the autumn of 1907 Gertrude was invited by her sister-in-law to meet two new Californian acquaintances, Harriet Levy and her friend, Alice Toklas. Gertrude must have been interested in the visitors, for she invited Alice, at least, to call on her shortly thereafter. Alice, who arrived slightly late on this second meeting, recalls Gertrude's formidable scowl of impatience, but she also remembers being overwhelmed, or so Gertrude has her remember in *The Autobiography of Alice B. Toklas*:

> I was impressed by the coral brooch she wore and by her voice. I may say that only three times in my life have I met a genius and each time a bell within me rang and I was not mistaken, and I may say in each case it was before there was any general recognition of the quality of genius in them. The three geniuses of whom I wish to speak are Gertrude Stein, Pablo Picasso and Alfred Whitehead.
> In that order.

Alice soon became a 'regular' at the Stein salon. Born in America of good middle-class bohemian stock, she accepted the goings-on in Paris with ease. Although the modern art appalled her ('The pictures were so strange that one quite instinctively looked at anything rather than at them just at first'), she did cut her own figure among an exceptional crowd. Mabel Dodge's description of her indicates the highly Romantic nature of her looks and style, and explains something of her appeal for Gertrude:

> She was slight and dark, with beautiful gray eyes hung with black lashes – and she had a drooping, Jewish nose, and her eyelids drooped, and the corners of her red mouth and the lobes of her ears drooped under the black folded Hebraic hair, weighted down, as they were, with long heavy Oriental earrings. . . . Alice wore

straight dresses made of Javanese prints – they are called batiks nowadays. She looked like Leah, out of the Old Testament, in her half-Oriental get-up – her blues and browns and oyster whites – her black hair – her barbaric chains and jewels – and her melancholy nose. Artistic.

During the summer of 1908 Alice and her friend Harriet Levy took a villa in Fiesole, near the one in which Gertrude and Leo habitually stayed. There she offered to take over the typing of *The Making of Americans*, on which Gertrude was working. By the winter of 1909–10 Alice had manoeuvred Harriet back to America, and herself into the Stein household. Alice had become indispensable. Mabel Dodge, who first met Gertrude around this time, noticed something odd about the presence of the new typist-companion: 'Alice Toklas', she later wrote, 'entered the Stein ménage and became a hand-maiden. She was always serving someone, and especially Gertrude and Gertrude's friends. She was perfect for doing errands and was willing to run all over Paris to get one a special perfume or any little thing one wanted. . . . She began by being so self-obliterating that no one considered her very much beside thinking her a silent, picturesque object in the background. . . .'

But those who considered Alice no more than this were soon shown to be very much mistaken. Already in 1908 Leo and Gertrude had begun to disagree about the importance of the work of Picasso. Nor did Leo show any real interest in Gertrude's writing. Passages in *The Making of Americans* show the beginnings of Gertrude's doubt about the character of Leo, a beginning resentment of his self-importance, of his indifference to her own interests. They indicate that domestic clashes were becoming more frequent between them, and that a tenseness and suspicion existed between brother and sister.

> Two knowing each other very well in being living might be thinking they are not knowing what the other one is thinking about the other one. Two knowing each other very well in living might be telling each one of them to some one what they are thinking of the other one. Two knowing each other very well in living might not be telling any one what they are each one of them thinking about the other one.

Another passage suggests the effects of Leo's disapproval of her writing:

> Disillusionment in living is the finding out nobody agrees with you not those that are and were fighting with you. Disillusionment in living is the finding out nobody agrees with you not those that are fighting for you. Complete disillusionment is when you realise no one can for they can't change. The amount they agree is important to you until the amount they do not agree with you is completely realised by you. Then you say you will write for yourself and strangers, you will be for yourself and strangers and this then makes an old man or an old woman of you.

Gertrude had, apparently, accepted that she would have to continue alone in her writing and in her conviction of her own worth. Leo, certainly, could not 'change'. But another passage on the page suggests that Alice had early on convinced Gertrude that she might be the one to replace him:

. . . You write a book and while you write it you are ashamed for every one must think you are a silly or a crazy one and yet you write it and you are ashamed, you know you will be laughed at or pitied by every one and you have a queer feeling and you are not very certain and you go on writing. Then some one says yes to it, to something you are liking, or doing or making and then never again can you have completely such a feeling of being afraid and ashamed that you had then when you were writing or liking the thing and not any one had said yes about the thing.

Throughout *The Making of Americans* there are signs, revealed in passages such as these, of a gradual and important change in Gertrude's affections. When, years later, she wrote of her disaffection from Leo, she explained it in terms of his ceasing to interest her, not as the case must have been, at least in part, of her work ceasing – along with Picasso's Cubism – to interest him. 'I think cubism whether in paint or ink is tommy-rot,' he wrote in 1913. 'As for Picasso's late work, it is for me utter abomination. Somebody asked me whether I didn't think it mad. I said sadly, "No, it isn't as interesting as that; it's only stupid." '

With his attack on modern art and on Picasso in particular, with whom Gertrude had discussed the significance of being a genius, Leo violated Gertrude's long-held belief in her brother's wisdom. She began to classify herself with Picasso not only in terms of aims, but in terms of importance as well. Alice – who told her often enough she was something even greater than the artist – played on her wounded vanity, and Leo was the one who suffered. The change in Gertrude's thinking about her brother and herself was expressed years later, not without a little guilt, in *Everybody's Autobiography*: 'It is funny this thing of being a genius, there is no reason for it, there is no reason that it should be you and should not have been him, no reason at all that it should have been you, no no reason at all.'

What Alice got out of her relationship with Gertrude is easier to understand. Her arrival in Paris coincided with what Braque later called the 'heroic age of cubism'. She began to meet the artists whose fame had already spread to San Francisco before she left. She even had French lessons from the mistress of the famous Picasso, Fernande, with whom she discussed French fashion and French perfume. Most important, she had become accepted as Gertrude's companion in time to be invited with her to the famous Banquet Rousseau.

The origins of this celebrated event are obscure. Leo claims to have had a large hand in it, though he was not among the admirers of the recently taken-up painter: 'I recognized a talent, a gift for composition and color,' he later wrote, 'but I don't want that sort of thing hanging on my wall and staring me in the face all the time. I like to talk with the people of the village, but I don't want to live with them.' In any event, it was, said Leo, because he asked to hear Rousseau play his violin, that the dinner was planned. Taking up Leo's request, Fernande asked the old painter to come and dine 'a week from Saturday, and I'll ask the Steins, and Braque and Apollinaire and Marie Laurencin'. 'That', said Leo, 'was agreed to, but when the news got about, so many others wanted to come that the dinner was changed to a picnic supper, famous through all the world as the Banquet Rousseau.'

According to Fernande, on the other hand, the whole thing was intended as an elaborate joke at the artist's expense: 'The project was received enthusiastically by the gang, who were overjoyed at the prospect of pulling the *douanier*'s leg.' Thirty people were invited to the studio at the Bateau Lavoir where a sort of throne for Rousseau was erected with a banner behind it reading *Honneur à Rousseau*. As it turned out, the dinner that Fernande had ordered from the nearby restaurant had not arrived by eight, by which time most of the guests had already arrived and begun their drinking. While they waited for Fernande to return from the shops with the ingredients for a new dinner, they went to a bar where they continued to drink, developing into a rowdy and hysterical crowd. According to Fernande's account of the evening:

> . . . poor Marie Laurencin . . . who was just making her début in this artists' world, became the object of determined attentions from some of the guests who had decided to make her drunk.
>
> It was not difficult. The first thing she did when she came back into the studio was fall onto the jam tarts which had been left on the sofa, and, with her hands and dress smothered in jam, start kissing everybody. She got more and more excited, and then found herself quarrelling with Apollinaire, until finally she was rather brutally packed off to mother.
>
> . . . Rousseau, who thought the food had arrived, installed himself gravely and tearfully on the dais that had been erected for him. He drank more than he was used to and finally fell into a peaceful sleep.

The dinner continued, with songs and poems from Apollinaire. Rousseau was woken up and played his violin. Gertrude and Alice were asked and refused to sing songs of the American Indians. 'There were the Pichots, the Fornerods, André Salmon and Cremnitz, who at the end of the evening did an imitation of *delirium tremens*, chewing soap and making it froth out of his mouth, which horrified the Americans. Jacques Vaillant, Max Jacob, Apollinaire and Leo and Gertrude Stein were there and many, many others.' Including Lolo, the pet Donkey from the café Lapin Agile, who ate the flowers off Alice Toklas's hat. Rousseau, at least, was deeply touched by the evening: 'Indeed, so happy was he that he accepted with the greatest stoicism the regular dripping of wax tears on to his brow from a huge lantern above him. The wax droppings accumulated to form a small pyramid like a clown's cap on his head, which stayed there until the lantern eventually caught fire.'

Rousseau was one of the few of Gertrude's acquaintances to take an interest in Alice, largely because she looked so much like his second wife. Others were a little suspicious of her, but accepted her because Gertrude did. Max Jacob, when he read her horoscope said she had 'a tendency to theft', and it was a characteristic reaction. But no one could doubt her devotion to Gertrude, or the fact that she earned her way.

Early in 1909, the year Alice moved in to the rue de Fleurus flat to transcribe the first part of *The Making of Americans*, she also dealt with the proofs of Gertrude's *Three Lives*, the three short stories Gertrude had finished in 1906. In 1907 Gertrude had tried to get them published through friends in New York. After several unsuccessful attempts, it was apparent that no commercial publisher would take them, and she was finally persuaded to pay for their printing herself. But not even the vanity press she chose was quite satisfied with the writing. A letter soon followed the proofs of the book to suggest that since the author was evidently not totally at ease with the English language, an editor ought to be sent to help out with the corrections. 'My proof-readers report that there are some pretty bad slips in grammar, probably caused in the type-writing,' it begins cautiously. 'I think, either you ought to go over these yourself very carefully correcting them all or else allow us to have some one do it here.' There soon followed a visit from one Mr Sanborn, the Paris representative of the Grafton Press, whom Gertrude quickly informed that 1) she was a perfectly well educated American, and 2) not one word of the text could be altered. In April, when the proofs had been returned and the book was being printed, Gertrude received another letter from the head of the Grafton Press: 'I want to say frankly that I think you have written a very peculiar book and it will be a hard thing to make people take it seriously. . . .'

In the event, some, though not many, did take it seriously. The book appeared with jacket blurbs by the then-known writer Neith Boyce, and her husband, Leo's friend, Hutchins Hapgood. By means of a clipping service, Gertrude soon discovered that some reviewers, at least, had been sympathetic to what they saw as a new 'naturalism', particularly in the depiction of Negro and immigrant life in Baltimore. Although she would have preferred to be recognised as something other than a 'naturalist' writer, Gertrude was pleased enough. She sent copies of the book to friends and relatives, and to various famous writers, one of whom was the writer H. G. Wells. More than three years later she received from him a reply: 'I have just read *Three Lives*. At first I was repelled by your extraordinary style, I was busy with a book of my own & I put yours away. It is only in the last week I have read it – I read it with a deepening pleasure & admiration. I'm very grateful indeed to you for sending it to me & I shall watch for your name again very curiously & eagerly.

Another late, but more important response came from her old friend and mentor William James, whom she had not seen since his visit to Paris some years ago. Then he had looked at her collection of modern painting and remarked, 'Well, I always did tell you to keep an open mind.' Now, in May 1910, from a sanatorium in Bad Nauheim, came his transparently kind letter:

I have had a bad conscience about 'Three Lives'. You know how hard it is for me to read novels. Well, I read 30 or 40 pages, and said 'this is a fine new kind of realism – Gertrude Stein is great! I will go at it carefully when the right mood comes.' But apparently the right mood never came. I thought I had put the book in my trunk, to finish over here, but I don't find it on unpacking. I promise you that it shall be read *some* time! You see what a swine I am to have pearls cast before him! . . .

James never did finish the book. He died three months later from a respiratory illness.

His letter, nevertheless, was received as encouragement by his former pupil.

While Gertrude's confidence in herself and her work increased after the publication of *Three Lives*, Leo's sense of his own failure deepened. Gertrude began to dominate the Saturday evenings, while Leo withdrew into his own world of doubts and jealousies, provoked no doubt by the relative achievements of his sister and Picasso and by the gradual takeover by Alice of the role of Gertrude's confidante. But mostly, it was the failure of his own work which upset him. Now that so many young artists were following the lead of Picasso, propaganda was no longer interesting. Painting was also less rewarding than it had been. In February 1910 Leo wrote to Mabel Weeks of his confusion: 'Quite lately I was explaining to Matisse, to Gertrude and others why I was going to stop painting entirely. I had an abundance of good reasons. The same night at twelve o'clock I began to do a big composition and have since done much the best things yet. It's hard to be so smart that the next minute can't fool you.'

Leo's confusion was also fostered by his recent involvement with a young artist's model of the district. In 1910 Nina Auzias had noticed Leo in a café and pointed him out to her friends: ' "See that man who is passing. He will be my husband. I know it." "Mad girl" they cried, laughing, "you do not know who he is – he is the great American Maecenas Leo Stein. Do not be angry, but fearful" ' – so ran Nina's account. Leo had then asked Nina to pose for him in the nude, but she had refused, saying she was too 'badly built'. According to Nina, Leo finally persuaded her, but after she had posed for a while, told her, 'yes, you are right, you are badly built and not at all inspiring'. Then Nina leapt up and kissed him. Leo reacted by spitting on the floor (all this, lovingly recounted by Nina). Then he gave her her modelling fee and dismissed her. The second episode of this extraordinary affair took place a short time later when Leo, pensive, though likely unashamed, once again approached the model, this time to ask her to act as a subject for psychological study (Leo had also been a pupil of William James). For a fee four times the modelling rate she would sit and talk to him while he listened. This proposition Nina accepted, and she began to tell Leo of her adventures, her three current lovers (one of whom she shared with Isadora Duncan), like, as she said, 'a modern Scheherazade to her modernistic sultan'. Leo's clinical distance must have both attracted and annoyed Nina. Later, as their affair advanced, Leo encouraged her not only to continue her outside liaisons, but to keep him informed as well. This is a typical passage from one of Leo's letters to Nina: 'Darling, . . . It is a little strange that you should have thought I would be angry because of the affair with S. How can you amuse yourself, indeed, if it is not thus? That is to say, if one is not lazy, one must act to be happy, and naturally one must act as one can. . . .'

It was a long time before Leo came to accept Nina as something more than a curious specimen of foreign morality (they finally married in 1921). But she did help him to work out his own attitudes to conventional sexual mores. It must be wondered what Leo's reaction to the prolonged appearance of Gertrude's female lover can have been.

Friends and Protégés

Gertrude Stein and Alice B. Toklas in Venice, 1908.

RIGHT Mabel Dodge at the Villa Curonia, *c.* 1912.
BELOW Isadora and Lisa Duncan, with Sergei Iessenine (who was also the lover of Nina Auzias who was later to marry Leo Stein).
BELOW RIGHT Isadora Duncan; poster by Van Dongen.

LEFT Henri Matisse by André Derain,
1905.
BELOW The 'Bal Van Dongen', 1912
(1 is Matisse and 6 Van Dongen).

ABOVE Juan Gris.

RIGHT Marie Laurencin, *Apollinaire and his Friends*, (*c.* 1908) which later Gertrude Stein exchanged with Kahnweiler for his portrait by Picasso. Gertrude Stein is on the far left, Apollinaire in the centre, next to Picasso and Fernande Olivier. Marie Laurencin is sitting on the right. BELOW Apollinaire with the Picabias in 1914.

ABOVE Douanier Rousseau, *Self-portrait*.

OPPOSITE Picasso in his studio on Boulevard Clichy.

The crowd at La Rotonde, 1916, by Gabriel Fournier.

It is likely that his long tolerance of the situation was due more to confusion and indecisiveness on his part, an awareness of his own deficiencies as a lover – which his long and soul-bearing letters to Nina clearly show – than to a conscientious indifference to sexual unconventualities.

But the situation cannot have been easy for Leo. He must have resented the constant presence of the 'typist' as he called her. By the autumn of 1912, after Gertrude and Alice had spent the summer in Spain, they all met up at Mabel Dodge's villa in Florence. Here Leo confided his feelings to Mabel. Leo, Mabel wrote later, was

> ... grieving over Gertrude and Alice. He had always had an especial disgust at seeing how the weaker can enslave the stronger as was happening in their case. Alice was making herself indispensable. She did everything to save Gertrude a movement – all the housekeeping, the typing, seeing people who called, and getting rid of the undesireables, answering letters – really providing all the motor force of the ménage. . . . And Gertrude was growing helpless and foolish from it and less and less inclined to do anything herself, Leo said; he had seen trees strangled by vines in the same way.

Whatever Alice's effect on Gertrude's character, the effect on her work was crucial. She was not only Gertrude's typist and protector from all the disagreeable and distracting elements of life. She was also, most important, Gertrude's audience – and for a long time, Gertrude's only audience. As Gertrude's experiments with language became more advanced in the years following the *Three Lives*, so they became more remote from normal usage. Much of the work of this period, culminating in the 'Portraits' and *Tender Buttons* of 1912, had been called unreadable, impenetrable, hopelessly obscure. Much of it demands of the reader an almost superhuman effort to understand, and raises the question of whether writing has the right to make such demands. Like all important writing, Gertrude's work, when it is successful, is a dance – but a dance that needs a partner. When her work is exciting, which it often is, it is not because of the mere presence of the writing, but because of its teasing half-presence, and its invitation to join this dance. Even when joining is impossible, the element of invitation remains. The seductiveness of this invitation could not have been present in Gertrude's work had she written for herself alone, or even for herself 'and strangers'. She wrote most of the time, in those early days, for Alice, who read each day what Gertrude called the 'daily miracle', and responded, typed each day. Like prisoners sending messages through cracks in a wall, Gertrude and Alice communicated in this strange language of thought and response to thought.

The year 1912 was an important one for Gertrude and her work. She had finished her long novel, *The Making of Americans*, now one thousand pages long, the previous autumn, and had been working at various shorter pieces which followed up the experiments the longer work had begun. Now she began to look for people who might publish some of these more 'difficult' works. With the publication of *Three Lives* in America in 1909 and with the continued reports of the importance of the Stein collection, her

E.A.—8

reputation as an eccentric member of the Paris avant-garde grew. In February 1912 Alfred Stieglitz wrote from New York that he would like to publish photographs of some of the work of Matisse and Picasso, accompanied by Gertrude's portraits of them. Although he could afford to pay nothing for the pieces, he did convince Gertrude that their appearance in his magazine *Camera Work* would greatly add to the prestige of both herself and the artists. To this she agreed, and she sent him the two pieces, both written in 1909.

'One whom some were certainly following was one who was completely charming', she begins her portrait of Picasso. 'One whom some were certainly following was one who was charming. One whom some were following was one who was completely charming. One whom some were following was one who was certainly completely charming.'

'You have undoubtedly succeeded in expressing Matisse and Picasso in words, for me at least,' wrote Stieglitz.

Gertrude's conquests of publishers was rarely so easy. She had sent some of the later, more abstract material to a recommended publisher in England. His reply, if cleverer than most (it is a good parody of one style of her work at the time) was to become the standard:

> 13, Clifford's Inn
> London, E.C.
> Apr 19, 1912

Dear Madam,

I am only one, only one, only one. Only one being, one at the same time. Not two, not three, only one. Only one life to live, only sixty minutes in one hour. Only one pair of eyes. Only one brain. Only one being. Being only one, having only one pair of eyes, having only one time, having only one life, I cannot read your M.S. three or four times. Not even one time. Only one look, only one look is enough. Hardly one copy would sell here. Hardly one. Hardly one.

Many thanks. I am returning the M.S. by registered post. Only one M.S. by one post.

> Sincerely yours,
> A. C. Fifield

Gertrude Stein's 'difficult' pieces of this time were, and remain, difficult. The more abstract portraits, for example, proceed by no logic other than an associational one, and they depend on rhythmical reading to sustain them. They coincide with the period of 'difficult' works which Braque and Picasso were engaged upon at this time, and I believe Gertrude was much encouraged by their experiments to pursue her own. Just as now the 'subject matter' of Picasso paintings becomes almost impossible to 'read', and the painter provides few clues as to the existence of the violin, or sitter, for example, so, too, the new works of Gertrude were providing few clues, few strains of narrative or logical succession of ideas. Total abstraction is a possibility in painting (although Gertrude later called abstract painting 'pornographic'), in writing it is hopeless. The reader searches and searches for meaning. It is the sole object of his reading and one which he cannot, as he can in painting, suspend indefinitely. Where there appears to be some sense as in the Portraits of this period, the effect of alternately suspending understanding in the most abstract sections, and grasping it eagerly where the writing shines forth – a beacon of comprehensibility' – the effect is dizzying. Here is a passage from the very 'difficult' 1912 *Portrait of Mabel Dodge at the Villa Curonia*: 'All the attention is' when there is not enough to do. This does not determine a question. The only reason that there is not that pressure is that there is a suggestion. There are many going. A delight is not bent. There had been that little wagon. There is that precision when there has not been an imagination. There has not been that kind abandonment. Nobody is alone.' Dizziness was the effect of Gertrude's prose (even of the relatively easy works of 1909) on those who had willingly followed her in *Three Lives* (written 1905–6). Berenson said exactly that in his letter acknowledging receipt of a copy of *Camera Work* (he also makes it a point of comparison between her and Picasso): 'As for your prose I find it vastly more obscure still. It beats me hollow, & makes me dizzy to boot. So do some of the Picasso's by the way.'

Henri-Pierre Roché, the long-time friend who had introduced Leo to Picasso in 1905, and who had praised *Three Lives*, wrote to Gertrude in February 1912 with great concern, and, I think, insight into the nature of the 1909–12 work – the style best exemplified in the later parts of *The Making of Americans*:

I start reading your style only when I feel very strong & want in a way to suffer.
– After a few minutes I am giddy, then sea-sick, though there are islands to be seen.
– It is no river, no sea, c'est une inondation l'hiver dans la campagne. . . .

Of course it is very enjoyable to let oneself go & write heaps – but – Why don't you finish, correct, re-write ten times the same chaotic material till it has it's very shape worthy of its fullness? A condensation of 60 to 90% would often do? . . .

Melanctha is great in my memory. I was quite at home with her, though I had already some toil. I thought your style would concentrate, it has enormously expanded. . . .

Are you not after all very lazy?

There is certainly an element of truth in Roché's charge. Passive and indulgent by nature, writing was a form of occupation that appealed to Gertrude. As she later wrote in *Everybody's Autobiography*: '. . . what is known as work is something that I cannot do it makes me nervous, I can read and write and I can wander around and I can drive an automobile and I can talk and that is almost all, doing anything else makes me nervous.' She also believed in the value of passivity. 'It takes a lot of time to be a genius, you have to sit around so much doing nothing really doing nothing.' She slept late every morning, she never hurried, and she allowed the slow, heavy rhythm of her life to find its natural expression in her work. She never altered a single word of what she wrote. Her work had to express her as she really, totally, exactly was. It was, she said, intended as 'an exact description of inner and outer reality'. Exact, as in a laboratory; and as in a laboratory, one could not tamper with the results.

She worked sitting alone at night, writing slowly and steadily until dawn when she went to bed. She never varied this routine, and when in the autumn of 1912 she went with Alice to stay with Mabel Dodge at the Villa Curonia, her methods of working fell under the sharp eye of her hostess. What we know about the manner of Gertrude's writing comes from such observations as hers:

> Gertrude always worked at night. After everyone was asleep she used to sit . . . writing automatically in a long-weak handwriting – four or five lines to the page – letting it ooze up from deep inside her, down on to the paper with the least possible physical effort; she would cover a few pages so and leave them there and go to bed, and in the morning Alice would gather them up the first thing and take them off and type them. Then she and Gertrude would always be so surprised and delighted at what she had written, for it had been done so unconsciously she'd have no idea what she'd said the night before.

It was like a baby's delight in its own physical processes, and Alice, like a mother, would be there to congratulate Gertrude on what had been produced. The process of creation was, for Gertrude at this stage, a sensuous, physical, almost 'automatic' thing. In painting, she thought, it could be the same, as she suggests in her 1909 'Portrait' of Picasso:

> One whom some were certainly following was one working and certainly was one bringing something out of himself then and was one who had been all his living had been one having something come out of him.
>
> Something had been coming out of him, certainly it had been coming out of him, certainly it was something, certainly it had been coming out of him and it had meaning, a charming meaning, a solid meaning, a struggling meaning, a clear meaning.

The lethargic pleasures of Gertrude's laborious night writing at the Villa Curonia were uninterrupted by the extraordinary comic sexual drama that raged about her, and to which she contributed.

Mabel Dodge, a charming and intelligent young American woman whom Gertrude had met the year before in Paris, was clearly enchanted by the writer. 'Why are there not more *real* people like you in the world?' she had written after their first meeting. Now she had invited Leo, Gertrude and Alice to spend the autumn at her villa in Fiesole. Here Gertrude wrote *The Portrait of Mabel Dodge at the Villa Curonia*, which Mabel had printed in an edition of three hundred and bound in Florentine wallpaper. Here, too, she met some of Mabel's friends, among them Constance Fletcher – the American author of *Kismet* – soon to become one of Gertrude's closest friends, and the young

André Gide. There was also a young blond tutor for Mabel's children, whom Gertrude watched pursuing Mabel while her husband Edwin was away. While Gertrude worked all night at her writing, Mabel would lie awake, trying to resist the advances of the young suitor, and to keep them out of Gertrude's hearing. One night when the suitor came again to her room, Mabel was torn between longing and duty. She allowed him as far as her bed, where she stopped him, according to her memoirs, repeating, ' "I can't – I can't – I can't . . ." and so we remained, for heaven knows how long – while Gertrude wrote on the other side of the wall, sitting in candle-light like a great Sibyl dim against the red and gold damask that hugh loosely on the walls. "And then there was that little wagon . . .".'

It was a curious assembly of characters that hot, end of summer in Florence. Leo, perturbed, talked endlessly in long, convoluted sentences about art and philosophy, the sexual demands of Nina, and, above all, the digestion that was once again troubling him. Gertrude, in ebullient spirits, crashed and bounded into every discussion, unsettling sensibilities with her great physical presence. Although Gertrude, like Picasso, was short (five foot two), people thought of her as monumental, as in Mabel Dodge's description of her: 'Gertrude Stein was prodigious. Pounds and pounds and pounds piled up on her skeleton – not the billowing kind, but massive, heavy fat. She wore some covering of corduroy or velvet and her crinkly hair was brushed back and twisted up high behind her jolly, intelligent face.' When Gertrude returned from a long walk, she would, according to Mabel,

> . . . arrive just sweating, her face parboiled. And when she sat down, fanning herself with her broad-brimmed hat with its wilted, dark-brown ribbon, she exhaled a vivid steam all around her. When she got up she frankly used to pull her clothes off from where they stuck to her great legs. Yet with all this she was not at all repulsive. On the contrary, she was positively, richly attractive in her grand *ampleur*. She always seemed to like her own fat anyway and that usually helps other people to accept it. She had none of the funny embarrassments Anglo-Saxons have about flesh. She gloried in hers.

Hovering in the background was the demure and sexually mimsing figure of Alice, quietly enticing. Again, Mabel has described her: 'She was forever manicuring her nails. Her hands were small and fine and almond shaped, painted glistening nails they looked like the hands of a courtesan. Every morning, for an hour, Alice polished her nails – they had become a fetish with her.' The oddness of the assembly was never so odd as at mealtimes, when Leo would sit picking at his food, worried about its consequences, while Mabel tried to ignore the eyes of the tutor, and Gertrude and Alice did their bizarre comestic duet: 'She loved beef,' Mabel wrote of Gertrude, 'and I used to like to see her sit down in front of five pounds of rare meat three inches thick and, with strong wrists wielding knife and fork, finish it with gusto, while Alice ate a little slice daintily, like a cat.'

Once, at least, the sexual atmosphere at the table became too much:

... One day at lunch, Gertrude, sitting opposite me in Edwin's chair, sent me such a strong look over the table that it seemed to cut across the air to me in a band of electrified steel – a smile travelling across on it – powerful – Heavens! I remember it *now* so keenly!

At that Alice arose hastily and ran out of the room on to the terrace.

Jealous as she was of Gertrude's feelings for Mabel, Alice was their helpless victim that autumn. Gradually, however, she managed to squeeze a wedge of mistrust between Gertrude and Mabel which was never removed.

For the time being, however, Mabel proved a useful friend. That winter she was in New York, where she and Edwin had decided to settle, and brought with her copies of Gertrude's beautifully bound *Portrait of Mabel Dodge at the Villa Curonia*. The New York intelligentsia were already familiar with Gertrude's 'Portraits' of Matisse and Picasso, published in Stieglitz's *Camera Work* the previous summer, and with *Three Lives*, which had appeared in 1909. Now when Mabel's 'Portrait' was circulated and read out at the various literary salons, it created a furore. Mabel Dodge soon became the height of fashion in New York, bearing on her shoulders the mantle of the European avant-garde and heralding the voice of the mysterious Gertrude Stein.

New York was alive with curiosity about the European art world. The great Armory Show was in the making, and Mabel was soon approached for advice by two of its organisers, the New York painters Walt Kuhn and Arthur Davies. Her job was to choose the important latest works from private collections and artists' studios all over Europe. In this capacity she excelled, though she insisted her real mission was to promote the work of Gertrude Stein. An article on Gertrude was soon commissioned by the magazine *Arts and Decorations*, to coincide with the opening of the Armory Show in February 1913. The article was a simple, clear piece of devotion: 'Life at birth is painful and rarely lovely,' it began. It was soon followed by an interview with Mabel in the *New York Times*, conducted by the young reporter Carl Van Vechten – later one of Gertrude's closest friends and staunchest champions. The article was to have photographs of both Mabel and Gertrude.

While the news of this imminent fame was transmitted in letters from Mabel to Gertrude ('I am your faithful and incomprehending Boswell,' Mabel wrote), Gertrude was making her own plans for her future. 'Don't be surprised Mabel,' she wrote early in 1913, 'but I may be going over to England to see if I can find a publisher. I don't know very well what I am to do when I get there but everyone tells me that I should go, ... if you know anyone who knows a publisher and can tell me how to meet him, will you let me know.'

Finally, that January, Gertrude and Alice did go to London, to see John Lane, publisher of Beardsley and the *Yellow Book*, and a man with a high reputation for interest in 'advanced' literary works. From the Knightsbridge Hotel Gertrude again wrote to Mabel in New York:

We are having a very amusing time here and as yet nothing is decided but John Lane and the English Review are nibbling. John Lane is an awfully funny man. He waits round and asks a question and you think he has got you and then you find he hasn't. Roger Fry is going to try to help him land me. . . . But the most unexpected interested person is Logan Pearsall Smith [Berenson's brother-in-law]. He went quite off his head about your portrait and is reading it to everybody. Never goes anywhere without it and wants to do an article on it for the English Review.

Among other things he read it to Zangwill and Zangwill was moved. He said, 'And I always thought she was such a healthy minded woman, what a terrible blow it must be for her poor dear brother . . . '

Nevertheless, as Gertrude described it, Pearsall Smith continued to read the Portrait to Zangwill. Zangwill got angry, and said to Logan: 'How can you waste your time reading and rereading a thing like that and all these years you have refused to read Kipling.' 'And,' Gertrude adds, 'the wonderful part of it was that Zangwill was not fooling.'

The time spent in London, although it did not result in the publication of her work, was a pleasure for Gertrude and Alice. From Gertrude's letters to Mabel it is clear that she was meeting all the right people in London, chiefly the Bloomsberries, and chief of them, for Gertrude, Roger Fry: 'Roger Fry is being awfully good about my work. It seems that he read Three Lives long ago and was much impressed with it and so he is doing his best to get me published. His being a quaker gives him more penetration in his sweetness than is usual with his type, it does not make him more interesting but it makes him purer.'

Gertrude's letters also give news of London society, still influenced by the nineties Aesthetes and given to Whistleresque refinements, as in Paul and Muriel Draper's dinner party for Gertrude and Alice: '. . . the table a complete scheme in white only broken by the vivid colour of food and wine. . . . They know a considerable number of amusing people and the place is attractive.' There was also news of a more modern set, the latest thing, in fact, from Italy: 'Also the futurists are in town. You know Marinetti and his crowd. He brought a bunch of painters who paint houses and people and streets and wagons and scaffoldings and bottles and fruits all moving and where they are not moving there are cubes to fill in. They have a catalogue that has a fiery introduction demolishing the old salons and they are exhibiting at Bernheims and everybody goes.'

The year 1913 witnessed the fruition of all the recent developments in painting and literature and music. Modernism was proclaimed everywhere – by the Cubists, Futurists, Vorticists, Imagists. Everywhere Gertrude looked she saw signs of the old order crumbling, and she recognised her own part in the creation of the new: 'Did I tell you that I heard Electra in London,' she wrote to Mabel in New York. 'I enjoyed it completely. It made a deeper impression on me than anything since Tristan in my youth. He has done what Wagner tried and couldn't, he has made real conversation and he does it by intervals and relations directly, without machinery. After all we are all modern.'

All that next year in Paris, the interest in Gertrude Stein that her trip to London and the publicity of Mabel Dodge in New York had aroused began to create for her an important reputation. People she had met in London now came as a matter of course to visit her in Paris, and they brought their friends – Roger Fry, Wyndham Lewis, the painters Henry Lamb and Augustus John, the sculptor Epstein, socialites like Nancy Cunard and Lady Ottoline Morrell, 'looking,' said Gertrude, 'like a marvellous feminine version of Disraeli'. There were also visits from new artists, whose names had been linked with hers at the New York Armory show, including Marcel Duchamp, whose painting *Nude Descending a Staircase* had been the scandal of that exhibition, and Francis Picabia, later to become an important friend of Gertrude's, but at the time impressive to her for 'the vulgarity of his delayed adolescence'. That year, too, Gertrude at last received her copy of Mabel Dodge's article. At first she was thrilled. 'I am delighted with it,' she wrote to Mabel, 'Hurrah for gloire.' But as the article began to work its effects, and as people sent from New York to meet her continued to talk enthusiastically about the charms of its author, Gertrude began to be annoyed. With Alice's encouragement, Gertrude grew resentful of Mabel's share of the limelight. Mabel had not, she thought, made it sufficiently clear 'who was the bear and who was leading the bear'.

Nonetheless, and in large part thanks to Mabel, Gertrude was soon the centre of flattering attention. In the winter of 1913–14 John Lane came to Paris, bearing with him a copy of Wyndham Lewis's magazine *Blast*, for which he sought a contribution from her. Although Gertrude did not promise this, she did arrange with him to make a second trip to England that summer, in order to get some of her work published. In February 1914, Donald Evans, a friend of Mabel Dodge's in New York, offered to publish some of the 'plays' Gertrude had been writing. Not wishing to have these published until they were produced (an unlikely event), she offered him instead the manuscript of her most abstract work *Tender Buttons*. When the work appeared in June that year, Gertrude's position in literary circles was assured. There had never been *anything* quite like it. *Tender Buttons*, written between 1910 and 1912 the year of her trip to Spain, when 'she first felt a desire to express the rhythm of the visible world', was a series of 'still life' descriptions. Divided into three parts, the book concerns itself ostensibly with definitions of objects, food, rooms:

A SOUND

 Elephant beaten with candy and little pops and chews all bolts and reckless reckless rats, this is this.

A PETTICOAT

 A light white, a disgrace, an ink spot, a rosy charm.

MILK

 Climb up in sight climb in the whole utter needles and a guess a whole guess is hanging. Hanging hanging.

Grammar Is As Disappointed

ASPARAGUS

Asparagus in a lean in a leap to hot. This makes it art and it is wet wet weather wet weather wet.

The care with which there is incredible justice and likeness, all this makes a magnificent asparagus, and also a fountain.

All of 1913 and 1914 Gertrude was courted and flattered as an important member of international modernism – as all of it was then generally called. Egged on by fame, and flattered by Alice, Gertrude must have been irritatingly ebullient – especially for Leo. At the Saturday evenings, now more and more filled with people who wanted to meet Gertrude as well as see the collection, Leo openly sulked. He was rarely willing to participate as he once had: 'I would rather harbour three devils in my insides than talk about art,' he wrote in 1913. The increasing fame of Picasso and the Cubists, and the linking in the public mind of their work with that of his sister was becoming more and more irksome to Leo. The encouragement of Alice began to seem to be at his expense; they were, he felt, ganging up on him. He had written a parody of the now-famous *Portrait of Mabel Dodge*, a series of nonsense sentences, and had shown it to them. Their reaction was disappointing: 'Gertrude and Alice even have the cheek to pretend that they understand this (which I can do in part sometimes),' he wrote to Mabel Weeks in February 1913, 'but as Gertrude thought it very nice and I had very sarcastical intentions we evidently didn't understand it in the same way.'

In a long letter to Mabel Weeks that same month, Leo wrote that his and Gertrude's points of view were irreconcilable:

One of the greatest changes that has become decisive in recent times is the fairly definite 'disaggregation' of Gertrude and myself. The presence of Alice was a godsend, as it enabled the thing to happen without any explosion. As we have come to maturity, we find that there is practically nothing under the heavens that we don't either disagree about, or at least regard with different sympathies. The crucial thing of course is our work. In my case this is of comparatively little importance because in the first place I never suspected Gertrude of having any interest in the criticism of ideas, and in the second place I have no desire for glory. . . . Gertrude on the other hand hungers and thirsts for *gloire*, and it was of course a serious thing for her that I can't abide her stuff and think it abominable. . . . To this has been added my utter refusal to accept the later phases of Picasso with whose tendency Gertrude has so closely allied herself. They both seem to me entirely on the wrong track. . . . Her artistic capacity is, I think, extremely small. I have just been looking over the Melanctha thing again. Gertrude's mind is about as little nimble as a mind can be. She can only express herself by elaborately telling all at full length. . . . It is the insistence on the facts that makes, to my thinking, the significance of the book. Well, Gertrude also wants to create a great and original form. . . . The *Portrait of Mabel Dodge* was directly inspired by Picasso's latest form. The last time but one that Picasso and I talked about art he said that once upon a time he had thought that an artist should be an animal with a talent, like Renoir, and should just go ahead and paint, but now he had changed his mind and felt that an artist should use his intelligence to develop his art. Picasso is a man of the finest sensitiveness, the keenest observation and a strong sense of man in his humours. Goethe said of Byron that he was a child when he thought, but Picasso is then a babe in arms. Both he and Gertrude are using their intellects, which they ain't got, to do what would need the finest critical tact, which they ain't got neither, and they are in my belief turning out the most Godalmighty rubbish that is to be found.

In the same month as this letter, Leo sold some of his Picasso paintings to buy a Renoir. He had not bought a Picasso work since 1910 ('. . . and that was one that I did not really want, but I had from time to time advanced him sums of money, and this cleared the account'). The news of the sale upset the artist. Leo's reaction against the painter had an element of vengeance in it. When Gertrude wrote to Leo about Picasso's reaction to the sale, Leo responded: 'You can tell Pablo that I regard my new Renoir as a little testimonial from what the art-conscious world would call the Spanish School of Painting. *Voilà España!*'

The selling of the Picassos was only the first step in the dismantling of the Stein ménage. Since 1897, when Leo and Gertrude had shared a house together in Baltimore, they had collected together prints, books, objects, furniture, and, in the last twelve years, the paintings which their joint finances allowed. The process of dividing the collected goods might have been arduous, but it followed easily. Most of the Gauguins and Matisses had already been sold. Since Leo now loathed the Picassos which they both owned, he agreed to give these, apart from a few drawings which had personal significance for him, to Gertrude. In exchange, she would allow him all the Renoirs, the Cézanne *Apples*, and the Renaissance furniture, for his new home in Florence. After all that was settled, some time in the spring of 1914, Leo wrote to Gertrude about their new arrangement: 'I very much prefer it that way, and I hope that we will all live happily ever after and maintain our respective and due proportions while sucking gleefully our respective oranges.'

Leo's departure wasn't the only change in Gertrude's life. Picasso had moved with his new mistress Eva to the fashionable suburbs, and although he continued to see Gertrude, his visits became rarer. So did those of Apollinaire, Marie Laurencin, and of course Fernande. Hélène, their cook since the first of the famous Saturday night dinner parties at rue de Fleurus, was also gone. But it was Leo's leaving that most altered Gertrude's life. He had been her protector and her mentor for forty years: 'We always had been together,' she wrote in *Everybody's Autobiography*, 'and now we were never at all together. Little by little we never met again.'

The last two years in Paris had been tremendously important years for Gertrude Stein; now on the eve of her summer trip to London, following the publication of *Tender Buttons*, her life in Paris had suddenly, irrevocably changed. As she wrote in *The Autobiography of Alice B. Toklas*, 'in the spring and early summer of nineteen fourteen the old life was over'.

5

The Last
Nineteenth-Century War

IN JULY 1914 Gertrude and Alice set off for a short trip to England to arrange for the publication of *Three Lives* with John Lane. They also intended to buy some furniture for the rue de Fleurus flat to replace that which Leo had taken away. 'We had to measure ourselves into the chairs and into the couch and to choose chintz that would go with the pictures, all of which we successfully achieved.'

After signing her contract with Lane, Gertrude and Alice went to Cambridge to stay with the mother of their friend Hope Mirlees. Here they met Alice's third genius, Alfred North Whitehead. Gertrude and Whitehead talked endlessly about philosophy and history, and Whitehead was obviously impressed. He invited the Americans to spend a weekend with him at his home in Lockeridge, Wiltshire. In the event, the weekend proved a long one. Ever since their arrival in England, there had been talk of little else than the coming war. Now on that weekend they heard about the invasion of Belgium. Simple social convention gave way in the face of the general anxiety and depression, and Alice and Gertrude were implored to stay in Wiltshire, at least until the situation became clearer. In *The Autobiography of Alice B. Toklas*, Gertrude describes through Alice those early days of the war: '. . . I can still hear Doctor Whitehead's gentle voice reading the papers out loud and then all of them talking about the destruction of Louvain and how they must help the brave little belgians. Gertrude Stein desperately unhappy said to me, where is Louvain. Don't you know, I said. No, she said, nor do I care, but where is it.'

Gertrude and Alice were by no means the oddest guests at that long house party in Wiltshire. Bertrand Russell was there, making everyone jumpy and irritable with his talk of pacifism. There was George Moore, whom Gertrude said looked like 'a prosperous Mellin's Food baby', and Lytton Strachey, with his 'silky beard and . . . faint high voice'. Lytton Strachey's sister was somewhere in Germany at the time, and Mrs Whitehead gave him the name of an official whom he might contact about her safety. 'But, said Lytton Strachey faintly, I have never met him. Yes, said Mrs Whitehead, but you might write to him and ask to see him. Not, replied Lytton Strachey faintly, if I have never met him.'

Those summer weeks at Lockeridge were tense for everyone, and there were constant arguments between the pacifist guests and the good citizens of the county. As an American living in France, Gertrude was continually asked for her views. Would the German population in the States keep the Americans from joining the Allies? Gertrude was pleased to deny it emphatically. She was less pleased, however, to answer questions on more specific issues. One day a bishop and his wife were dining with them at the Whiteheads. The wife, according to *The Autobiography of Alice B. Toklas,*

> . . . said solemnly to Gertrude Stein, Miss Stein you are I understand an important person in Paris. I think it would come very well from a neutral like yourself to suggest to the french government that they give us Pondichéry. It would be very useful to us. Gertrude Stein replied politely that to her great regret her importance such as it was was among painters and writers not with politicians. But that, said Mrs Bishop, would make no difference. You should I think suggest to the french government that they give us Pondichéry. After lunch Gertrude Stein said to me under her breath, where the hell is Pondichéry.

When England finally declared war on Germany, on the fourth of August, there was general relief. Alice and Gertrude went at once to London to arrange their finances from America and to get their visas. But on their return to Wiltshire, they heard terrified reports from the Whiteheads that their son, North, had just enlisted. It did not take long, however, for Mrs Whitehead's friend, Lord Kitchener, to arrange a safe commission for him.

The scrambling, muted panic of the first days of the war made Gertrude and Alice very nervous. They were far from home, and the news from France was not good: 'The germans were getting nearer and nearer Paris and the last day Gertrude Stein could not leave her room, she sat and mourned. She loved Paris, she thought neither of manuscripts nor of pictures, she thought only of Paris, and she was desolate. I came up to her room, I called out, it is alright Paris is saved, the germans are in retreat. She turned away and said, don't tell me these things. But it's true, I said, it is true. And then we wept together.' Finally that October, many weeks after the original weekend invitation, Gertrude and Alice were able to leave for Paris – accompanied by Mrs Whitehead, bearing papers from Lord Kitchener and an overcoat for her son at the Front.

On the crossing from England to France, Gertrude and Alice had noticed the Belgian soldiers, with 'tired but watchful eyes'. They came back to a changed Paris, with its silent streets and male-less population. The emptiness was frightening. One of the few painters who was still in the capital, the American Alfred Maurer, described what the evacuation had been like: 'I was sitting said Alfy at a café and Paris was pale, if you know what I mean, said Alfy, it was like pale absinthe. Well I was sitting there and then I noticed lots of horses pulling lots of big trucks going slowly by and there were some soldiers with them and on the boxes was written Banque de France. That was the gold going away just like that, said Alfy, before the battle of the Marne.' Gertrude soon took similar precautions. She sent off her manuscripts in large bundles to friends in New York, and prepared the rue de Fleurus for the war.

That first winter of the war was a shock for most of them. There was a new austerity, a new hunger. There were trucks and guns and daily news of deaths. But there was, too, the odd consolation:

> The first year of the war, Picasso and Eve, with whom he was living then, Gertrude Stein and myself, were walking down the boulevard Raspail a cold winter evening. There is nothing in the world colder than the Raspail on a cold winter evening, we used to call it the retreat from Moscow. All of a sudden down the street came some big cannon, the first any of us had seen painted, that is camouflaged. Pablo stopped, he was spell-bound. C'est nous qui avons fait ça, he said, it is we that have created that, he said. And he was right, he had. From Cézanne through him they had come to that.

Paris, which had been the most cosmopolitan city in Europe before the war, was now divided between patriots and aliens, combatants and non-combatants, and non-combatants did not count. Braque, Derain, and Léger were all at the Front; it was where everyone wished to be. Apollinaire, though he was of Polish-Italian descent, managed to enlist in the French army, as did the Armenian Marcoussis, whose mistress Eva had recently left him to live with Picasso. But many of Gertrude's friends could not enlist. Among these were Picasso and Juan Gris, both Spaniards, Lipchitz, a Russian, and Daniel Kahnweiler, a German, who was now forced to surrender his collection of art-works and remain in exile in Switzerland. Even Frenchmen who were unacceptable to the French army were held in suspicion. So, for example, the Cubist painter Herbin, too small to carry a knapsack, was left alone in Paris to scrape up what living he could in the deserted capital. The plight of these painters was severe. Picasso was by now wealthy enough to look after himself and his mistress Eve, and established enough to remain safely indifferent to the patriotic hysteria around him, but for the others the war years were ferocious. Herbin was only rescued, with Gertrude Stein's help, by Roger Fry, who was able to sell his work in England. Juan Gris, now penniless in the South of France, had to live off the charity of friends like Kahnweiler and Gertrude, who in October 1914, agreed to join the American Michael Brenner, another patron, in sending Gris 125 francs a month. 'Of course Gertrude and Brenner expect to get pictures in exchange', Gris wrote Kahnweiler at the time. Gris remained touchy about the arrangement, and in the end it was abandoned. In January 1915 Gertrude and he quarrelled when he insisted on repaying 200 francs of the advanced money. It was well known that he could hardly afford to be so particular.

Gris's letters from Collioure, where he later met Matisse, who was serving there as a guardian of railway bridges, describe the plight of the artist stranded in the French provinces. They also give a clear picture of the way the war was to change the lives of artists who had produced so much in the preceding years. These were friends Gertrude was not to see, except sporadically, until the end of the war. Here is a passage from Gris's letter to Kahnweiler of 30 October 1914:

> Matisse also writes from Paris that: he has seen Mme Derain, who is rather hard up, and Derain is in the front line; that Vlaminck is painting for the army at Le Havre, and that Picasso, from whom I have heard nothing for two months although I have written to him, withdrew a large sum – they say one hundred thousand francs – from a bank in Paris on the outbreak of war. People are surprised he sent me 20 frs. Gleizes wounded. Segonzac also. De la Fresnaye, who volunteered, is sick at base camp. I have no news of Braque, the one who interests me most.

From a letter of 15 February 1915 to Maurice Raynal at the Front:

> Marcous is in the artillery. He came to see me yesterday to show off his sergeant-major's stripes. He was furious, what's more, because in my ignorance I called him 'corporal'. He swears like a trooper and is deep in ballistics because he's determined to become a Second Lieutenant of the Reserve, which was the rank he had in Russia.

15 May to Maurice Raynal:

> As for news of friends: Braque has been seriously wounded but there is no news of him. [Braque was wounded in the head at Carency, and was eventually trepanned.] Vaillant is going for a month's convalescence to Brittany. He has a dislocated shoulder. Metzinger is a medical orderly at Saint Ménéhould, and Max [Max Jacob, who had seen Jesus in Montmartre in 1909, had seen him again in 1914 in a cinema, and who had recently been converted to the Catholic Church] treats the Sacré-Coeur as his office.

May 1915 to Maurice Raynal:

> Max, who gets sillier everyday since his conversion, is always at either the Sacré-Coeur or St Pierre. He even goes there at night so that he can be a perpetual worshipper.

4 August 1915 to Kahnweiler:

> There are times now when I think that everything is finished, and that after the war it will be impossible to sell a single picture.

Meanwhile, as another alien, Gertrude Stein was having her own difficulties. The war made everything exciting, but the absence of most of her friends also made life deathly dull. 'It was a strange winter,' she wrote of those first months of the war, 'nothing and everything happened.' Finally, in the spring of 1915, the boredom and strangeness became unbearable, and Gertrude and Alice decided to leave Paris, to stay with an American friend, William Cook, who was sitting out the war in the then-unknown resort of Palma de Mallorca.

The two women settled quite comfortably into life in Mallorca, where they were soon joined by a new French cook, and their first dog, a Mallorcan hound called Polybe. Every day they read the news of the war, and worried letters from friends in America. There was sporadic news, too, from Paris, of recent poetry readings or piano recitals, and in December 1915, of the death of Picasso's mistress Eva. Gertrude also received the American reviews of *Tender Buttons*, which had appeared in June 1914. Most of the reviews were hostile and ridiculing, content to dismiss the writer by means of parody. Unperturbed, Gertrude continued to write her abstract prose, and to watch from a safe distance the progress of the war.

Gertrude and Alice enjoyed their easy life in Palma. There was good food and sunshine and bullfights. But they did not remain unaware of the war that was taking place in France, and with news of the losses at the Battle of Verdun in the spring of 1916, their fears for their adopted country became acute. Despite their terror of the Zeppelin raids in Paris, Gertrude and Alice quickly decided they had had enough of their refugee's life and set off to join the war effort at home.

Gertrude was delighted to be back in Paris; she found it changed: 'It was no longer gloomy. It was no longer empty.' Picasso was there, with his new high-society Chilean mistress, and his new friends Erik Satie and Jean Cocteau, whom Gertrude soon took up. They heard news of friends, of Braque's successful convalescence, of Apollinaire who had been trepanned in May 1916, after a superficial head wound. But complications had set in, and none of his friends was sure what the extent of the damage would be. Apollinaire's recent collection of poems had been published that April. Called *Le Poète assassiné*, there were fears the title might turn out to be prophetic.

Meanwhile, Gertrude had joined the American Fund for French Wounded, and was learning to drive. William Cook, who had followed the women to Paris, and was now earning his living driving a taxi, gave Gertrude her lessons every night outside the fortifications of the city. Gertrude had been informed by the woman who ran the American Fund that if she wished to help she would have to have a car. Duly, Gertrude sent off a request to cousin Fred Stein in America, and early in 1917, the car, soon to be called 'Auntie' after Mrs Solomon Stein, who always kept her head in a crisis, arrived. Here is Gertrude's account from *The Autobiography of Alice B. Toklas* of that memorable encounter between herself and her first automobile:

We went outside of Paris to get it when it was ready and Gertrude Stein drove it in. Of course the first thing she did was to stop dead on the track between two street cars. Everybody got out and pushed us off the track. The next day when we started off to see what would happen we managed to get as far as the Champs Elysées and once more stopped dead. A crowd shoved us to the sidewalk and then tried to find out what was the matter. Gertrude Stein cranked, the whole crowd cranked, nothing happened. Finally an old chauffeur said, no gasoline. We said proudly, oh yes at least a gallon, but he insisted on looking and of course there was none. Then the crowd stopped a whole procession of military trucks that were going up the Champs Elysées. They all stopped and a couple of them brought over an immense tank of gasoline and tried to pour it into the little ford. Naturally the process was not successful. Finally getting into a taxi I went to a store in our quarter where they sell brooms and gasoline and where they knew me and I came back with a tin of gasoline and we finally arrived at the Alcazar d'Eté, the then headquarters of the American Fund for French Wounded.

Auntie was to be the first of a series of Fords, proudly owned and recklessly driven by Gertrude Stein. Fords had a special significance to her. They formed part of her theory of modernism and repetitions. The first Fords had all been repetitions of a prototype, identical in body as in colour (Henry Ford told prospective customers they could have any colour as long as it was black), and they were examples of the American invention of 'series manufacturing', which had made America the first twentieth-century nation. Also they were all the same but different. Now Gertrude owned one of these symbolic objects: American and modern, and a repetition.

In the Ford, Gertrude and Alice were soon sent to Perpignan in the south west of France, to deliver supplies for the wounded. On this long drive through the French countryside ('. . . we had never been further from Paris than Fontainebleau in the car and it was terribly exciting'), Gertrude began to give lifts to soldiers, a custom she kept up any time of day or night, and quite fearlessly. She began, too, her habit of interviewing. She asked them all searching questions about their education, their girlfriends, their fathers' business. Her interest in soldiers also related to her philosophy of repetition and identity, since they were all dressed uniformly, functioned identically, yet were each different from the others. But her friendships with soldiers, maintained through long correspondences, were genuine enough – though she, like Alice, in *The Autobiography* was not always as careful as she might have been in answering their letters: '. . . One had to remember all their family histories,' she writes in Alice's voice, 'and once I did a dreadful thing, I mixed my letters and so I asked a soldier whose mother was dead to remember me to his mother, and the one who had the mother to remember me to his wife. Their return letters were quite mournful.'

When the American troops arrived in France at the end of 1917, Gertrude was delighted. She had not seen so many Americans since her last visit to New York in 1904, and had never met so many from so many different states. 'It was quite a thrilling experience. Gertrude Stein of course talked to them all, wanted to know what state and what city they came from, what they did, how old they were and how they liked it. She talked to the french girls who were with the american boys and the french girls told her what they thought of the american boys and the american boys told her all they thought about the french girls.'

The American doughboys were not as wonderful a sight to the French army as they were to Gertrude Stein. The word 'doughboy' fitted many of them admirably. They were thought of as heavy and naive, young calves in uniform who were as likely as not to get into trouble. In *Everybody's Autobiography*, Gertrude repeats a story told to her by a French soldier at the time:

A young French soldier who was one of those who taught the American soldiers how to use the mitraleuse told me that to his surprise the Americans understood very quickly the mechanics of the gun but their physical reaction in action was very slow very much slower than the French one, consequently it took more Americans to do anything than it did Frenchmen and so of course it was done less quickly. He also told a story of when he posted the Americans as sentry he told them that when they heard a sound like quack quack it was not a duck it was a German and he said he told them this and they always understood and then when it was the German they did not disappear quickly enough and the German got them.

Another characteristic of the young Americans in France was their bafflement at the old-fashioned machinery and life-style of the French. Their complacency about the superior skill and speed of American machinery was sometimes fatal, as in the case of a young doughboy whom Gertrude visited in hospital: 'One of them fell off the train. He did not believe the little french trains could go fast but they did, fast enough to kill him.'

After their work in Perpignan was finished, Gertrude and Alice returned to Paris, where they heard more news of friends, and of the latest events in the arts. The combined talents of Cocteau, Satie and Picasso, who had all been working recently with the Russian Ballet in Italy, had produced one of the delights of the Paris season in the ballet *Parade*. It was a rare pleasure for an art world devastated of its talents, and it served to remind a beleaguered population of what its artists could do. In Juan Gris's letter to Maurice Raynal in May 1917, he writes of what he saw as another triumph for Cubism:

> I like *Parade* because it's unpretentious, gay and distinctly comic; Picasso's *décor* has lots of style and is simple and Satie's music is elegant. . . . It's a sort of musical joke in the best of taste and without high artistic pretensions. . . . I even believe that it is an attempt to do something quite new in the theatre. It had quite a lot of success although a group was organized to boo it. The idea of course was to boo Cubism, but the unprejudiced people were nevertheless swung over and it was the applause which prevailed.

In reality, however, Cubism as a revolutionary art form, had long been dead. A month after Gris's letter to Raynal, an event was to herald the succession of the new art-philosophy, Dada, born among the exiles of Zurich and proclaimed by Tristan Tzara when he fired a pistol at the first-night performance of Apollinaire's *Les Mamelles de Tirésias,* called by one critic a 'cubist play' and hitherto accepted as the last word in avant-garde.

Besides his designs for *Parade*, Picasso had brought something else back from his stay in Italy with the Russian Ballet: Olga Koklova, a ballerina in the company and now Picasso's wife. He had sent Gertrude 'a wedding present of a lovely little painting and a photograph of a painting of his wife'. For Picasso, his marriage was a real step into the establishment, and his friends were sceptical. Braque, convalescing near Avignon, where

E.A.—9

Gertrude and Alice visited him in 1918, referred to her scathingly as a 'real young lady'. Apollinaire, he told them, had also just married a 'real young lady'.

The news of Apollinaire which Gertrude, now stationed at Nîmes, heard from Paris was not good. The trepanning operation had not been a success, and he was now in constant pain. In October 1918, Guillaume Apollinaire began to decline quickly. He died on 10 November, the day before the Armistice, to the sounds of patriotic Frenchmen decrying the Kaiser with the words *à bas Guillaume*.

Following the news of the Armistice, Gertruce and Alice returned from Nîmes to Paris. War work was proving expensive and they were now forced to sell the last remaining Matisse, the formerly scandalous *Femme au chapeau*. Sally Stein bought the painting for some five hundred dollars, and with the extra money the women were now able to volunteer for relief work in Alsace.

It was here that Gertrude and Alice had their first glimpse of a battle-field, with its lines of trenches and muddy, burnt-out landscape. 'To any one who did not see it as it was then,' she later wrote in *The Autobiography*, 'it is impossible to imagine it. It was not terrifying it was strange. We were used to ruined houses and even ruined towns but this was different. It was a landscape and it belonged to no country.' Gertrude also found working among the Alsatians strange. They were very eager to be French, but they were not French: 'The french whatever else they may be are frank. They are very polite, they are very adroit but sooner or later they always tell you the truth. The alsatians are not adroit, they are not polite and they do not inevitably tell you the truth. Perhaps with renewed contact with the french they will learn these things.' After two years of war work in France, and some fifteen years as a French resident, Gertrude Stein had become a chauvinist. And France, in turn, was to recognise her services. At the end of the war both she and Alice Toklas were awarded the *Reconnaissance Française*.

On their return to Paris, in May 1919, Gertrude and Alice tried to resume the life they had led before the war. 'But it was a restless and disturbed world,' as Gertrude wrote in *The Autobiography*. Everyone was edgy, she and Picasso quarrelled, there were strange new people in the city. Paris was taken over by the members and followers of the Peace Commission: 'We saw a tremendous number of people but none of them as far as I can remember that we had ever known before. Paris was crowded. As Clive Bell remarked, they say that an awful lot of people were killed in the war but it seems to me that an extraordinary large number of grown men and women have suddenly been born.'

The artists had returned to Paris, but as Gertrude wrote in *The Autobiography*, 'It was a changed Paris. Guillaume Apollinaire was dead.' Daniel Kahnweiler's collection of Cubist paintings, which had been taken over by the government during the war, was now to be sold. It 'was the first occasion after the war where everybody of the old crowd met ... '. But no one was interested in Cubism any longer: 'All the pictures except those of Derain went for little. Poor Juan Gris whose pictures went for very little tried to be brave. They after all did bring an honourable price, he said to Gertrude Stein, but he was sad.' According to Gertrude, the sale had been part of a conscious effort on the part of the dealers 'to kill cubism', but more likely Paris just wished to forget everything that had preceded the war. In the event, however, the 'old crowd', as Gertrude called them, was ill-treated by the post-war desire for the new. Of the Kahnweiler sale, wrote Gertrude in *The Autobiography*: 'Matisse said, and it was a Matisse way to say it, Braque a raison, celui-là a volé la France, et on sait bien ce que c'est que voler la France.'

It was not just the Cubists, now bereft of their leader Apollinaire, and deprived for five years of their dealer and friend Kahnweiler, whom the war had devastated. Others had also been permanently affected. Leo Stein came back to Europe greatly weakened and aged. He had gone to America for psychoanalysis in 1915, and, as the son of a German-born, was not allowed to return to Europe until the end of the war. Nor was he able to send for Nina, who remained in France. Their letters during the war years indicate the great suffering that this separation caused. Leo's psychoanalysis was not going well. Furthermore, his finances were immeasurably weakened by his prolonged stay in America, and on his return to Italy in 1919 he was forced to sell his collection of Renoirs. Leo was also much altered physically by the war years. While Gertrude had grown stronger and tougher and more vocal in all her activities during those years, Leo had grown thinner and weaker, suffering from poor health, both mental and physical, and from an increasing deafness which cut him off from former friends. In 1921, Leo finally married Nina, but he was by then almost totally deaf, and completely defeated by what he saw as his failure to achieve anything, even to undergo analysis successfully. In 1922 he summed up the results of his long self-exploration: 'My life had been such an utter failure because the foundations had been entirely bad. I have finally cleared away the debris, but there was so much of it bad that when it is all cleared away, it left nothing but the bare ground. This would be quite perfect if I were twenty years younger, or even ten years younger. At fifty, and with rotten health and very little energy, it is quite too big an order to commence building from the ground up.'

Yet there were survivors, people like Gertrude and Picasso, who had been able to grow as people and as artists during the war, and the long procession of allies who marched under the Arc de Triomphe made for Gertrude a victorious ceremony for the end of the war:

> Everybody was on the streets, men, women, children, soldiers, priests, nuns, we saw two nuns being helped into a tree from which they would be able to see. And we ourselves were admirably placed and we saw perfectly.
>
> We saw it all, we saw first the few wounded from the Invalides in their wheeling chairs wheeling themselves. . . .
>
> All the nations marched differently, some slowly, some quickly, the french carry their flags best of all. . . .
>
> However it all finally came to an end. We wandered up and we wandered down the Champs-Elysées and the war was over and the piles of captured cannon that had made two pyramids were being taken away and peace was upon us.

6

Such Nice Young Men

GERTRUDE STEIN had been some five years away from Paris when she returned to the capital in 1919. It was, as she said, 'a changed Paris'. Apollinaire was dead and with him the communality of artists that had characterised life before the war. 'Guillaume would have been a bond of union,' Gertrude wrote in *The Autobiography*, 'he always had a quality of keeping people together, and now that he was gone everybody ceased to be friends.' The old crowd quarrelled with each other and dispersed. Some, like Matisse and Picasso, went to live and work in the provinces, others remained in Paris disoriented both by the war and by the artistic events which had superseded Cubism – chief among them the nihilistic activities of Dada and Surrealism. The war brought other changes to Paris, new people – some of them the bureaucrats and journalists drawn to Paris by the Peace Conference, some of them the disaffected young Americans, torn from their roots by the war, too bitter or too tired to go home. It was to these young men, soon to dominate the social and literary life of the twenties, that Gertrude was to apply the term 'the lost generation'.

To the American writers who remained in Europe after the war, or who came throughout the early twenties to renew their relationship with the 'old world' and take advantage of the favourable rates of exchange for the dollar, Paris was known, among other things, as the home of Gertrude Stein. Her reputation was far greater than could have been guessed from the slender works of hers that were then known to the American literary public. Apart from *Three Lives*, which had been published in 1909, the Portraits of Picasso and Matisse, published in Stieglitz's *Camera Work* in 1912, and *Tender Buttons*, which appeared in limited numbers in 1914, little of her work was known. But numerous parodies of her writing had appeared in magazines such as *Life* and *Vanity Fair*, and together with her own short pieces published in these magazines, they created for her an important, though hardly understood reputation. While to most she remained an unapproachable enigma, or even an unassailable balloon of pretentious mystification, there were many in America who took her work seriously, and some who could claim to have been influenced by her writing.

Chief among these was the American novelist Sherwood Anderson, whose book *Winesburg, Ohio* had had a great critical success when it appeared in 1919. Marked by a stark 'naturalism', his work was seen by some as the successor to Gertrude's 'Melanctha', the chief story of *Three Lives*. Certainly Anderson himself acknowledged his debt to Gertrude, and when in 1921 he arrived in Paris with his wife, Tennessee, he found means of presenting himself to his mentor.

Such a presentation was not a straightforward matter in those days. There were certain channels for approaching the 'Sybil of Montparnasse'. One of these was through the kindly offices of Sylvia Beach, whose English bookshop Shakespeare and Company, around the corner from Adrienne Monnier's Les Amis des Livres, the haunt of the French Surrealists, was a natural meeting-place for the English-speaking colony in Paris. Gertrude Stein had been the first subscriber to the lending library which Sylvia had instituted when the bookshop opened in November 1919. She had been pleased to see that it possessed two copies of *Tender Buttons*, among other works of recent literature – some of it unobtainable in the States, most of it unique to Paris. On the other hand, according to Sylvia's memoir *Shakespeare and Company*, Gertrude had chastised her for the absence of certain works from her library. 'Where, she asked indignantly, were those American masterpieces *The Trail of the Lonesome Pine* and *The Girl of the Limberlost*?' – titles of favourite books among her recent doughboy acquaintances. Nevertheless, the two women became friends for a while (until Sylvia Beach published James Joyce's *Ulysses* in 1922), and letters from Sylvia began to arrive at the rue de Fleurus, announcing the appearance of one or another new American devotee. As Sylvia Beach recalls, 'Gertrude Stein's admirers, until they met her and discovered how affable she was, were often "skeered" to approach her without proper protection. So the poor things would come to me, exactly as if I were a guide from one of the tourist agencies, and beg me to take them to see Gertrude Stein.'

The letters of introduction from Sylvia to Gertrude were always a little obsequious. Together with James Joyce – whose existence in the city she barely acknowledged – Gertrude Stein was *the* person to know in Paris. Sylvia's letter of introduction for Sherwood Anderson, was not, however, mere flattery. 'He is so anxious to know you,' she wrote, 'for he says you have influenced him ever so much & that you stand as such a great master of words.' So began a friendship which was to last twenty years, until Sherwood's death in 1941. It inspired a long correspondence, essays by each on the other's work, pieces from Gertrude with titles such as 'Sherwood's Sweetness' and 'A Valentine for Sherwood Anderson', and above all, works from Sherwood Anderson in which it was evident he continued to learn from the writings of his mentor. His devotion to her, and his adaptation of her ideas on language in his own work, gave her a needed, living proof that she was who she thought she was. Sherwood Anderson, in turn, had his own admirers in the States. One of these, a handsome young journalist and writer of unpublished poetry and short-stories, he sent to meet Gertrude in 1922.

Ernest Hemingway, when he arrived in Paris at the age of twenty-two was a likeable callow fellow, what Gertrude would have called 'winsome'. He was gauche, sometimes brash, but quite evidently talented, and there were many people who thought he was special. He also told tragic tales, according to Sylvia Beach, of a father who had died when he was in high school, 'leaving him a gun as sole legacy', and of his struggle to bring up his brothers and sisters by himself, earning his 'first money in a boxing match' – all of these becoming lies which were to sow, even then, the seeds of the Hemingway legend. If pressed about his heroic exploits, Hemingway could always resort to palpable evidence. Early in their acquaintance, as his life-long admirer Sylvia Beach recalls, Hemingway pulled up his trouser legs to reveal the terrible scars which his wartime activity in Italy had left him.

In March 1922 Hemingway and his wife Hadley turned up at 27 rue de Fleurus to present themselves to Miss Stein and Miss Toklas. Like Tennessee Anderson, Hadley resented the custom which then existed at such meetings, where wives were not allowed to join in conversation with Gertrude Stein, but had to content themselves with feminine smalltalk with Alice. Probably it was Sylvia Beach who instructed them on the protocol: 'I knew the rules and regulations about wives at Gertrude's,' she wrote in *Shakespeare and Company*. 'They couldn't be kept from coming, but Alice had strict orders to keep them out of the way while Gertrude conversed with the husbands.'

Soon after this first visit, Alice and Gertrude returned the call, walking up the long flights of stairs to the dingy little flat above a sawmill where the Hemingways lived. There they sat on the corner of the large bed which filled the room and exchanged pleasantries, nodding in approval of this charming, and charmingly poor, young couple.

In a short time, Hemingway took to calling regularly on Gertrude to discuss both the writing he was doing outside his regular job as reporter for the *Toronto Star*, and the pictures for which the flat was now famous in America. Probably it was due to Gertrude that he began to look regularly at the Cézannes in the Tuileries – from which, as he later wrote, he learned the principles of composition, just as Gertrude had claimed to have done many years earlier. Encouraged by the intelligent conversation and the pedagogic interest which emanated from Gertrude, as well as by the comforts and elegance of the rue de Fleurus – 'It was like one of the best rooms in the finest museum except there was a big fireplace and it was warm and comfortable and they gave you good things to eat and tea and natural distilled liqueurs made from purple plums, yellow plums or wild raspberries' – Hemingway began to put himself in the hands of the older writer. She read all of his early work, and she told him to 'begin over again and concentrate'. One story, which dealt explicitly with a sexual encounter, she told him was 'inaccrochable', like certain paintings which may be well painted but cannot be exhibited, or *accroché* – hung up. She taught him something about taste in writing, and control, the virtues of discipline for a young writer, and the power of simple statement. She warned him against mere cleverness: 'Hemingway, remarks are not literature.' She played games with him that would stretch his imagination, and there are references to these in her own work of the period: 'Imitate a cheese if you please. We are very well pleased with gold coin and ribbons. . . . We were not pleased with the imitation of the lamb.'

That Hemingway could put himself so docilely in the hands of Gertrude is surprising only in the light of the much later legend. During his early years in Paris he was apparently vulnerable and willing to learn from people whom he recognised as greater than himself. Both James Joyce and Ezra Pound, as well as Gertrude, found him a nice, well-mannered, and earnest young man, trying to disguise his sensitivity, but not yet pretentiously tough. Besides, Hemingway genuinely admired, and was told to admire, Gertrude's writing. Even many years later, after a good deal of bitterness and renunciation on both sides, and notorious as he was for bearing grudges, Hemingway was able to praise Gertrude's work in *A Moveable Feast*, a memoir of his early days in Paris and one notable chiefly for its high romanticism and an appalling condescension to former friends:

> . . . *Melanctha* was very good, and good samples of her experimental writing had been published in book form [*Geography and Plays* of 1922] and had been well praised by critics who had met her or known her. She had such a personality that when she wished to win anyone over to her side she could not be resisted, and critics who met her or saw her pictures took on trust writing of her that they could not understand because of their enthusiasm for her as a person, and because of their confidence in her judgement. She had also discovered many truths about rhythms and the use of words in repetition that were valid and valuable and she talked well about them.

Most of all, Gertrude gave Hemingway enormous confidence in himself as a writer. When Hadley, horror-struck, told Hemingway that she had left his entire written output – with the exception of two short stories – in a suitcase on a train, it was Gertrude who consoled him and promised him that this loss would prove a valuable liberation. And when in 1922 Hadley was pregnant and wished to return to Canada to have her baby, it was Gertrude who advised Hemingway to work hard at journalism for a year so that he need not do anything but write for himself when he returned, that he was good enough not to do anything but write for himself. For all these reasons, it was Gertrude Stein, who, together with Alice Toklas, stood as godmother to the Hemingway's first child, Bumby, when the Hemingways returned to Paris in 1923.

Gertrude Stein's morale was very much lifted by the attentions of young writers like Sherwood Anderson and Ernest Hemingway in the early nineteen twenties. Although she worried constantly about all the unpublished work that was mounting at the rue de Fleurus, she was very much aware of her reputation as an important Parisian figure. She had recently been sculpted by Lipchitz ('. . . although she does not like sculpture and told Lipchitz so . . .') and by Jo Davidson (who made her, she thought, look like 'the goddess of pregnancy'), and had been photographed by the young American Surrealist Man Ray; but it was for her work rather than for her special looks and reputation that she wished to be known, and now once again she began earnestly to look for publishers.

For most of 1921 literary talk in Paris had centred chiefly on James Joyce's *Ulysses*, parts of which had been appearing in the American *Little Review*. James Joyce and

Henri Matisse, *Portrait à la raie verte*.

The First World War

OPPOSITE Gertrude Stein and Alice B. Toklas with nurses and soldiers at the Hôpital Simon Violet.

RIGHT In 'Auntie', Gertrude's first Ford automobile.
BELOW Gertrude Stein and Alice B. Toklas with some of the staff of the American Fund for French Wounded, *c.* 1917.

Portrait of Gertrude Stein by Francis Picabia, 1933.

Gertrude Stein were the two pillars of the literary avant-garde in Paris, and Gertrude was extremely jealous of her rival. As Hemingway remembers, 'If you brought up Joyce twice, you would not be invited back. It was like mentioning one general favourably to another general.' When *Ulysses* was published in book form by Sylvia Beach in February 1922, Gertrude was furious with her former friend. She arrived one day at the bookshop with Alice to announce in a regal huff the transference of her subscription to the American Library on the Right Bank.

Of *Ulysses* itself, she apparently thought very little, according to Alice's letter of 1947 to Donald Sutherland. '. . . She once said it was rather more than she could manage of the Irish fairies – that Irish fairies were even less palatable than German fairies.' She took comfort in childish sniggering with Picasso at their separate rivals. She tells the anecdote with evident relish in *The Autobiography*: 'Picasso said once when he and Gertrude were talking together, yes Braque and James Joyce, they are the incomprehensibles whom anybody can understand. Les incompréhensibles que tout le monde peut comprendre.'

Still, all the current fuss about *Ulysses* was plainly irritating to Gertrude, and she renewed her efforts to find her own appreciative public. Her short pieces were easier to get into print, not surprisingly, than the work she dreamed of publishing, the long *Making of Americans*. Early in 1922 the Four Seas Company of Boston agreed to bring out a collection of short works written over the past decade, to be called *Geography and Plays*. It was to have an Introduction by Sherwood Anderson.

It was an interesting collection of work. It included some lyrical love poetry written to Alice: perhaps the best known is 'Susie Asado' of 1913, with its punning refrain:

Sweet sweet sweet sweet sweet tea.
 Susie Asado.
Sweet sweet sweet sweet sweet tea.
 Susie Asado.
Susie Asado which is a told tray sure.

And also more erotic verse, safely hermetic: 'Pink Melon Joy', for example:

 Pillow.

 I meant to say.
 Saturday.
 Not polite.
 Do satisfy me.
 This is to say that baby is all well. That baby is baby. That baby is all well.
 That there is a piano. That baby is all well. That there is a piano. That
 baby is all well. This is to say that baby is all well. This is to say that
 baby is all well.

 Come in.

Splashes splashes of jelly splashes of jelly.

Brutes.

I said whisper.

Anyway Pink melon or joy.
Is that the same.
Pink melon and enjoy.
Pink melon by joy.
Is that in him.
Is that in.
Positive . . .

And the interesting 'Play', 'Ladies Voices' of 1916, whose Act II suggests the 'Goodnight ladies' passage of Eliot's later *Wasteland*:

Act II

Honest to God Miss Williams I don't mean to say that I was older.
But you were.
Yes I was. I do not excuse myself. I feel that there is no reason for passing
    an archduke.
You like the word.

You know very well that they all call it their house.
As Christ was to Lazarus so was the founder of the hill to Mahon.
You really mean it.
I do.

'I assure you', the book's publisher had written, 'that even if we never succeed in making any great amount of money on this book, we appreciate the value of having your name on our list. . . .' Although the book was partly subsidised by Gertrude, this was a gallant and unusual statement from a man of commerce. Better still, Sherwood Anderson had expressed in his Introduction a wish foremost in Gertrude's mind in the year of the *Ulysses* publication: 'Would it not be a lovely and charmingly ironic gesture of the gods, if, in the end, the work of this artist were to prove the most lasting and important of all the word slingers of our generation!'

In the summer of 1922, exhausted by the long preparation of the manuscript of *Geography and Plays*, Gertrude and Alice went to spend some time in St Rémy. It was there they realised they were tired, 'just tired', and they decided to stay for most of the year. Here, too, Gertrude began to think about the things she and Hemingway had discussed recently: 'It was during this winter,' she wrote in *The Autobiography*, 'that Gertrude Stein meditated on the use of grammar, poetical forms and what might be termed landscape plays.' Among these meditations was the hopelessly obscure 'An Elucidation', 'her first effort to state her problems of expression and her attempts to answer them'. When it was published in 1927 in *Transition*, it hardly made her work clearer to her readers.

It begins:

'Halve Rivers and Harbours'

Elucidation.
First as Explanation.
Elucidate the problem of halve.
Halve and have.
Halve Rivers and Harbours.
Have rivers and harbours.

You do see that halve rivers and harbours, halve rivers and harbours, you do see that halve rivers and harbours makes halve rivers and harbours and you do see, you do see that you that you do not have rivers and harbours when you halve rivers and harbours, you do see that you can halve rivers and harbours.

I refuse have rivers and harbours I have refused. I do refuse have rivers and harbours. I receive halve rivers and harbours, I accept halve rivers and harbours.

I have elucidated the pretence of halve rivers and harbours and the acceptation of halve rivers and harbours.

Tantalising as this was, it was hardly 'an elucidation'. But it did offer for the first time the line 'a rose is a rose is a rose is a rose', soon to become a catchphrase for her work in Paris and America.

Transition was one of several inadequately financed and highly ambitious little magazines that published Gertrude's work in the twenties. These small reviews, most of them short-lived, were fundamental to the literary life of Paris. In these the English-speaking colony could have its work published and read the writings of its rivals in the avant-garde. Gertrude Stein did not always take the reviews or their editors as seriously as they might have wished. Harold Loeb, the editor of *Broom*, who was cruelly caricatured by Hemingway as Robert Cohn in *The Sun Also Rises* of 1926, came one day to ask Gertrude for a contribution to his magazine. What he wanted, he said, was something 'as fine as "Melanctha" '. What he got, an abstract experiment, was entitled just that: 'As Fine as Melanctha'. Another editor, T. S. Eliot, came, reluctantly, on behalf of Lady Rothermere, a friend of Gertrude's friend Muriel Draper, to solicit a piece for her London magazine, *Criterion*. Eliot had been to visit Gertrude once before, when he had made it plain that he was disturbed by her style. As Alice recorded that meeting in her memoir *What is Remembered*, Eliot said, 'Can you tell me, Miss Stein, what authority you have for so frequently using the split infinitive?' The reply was startling, but correct: 'Henry James, said Gertrude.' Eliot agreed to publish something of Gertrude's work, but asked particularly that it be her very latest piece. She gave him something written the same day as his request and titled: 'A Description of the Fifteenth of November. A Portrait of T. S. Eliot.'

Short pieces by Gertrude now appeared fairly regularly in the important magazines of the day – Jane Heap and Margaret Anderson's *Little Review*, and *Vanity Fair*, both published in America, and after 1927, in *Transition*, edited by Eugene Jolas and Elliot Paul, and which, according to Leo Stein, used to print in its list of contributors: 'And Gertrude Stein sends what she wishes and when she wishes and she is pleased and we are pleased.' But in 1924 there was still no one who would take on the publication of Gertrude's major work, *The Making of Americans*. Now, thanks to Hemingway, something was to be done.

In 1923, when the Hemingways returned from Canada, Hemingway had been offered the post of assistant editor of *The Transatlantic Review* by Ford Madox Ford, who had recently come to Paris to establish the magazine. Ford, whom Hemingway then called 'the golden walrus', later satirised in *The Sun Also Rises* as the tiresome and pretentious Major Braddocks, and much later flayed in *A Moveable Feast* ('I had always avoided looking at Ford when I could and I always held my breath when I was near him in a closed room . . .'), was already devoted to the young writer. 'I did not read more than six words of his before I decided to publish everything he sent me,' Ford remarked, according to Hemingway's biographer Carlos Baker. In such a situation it was possible for Hemingway to help Gertrude, and early in 1924, he arranged with Ford for the serialisation of *The Making of Americans*.

I made it clear it was a remarkable scoop for his magazine, [Hemingway wrote to Gertrude that February] obtained only through my obtaining genius. He is under the impression that you get big prices when you consent to publish. I did not give him this impression but did not discourage it. . . . Treat him high wide and handsome. I said they could publish as much of the six volumes as they wished and that it got better and better as it went along.

It is really a scoop for them you know. They are going to have Joyce in the same number. . . .

The letter was – apart from that last sentence – all that Gertrude could have wished. At long last, after some thirteen years, her *magnum opus* was to be taken to the public.

But Gertrude's triumph was to be short-lived. In the event, only two instalments of the work ever appeared in *The Transatlantic Review*. The financial backing of John Quinn ceased after Quinn's death that year, and Ford and Hemingway soon fell out. Ford claimed that Hemingway had given him the impression that *The Making of Americans* was a short work, and that Hemingway had overreached himself by committing the magazine to such a long-term project. Hemingway felt that Ford was not only breathing down his neck in his job as assistant editor, but now calling him a liar as well. By the summer of 1924, they were hardly speaking to one another.

Meanwhile, Hemingway did not abandon his mentor. As he wrote in *A Moveable Feast*, he had early on vowed to assist her: '. . . and I thought, I will do my best to serve her and see she gets justice for the good work she has done as long as I can, so help me God and Mike Ney.' Somewhat less melodramatically he approached Lady Rothermere to ask if she and The Major, as he called Eliot, would carry on the publication in the *Criterion*. This, thanks to Eliot, never happened, but when Ford heard about the proposal in September 1924, he wrote gallantly to Gertrude Stein. It was clear, however, he was still nursing his wounds: 'I should be very sorry to lose you, but I was never the one to stand in a contributor's way: indeed I really exist as a sort of half-way house between non-publishable youth and real money – a sort of green baize swing door that everyone kicks both on entering and on leaving.'

In the end, *The Transatlantic Review* was bailed out by the funds of the American Krebs Friend, but it did not resume the publication of Gertrude's novel. For that she had to look elsewhere. Robert McAlmon, whose New York firm, Contact Editions, had published Hemingway's first book, *Three Stories and Ten Poems* in 1923, had now moved with his publishing venture to Paris. In 1921, he had written to Gertrude from New York about some of her submitted work: '. . . It doesn't mean much to me, but a whimsical emotion now and then at some neat phrase, or an irony upon unfinished thought, and situation. . . . I take your work – how shall I say, seriously, or at least with a potential or suspended respect. I don't get it, and believing that you have conviction to go on in your manner, simply have a waiting frame of mind.' Now, in Paris, and at the centre of the American community there, McAlmon and his 'waiting frame of mind' surrendered under pressure of Gertrude's personality and reputation, and probably most of all, of his friend Hemingway's soliciting on her behalf. Early in 1925 he agreed to take on the publication of the thousand-page-long *The Making of Americans*.

Meanwhile, Gertrude's friendship with Hemingway and the literary instruction continued pleasantly. Even her friendship with Ford continued, soldered by Ford's request to dedicate to Gertrude his forthcoming book, *A Mirror to France*. New and interesting literary figures came to the rue de Fleurus flat, young Americans like William Carlos Williams and John Dos Passos – whom Gertrude thought charmingly Spanish though his brains 'were addled' – the Imagist poet Hilda Doolittle, the painter and poet and ex-lover of Mabel Dodge, Marsden Hartley, exotics like Mina Loy, Djuna Barnes, and the then fashionable aesthete poet, Glenway Wescott, of whom Gertrude remarked, 'He has a certain syrup but it does not pour'.

Of the more famous writers, Gertrude did not always hold the common view. Not only Joyce and Eliot, but even the generally loved Ezra Pound failed to impress her. 'He came home to dinner with us,' she wrote in *The Autobiography*, 'and he stayed and he talked about japanese prints among other things. Gertrude Stein liked him but did not find him amusing. She said he was a village explainer, excellent if you were a village, but if you were not, not.' Worse, he would gesticulate wildly when talking, and as a result broke one of Gertrude's chairs. After that, she did not see very much of him, although she continued to know his friend of the fine Shakespearian name, Kate Buss.

Wyndham Lewis, on the other hand, whom no one really liked, but most respected for the sharpness of his views on art and literature, Gertrude found charmingly naive. She called him the 'Measuring Worm' because he would arrive to look at the paintings at the rue de Fleurus flat with ruler and pencil, measuring on his thumb angles and distances in the Cubist compositions, and returning to London to paint, said Gertrude, exactly as he had seen. She was to like him less after 1928, however, when his essay on her writing appeared in *Time and Western Man*. He not only called her 'a Monument sitting upon patience', but accurately pointed to the childlike nature of her work, although he wrongly accused her of a false naivety. But his description of her prose was, in its totally negative way, close to a certain truth about what was revolutionary, important and Cézanne-derived in Gertrude's writing:

> It is in a thick, monotonous prose-song that Miss Stein characteristically expresses her fatigue, her energy, and the bitter fatalism of her nature. Her stories [*Three Lives*] are very often long – all the longer, too, because everything has to be repeated half a dozen times over. In the end the most wearisome dirge it is possible to imagine results, as slab after slab of this heavy, insensitive, common prose-song churns and lumbers by. . . .

> . . . Gertrude Stein's prose-song is a cold, black suet-pudding. We can represent it as a cold suet-roll of fabulously-reptilian length. Cut it at any point, it is the same thing; the same heavy, sticky, opaque mass all through, and all along. It is weighted, projected, with a sibylline urge. It is mournful and monstrous, composed of dead and inanimate material. It is all fat, without nerve. Or the evident vitality that informs it is vegetable rather than animal. Its life is a low grade, if tenacious, one; of the sausage, by-the-yard, variety.

Of all the writers and painters that Gertrude met in the early twenties, the one she liked best, and continued to like despite the rarity of their meetings, was Scott Fitzgerald. Fitzgerald, when Gertrude met him in 1925, was the kind of novelist Hemingway wished to be. He was handsome, charming, rich, and his writing was a critical, as well as a commercial, success. Above all, Hemingway infinitely admired *The Great Gatsby*, which had just been published and was now universally acclaimed. Scott and his wife Zelda were already legendary in Paris when Gertrude met them. According to Sylvia Beach, 'Poor Scott was earning so much money from his books that he and Zelda had to drink a great deal of Champagne in Montmartre . . .' They were also impressively cavalier with their money, which they used to leave '. . . on a plate in the hall of the house where they lived, so that people coming with bills or those to be tipped could simply help themselves'. And once, according to Sylvia, Scott '. . . spent an entire publisher's cheque on a pearl necklace for [Zelda]. She made a present of the necklace to a Negress with whom she was dancing in one of the nightclubs up there; but the girl returned it to her early next morning.' They gave wild parties, mostly in the South of France, but one of them in Paris. According to Janet Flanner in *Paris Was Yesterday*, '. . . their famous dinner party on the houseboat anchored in the Seine was the only social American event that achieved a kind of historical importance, almost as if it had been French'.

But more than any of this, the character of Scott Fitzgerald made him legendary in

Paris. Charming, gentle, with 'the visage of a poet', as Janet Flanner wrote, he was always willing to praise or learn from or to help other writers. For Hemingway, he procured the services of his publisher, at the time the most distinguished of fiction editors, Maxwell Perkins of Scribner's. For Gertrude he offered the devotion and tribute of someone she recognised as a genuinely gifted writer. After he had met her, and after she had written in praise of his earlier novel *This Side of Paradise* – she later called it the book 'that really created for the public the new generation' – he wrote her this letter:

My wife and I think you a very handsome, very gallant, very kind lady and thought so as soon as we saw you. . . .

I am so anxious to get *The Making of Americans* & learn something from it and imitate things . . . out of it which I shall doubtless do.

You see, I am content to let you, and the one or two like you who are acutely sensitive, think or fail to think for me and my kind artistically (their name is not legend but the word like it), much as the man of 1901, say, would let Nietche (sp.) think for him intellectually. I am a very second rate person compared to first rate people – I have indignation as well as most of the other major faults – and it honestly makes me shiver to know that such a writer as you attributes such a significance to my factitious, meritricious (metricous?) *This Side of Paradise*. It puts me in a false position, I feel. Like Gatsby I have only hope.

Thank you enormously for writing me.

Scott Fitzg–.

While they saw each other in Paris, Gertrude was a support to Fitzgerald, and in her matter-of-fact way helped to dispel some of the gloom which his bouts of drinking and his depressions about his work produced. In *What is Remembered* Alice says that Scott was always sober when he visited the rue de Fleurus, but he was also often depressed: 'One afternoon he said, You know I am thirty years old today and it is tragic. What is to become of me, what am I to do? And Gertrude told him that he should not worry, that he had been writing like a man of thirty for many years. She told him that he would go home and write a greater novel than he ever had.'

Although Fitzgerald valued to a surprising degree the praise of lesser known writers such as Hemingway and Gertrude Stein, he could not always bring himself to accept their praise when it was offered. In *The Autobiography*, Gertrude wrote: 'She thinks Fitzgerald will be read when many of his well known contemporaries are forgotten. Fitzgerald always says that he thinks Gertrude says these things just to annoy him by making him think that she means them, and he adds in a favourite way, and her doing it is the cruellest thing I ever heard.'

By the late summer of 1925, while Gertrude laboured over the proofs for her novel which was to appear that October, Gertrude's influence on the young American writers was well known. A letter from a painter friend in London expressed a fairly general view: 'I find you have had a great influence on many of the story writers,' wrote Harry Phelan Gibb, 'some of whom have really got something worthwhile entirely through you. I think this should be some return, some satisfaction to you. For it means that you have done good & shown a road clearly which is so well worth treading. . . .' Earlier, Edmund Wilson had written a review of Hemingway's two books, *Three Stories and Ten Poems*, and the collection of stories, *In Our Time*, in which he had spoken of the writer as a disciple of both Sherwood Anderson and Gertrude Stein.

At the time, Hemingway was well pleased with the review. He continued to reassure Gertrude of how much he had learned from her while reading proofs for the part of *The Making of Americans* which *The Transatlantic Review* had serialised, and of how much he valued their discussions of writing. That summer from Spain, where she had sent him to look at the bullfights, he wrote to Gertrude about the novel, *The Sun Also Rises*, on which he was then working:

> . . . I'm trying to do the country like Cézanne and having a hell of a time and sometimes getting it a little bit. It is about 100 pages long and nothing happens and the country is swell, I made it all up, so I see it all and part of it comes out the way it ought to, it is swell about the fish, but isn't writing a hard job though?
>
> It used to be easy before I met you. I certainly was bad, gosh, I'm awfully bad now but it's a different kind of bad. . . .

Hemingway's willingness to acknowledge his debt to Gertrude, and his humility in the face of his teachers were soon to wear off. As Hemingway worked that year on the second draft of this first novel, he began to feel he had his own voice and to wish once and for all to rid himself of inevitable comparisons with other writers. Gertrude Stein was too obscure for attack, but when that autumn Sherwood Anderson's novel *Dark Laughter* was published, Hemingway conceived a plan. He began to write a parody of Anderson's style in the book that was to be called *The Torrents of Spring*.

Hemingway's book was a stab in the back for several reasons. Not only was Anderson a close and trusting friend, he had been among the very first to befriend the Hemingways in America, and had assured his welcome in Paris with various letters of introduction to prominent figures such as James Joyce and Gertrude Stein. Furthermore, he had got his own publisher, Boni & Liveright, to bring out Hemingway's first big collection of short stories, which appeared in 1925 with a jacket review by Anderson himself. Hemingway's attack was against Anderson's publisher as well. It was part of the contract that Hemingway held with Boni & Liveright – and normal publishing practice – that Hemingway would offer them the first three novels he wrote. Only their refusal of the next work could release him from that contract. Having taken some financial risk in bringing out Hemingway's short stories – always less saleable than novels – Boni & Liveright were eagerly awaiting what they were sure would be the commercial and critical success of Hemingway's first novel, *The Sun Also Rises*. Hemingway, on the other hand, had by this time met and conquered Scott Fitzgerald, who had convinced his own publisher, Scribner's, that they should get Hemingway as their writer. If Hemingway could be released from his contract with Liveright, Scribner's was prepared to offer him more money, and certainly more prestige. Hemingway now played a clever but shabby trick. Instead of *The Sun Also Rises* which Liveright had been expecting, Hemingway sent his publishers the new book, his cruel parody of their prized author Anderson. Legally, they would be bound to accept whatever book Hemingway offered, or else have to release him from his contract. Their plaintive telegram arrived that winter in Austria, where the Hemingways were skiing: 'REJECTING TORRENTS OF SPRING ... PATIENTLY AWAITING MANUSCRIPT SUN ALSO RISES.'

There was nothing the publisher could do in such a trap. Released from his contract with Liveright, Hemingway was free to give both books to Scribner's. Just before *The Torrents of Spring* was published in May 1926, Hemingway wrote a cover letter to Sherwood Anderson, explaining why he felt Anderson's work should be attacked. It was a gesture of bravado, but it was clear that Hemingway felt a little sheepish about his actions. As Carlos Baker remarks, most of his friends thought the work was a vicious attack and warned him against publishing it. Hadley had 'found the whole idea detestable'. For Gertrude Stein, it was the end of their friendship.

As Hemingway saw it, Gertrude was angry because 'I had attacked someone that was part of her apparatus'. But Gertrude was incensed both by the attack on a close friend and by the shabbiness which it revealed in someone she had always liked and admired. As Hemingway thought, Gertrude did not really care about Sherwood as a writer, 'but spoke glowingly of him as a man and of his great, beautiful warm Italian eyes and of his kindness and charm'. These things, Hemingway obviously felt, did not count. But they counted to Gertrude. She felt it was as a friend, not as a writer, that Anderson had been betrayed by Hemingway's humiliating parody. But it was also true that Hemingway's book had drawn Gertrude as well into its range of fire. Part of it was entitled 'The Making and Marring of Americans', by 1926 a well-understood reference. Six years later, in *The Autobiography of Alice B. Toklas*, Gertrude was to take her revenge.

In the few months before the Hemingway-Anderson storm broke around her, Gertrude was heavily preoccupied with her own work. When *The Making of Americans* had appeared in Robert McAlmon's Contact Editions in October 1925, she had been delighted. As she had written in 'Publishers', one of the pieces in *Geography and Plays*, there was nothing so exciting as seeing yourself in print: 'and then comes the time to look and there it is, there is the writing'. Besides, as she later wrote, 'The Making of Americans is a very important thing and everybody ought to be reading at it or it . . .'. Friends had been quick to acknowledge its importance. Earlier Carl Van Vechten had written to her: '. . . my feeling is that you have done a very big thing, probably as big as, perhaps bigger than James Joyce, Marcel Proust, or Dorothy Richardson [a then-known writer of the stream-of-consciousness novel, author of a sequence entitled *Pilgrimage*]. . . . To the average reader, the book will probably be *work*. I think even the average reader will enjoy it, however, once he begins to get the rhythm, that is so important. To me, now, it is a little like the Book of Genesis. There is something Biblical about you, Gertrude. . . .'

Sherwood Anderson also wrote, to reassure her of the continued importance of her work for his own writing: 'I find the same music I always find in your prose, the thing that always stirs me in everything you write. The music is only more complete, more sustained. . . . When I got up here I got at once into a new novel. That has absorbed me. I keep your book here on my desk. I steal from it.' Although their praise was necessary to her, and generously given – it was still just the word of friends. What Gertrude longed for was wider recognition.

The spring after the book was published was a disappointment to Gertrude. Although Janet Flanner had written in her Paris column for *The New Yorker* of 'the intellectual success of her *The Making of Americans*', and that 'No American writer is taken more seriously than Miss Stein by the Paris modernists', the kind of acclaim she had expected was not forthcoming. Nor were the book's sales figures very good. Whereas *Ulysses* had sold out in the first few weeks of its publication and was well into its eighth printing by this time, *The Making of Americans* was moving slowly. In fact, she had recently received an angry letter from McAlmon himself, accusing her of laziness in publicising the book, and threatening to pulp the remainder of the edition. It was with these disappointments in mind that in the spring of 1926 Gertrude decided to accept an offer to lecture in England.

The idea had come originally from Edith Sitwell, a passionate devotee and literary disciple of Gertrude Stein, and a recent friend. In 1924 Edith Sitwell had reviewed at length, but according to Alice, a little condescendingly, Gertrude's 1922 *Geography and Plays*. The following year, however, Edith was whole-hearted. As she wrote in *Vogue* magazine, she had recently been reading nothing but Gertrude Stein and had found her work magnificent. She came from London to do an interview with Gertrude for *Vogue*, and the two soon became friends. Gertrude saw at once that Edith was an original, and she very much liked her looks, as she described them in *The Autobiography*: 'Very tall, bending slightly, withdrawing and hesitatingly advancing, and beautiful and with the most distinguished nose I have ever seen on any human being.' Alice was also taken by Edith's dress, 'like a gendarme, she wore double-breasted coats with large buttons', but most of all by her ardour on behalf of Gertrude's work. Edith had recently tried, unsuccessfully, to get Leonard and Virginia Woolf to publish the English edition of *The Making of Americans* at their Hogarth Press, but she was not defeated by their refusal. As she wrote to Gertrude in January 1926: 'I am still working hard at propaganda [a phrase which must have reminded Gertrude of Leo's campaign on behalf of Cézanne, Matisse and Picasso more than twenty years ago]. It is miserably disappointing, Virginia Woolf not taking the book. – However . . . a great writer like yourself is absolutely bound to win through. There can't be any question about it.' But what was needed, said Edith, was a campaign publicising Gertrude and her work, personal appearances and letters for the cause. For Gertrude, of course, such open fighting on her own behalf was out of the question, and she wrote at once to tell Edith so. But Edith persisted and eventually – swayed also by the poor sales of *The Making of Americans* – Gertrude gave in. She would give a lecture in Cambridge.

Such Nice Young Men

The first thing Gertrude needed was a subject to lecture on. For this she went out, as was her habit, to her Ford car and began to write under its inspiration. As it happened, the Ford was then being repaired, and as she remembers in *The Autobiography*, it was watching her car being taken to pieces and put back together that inspired her to write about the construction of her own work: 'She stayed there several hours and when she came back chilled, with the ford repaired, she had written the whole of Composition as Explanation.' She had often used the car for her writing before, listening as she drove to its rhythm, to repetitious sounds like the movement of windscreen wipers, odd sounds like the lurching forward in steady traffic, the sound of the horn, the crunching of the gears, etc. Now, as she watched her car being taken apart, she thought of grammatical constructions, and of car parts, what made one Ford different from other identical Fords, and with these not altogether clear speculations on rhythm, identity, and repetition, she composed her lecture.

After it was written, Gertrude set about reading it to select audiences. Different people gave her different advice on its delivery. Some said to speak slowly and never look down at the notes, others advised her to talk quickly and never look up. Baffled, and unsure of herself, but with new clothes and a new passport, Gertrude set out for Cambridge with Alice Toklas in May 1926, to deliver the first lecture she had ever given.

There, despite the parties that the Sitwells gave for her, Gertrude Stein's nervousness increased. Osbert Sitwell, as she remembers in *The Autobiography*, was exceptionally kind: 'He so thoroughly understood every possible way in which one could be nervous that as he sat beside her in the hotel telling her all the kinds of ways that he and she could suffer from stage fright she was quite soothed.' Gertrude liked Osbert very much, although she did not much like his younger brother Sacheverell, but Osbert was '. . . like an uncle of a king. He had that pleasant kindly irresponsible agitated calm that an uncle of an english king always must have.'

There was only a small audience, around a hundred students, at The Literary Society which met at Jesus College, and the regal Sitwells were to sit on the platform where the lecture was to be delivered; but as Gertrude entered the room she must have felt she was taking part in a beheading. Once Gertrude got through the reading, however, her nervousness ended, and she answered quite calmly the questions the students asked of her. The Sitwells assured her it was a success, and by the time she arrived in Oxford for her second performance, she was actually looking forward to it. She began to feel, as she later wrote, 'just like a prima donna'.

That she had agreed to lecture at Oxford as well as Cambridge was due to the beseeching of young Harold Acton. Acton, a friend of the Sitwells and a prominent undergraduate and literary aesthete from Christ Church, had remembered meeting Gertrude as long ago as 1912, when as a child he had come to tea with his father at Mabel Dodge's Villa Curonia. He was also much impressed by what he knew of Gertrude's work, and believed with Edith in the importance of her part in the struggle for 'modernism'. But there was also a part of his invitation that was motivated by mischief. He greatly looked forward to the effect of Gertrude Stein's appearance on the philistine

131

undergraduate body of the university. As Harold Acton wrote years later in his *Memoirs of an Aesthete*, her appearance in Oxford that May 1926 was in itself a *coup de théâtre* for those many hundreds of students who had crowded into the hall hired by Acton's Ordinary Society:

Owing to the critics, the popular conception of Gertrude Stein was of an eccentric visionary, a literary Madame Blavatsky in fabulous clothes, the triumph of the dream and escape from life personified, with bells on her fingers as well as her toes, or a mermaid swathed in tinsel, smoking drugged cigarettes through an exaggerated cigarette holder, or a Gioconda who had had her face lifted so often that it was fixed in a smile beyond the nightmares of Leonardo da Vinci.

Imagine the devastation of these expectations as Gertrude entered: '. . . a squat Aztec figure in obsidian, growing more monumental as soon as she sat down. With her tall bodyguard of Sitwells and the gipsy acolyte [Alice]. . . .' Then Gertrude began to read her lecture: 'The litany of an Aztec priestess . . . uttered in a friendly American voice that made everyone feel at home until they pondered the subject-matter. What a contrast between manner and matter, between voice and written page! . . . Though we had heard dozens of lectures, nobody had heard anything like this before.'

'Everything is the same except composition and as the composition is different and always going to be different everything is not the same. Everything is not the same as the time when of the composition and the time in the composition is different. The composition is different, that is certain,' she read in her rich, matter-of-fact, slightly Baltimore voice. It was a voice that made it impossible to snicker, sensuous, highly intelligent, comforting – and hypnotic. As Harold Acton recalls, '. . . it was hard not to fall into a trance . . . to concentrate on so many repetitions. . . . The illusion that we were living in a continuous present was certainly there, a little too continuous for my taste.'

Gertrude read some of her word Portraits, including 'Sitwell Edith Sitwell', which was as strange as it was beautiful:

Introduces have and heard.
Miss Edith Sitwell have and heard.
Introduces have and had.
Miss Edith Sitwell have and had.
Introduces have and had introduces have and had and heard.
Miss Edith Sitwell have and had and heard.
Left and right.
Part two of Part one.
If she had a ball at all, if she had a ball at all too.
Fill my eyes no no.
It was and held it.
The size of my eyes
Why does one want to or to and to, when does one want to and to went to.

The Portrait of Edith Sitwell was a good piece for Gertrude to have chosen to illustrate her lecture. It used repetition with slight variation and played with the idea of similarity and difference in sense and sound, in past and present tenses. Words were looked at like objects or people, they are 'introduced'. 'Miss Edith Sitwell have and heard' is similar to 'Miss Edith Sitwell have and had', in sound, but not at all in sense. So is 'eyes' like 'size' or like ayes when contrasted to nose or 'noes'. 'Ball' was like 'eyeball'; there were two or 'too', 'left and right'. 'One' leads to two or 'to'. 'Want to' becomes progressively, like 'to and to', 'went to'. It was fairly understandable Steinian word-play. But as a portrait of one of the people on the platform, the piece had its own effect. As Harold Acton recalls, 'While she read Edith Sitwell's portrait I glanced at the model. No, I could not see the likeness, nor apparently could Edith, for she was trying not to look as embarrassed as she felt. Sachie looked as if he were swallowing a plum and Osbert shifted on his insufficient chair with a vague nervousness in his eyes.'

At last the reading came to an end. For some it had been a momentous experience. Maurice Bowra told Acton 'it had sounded like Kant's Critique of Pure Reason'. But others, Acton said, were 'burning with indignation and felt personally affronted by this new experience'. The tensions which had been produced by prolonged exposure to that droning southern voice, and the boredom and teasing of statements just outside the reach of understanding, now exploded in violent questioning and attack. But to these Gertrude responded in her characteristic calm manner, and above all with her good nature:

> Gertrude Stein's deep abdominal chuckle . . . burst forth frequently as she answered each question in reassuring motherly tones, patting and soothing the obstreperous with gusty sallies, and everybody joined in her laughter. Her answers were suggestive yet full of common sense as when, after David Cecil and Robbie Calburn had jumped up in rapid succession with questions, Robbie asked what she meant by saying that everything being the same everything is always different. 'Consider the two of you,' she replied, 'you jump up one after the other. That is the same thing and surely you admit that the two of you are always different.' 'Touché,' said Robbie.

There was no doubt that after two hours of questions and answers Gertrude had won over her audience. 'Those who came to scoff were disarmed and charmed,' wrote Acton. The lecture was published at Oxford, and later by the Woolfs at the Hogarth Press. For a long time afterwards, discussion at Oxford centred around the appearance and triumph of Gertrude Stein, and imitations of her work dominated the literary magazines.

Gertrude and Alice returned to Paris with the pleasing memory of a resounding success. Soon their flat in the rue de Fleurus was full of Oxford and Cambridge men eager to pay homage. The American publisher Joseph Brewer came from Oxford to ask for a collection of short pieces, which eventually appeared in 1928 as *Useful Knowledge*. John Lane wrote early in February 1927 to ask if he could bring out a second edition of *Three Lives*. But more important for Gertrude than this revived interest in her work in England, were the favourable reviews of *The Making of Americans* that were now coming from America, Marianne Moore's review in *The Dial* (which also published her lecture in October 1926), and Katherine Anne Porter's review in 1927: 'I doubt if all the people who should read it will read it for a great while yet . . . and reading it is a sort of permanent occupation. Yet to shorten it would be to mutilate its vitals, and it is a very necessary book.' That year Edith Sitwell wrote as well: 'Your reputation grows every day, it seems to me. It is such a happiness to me to see this happening, under our eyes, as it were.' And, she added, 'I'm having my own new book sent to you from the publishers. It contains a Variation ['Jodelling Song' in *Façade*] on a theme from [Gertrude's] "Accents in Alsace". I do *hope* you like it.'

As Gertrude Stein often said, 'no artist needs criticism, he only needs appreciation'. At long last she was beginning to receive it.

7

Saints and Landscapes

WHILE GERTRUDE'S POSITION as an important 'modernist' writer strengthened throughout the twenties, her reputation as an art collector continued to rest on those acquisitions that had been made before World War I. Even so, hers was a formidable reputation. Bravig Imbs, a young American writer whom Gertrude took up in the mid-twenties, was greatly impressed when he accompanied Gertrude and Alice to exhibitions: 'She became an official pontiff,' he wrote in his *Confessions of Another Young Man*, 'and the merchants dreaded her visits, for she could make or mar an exhibition, with little more than a movement of her thumb. If she approved of an exhibition, she naturally carried off the best painting of the lot at a bargain price; if she disapproved, there was a whole coterie of American buyers who would follow her hint.'

But though visitors from all over the world continued to call at the rue de Fleurus in order to view what was by then almost a private museum of modern art, they no longer expected to see the very best of the current avant-garde. Instead, she was known as one of the last supporters of Cubism, a style which most critics associated with the pre-war years. In 1921 she had made up her quarrel with Juan Gris, almost the last of the Cubists to continue in the style of that school, and together with Gris's dealer Kahnweiler, she supported the artist in his work. Most of the other Cubists had by then become too successful to need her patronage (and their paintings had become too expensive for her to buy), but Gris had suffered for a long time from both poverty and ill-health and very much depended on Gertrude and Kahnweiler's support to stay alive. With a good deal less money to spend on pictures than she had had formerly, Gertrude continued to collect his work. In 1925, for example, she exchanged with Kahnweiler the Marie Laurencin group portrait of Apollinaire, Marie, Picasso, and Fernande – a work of great sentimental value, and the first painting Marie Laurencin had ever sold – for a painting by Gris. By then, however, Gris's fortunes had begun to change. As Kahnweiler wrote to Gertrude that year, Gris's pictures were now 'selling exceedingly well: lots of people that did not like him, till now, are liking them, and buying them, too. At last, success has come.' But it had, in the event, come too late. For a long time ill, and under the strain of poverty, Juan Gris finally died in May 1927.

Gris's death shattered Gertrude. Not only was he a dear friend, and for her one of the most intelligent and noble of her painter acquaintances – 'He understood and knew everything,' wrote Alice in a letter of 1949, '. . . and not at all only about painting. . . . And he loved to laugh and make merry and dance (none too well) . . .' – but he was also her special find. She had bought three of his paintings in 1914, at his first exhibition at Kahnweiler's gallery. Leo had had nothing to do with that discovery, nor Picasso. She – almost alone with Kahnweiler – had supported him when no one else would, or so it seemed to her. Now he was recognised as one of the great painters of his time. It was like the death of one of Gertrude's greatest creations.

So possessive of Gris was Gertrude that when Picasso, who she thought had always been jealous of Gris, came to the rue de Fleurus to talk about his death, Gertrude had attacked him. As she tells the story in *The Autobiography*: 'Gertrude Stein said to him bitterly, you have no right to mourn, and he said, you have no right to say that to me. You never realised his meaning because you did not have it, she said angrily.'

In July that year *Transition* published what Gertrude said was 'the most moving thing' she ever wrote, 'The Life and Death of Juan Gris':

. . . Juan Gris was a brother and a comrade to every one being one as no one ever had been one. . . . He had his own Spanish gift for intimacy. We were intimate. . . . Juan knew what he did. . . . As a Spaniard he knew cubism and he stepped through it. There was besides this perfection. To have it shown you. Then came the war and desertion. There was little aid. Four years partly illness much perfection and rejoining beauty and perfection and then at the end there came a definite creation of something. This is what is to be measured. He made something that is to be measured. And that is something.

By 'something to be measured', Gertrude meant not only the substance of Juan's achievement, but also, more specifically, his exact, or 'measurable' picture of the real world. That concrete understanding and the ability to transmit it, 'have it show you', she called 'perfection', it demonstrated a greater intelligence – or 'clarity' than Picasso's – so she told Picasso in the angry exchange just quoted, and so she wrote in *The Autobiography* when she said, '. . . the only real cubism is that of Picasso and Juan Gris. Picasso created it and Juan Gris permeated it with his clarity and his exaltation [that is, mysticism].' That mystic vision of reality which Gris had, Gertrude felt, gave them a common gift and a common basis to their work. She wrote in *The Autobiography*, in an important passage for an understanding of Gertrude's own intentions, as well as her artistic affiliations:

Gertrude Stein, in her work, has always been possessed by the intellectual passion for exactitude in the description of inner and outer reality. She has produced a simplification by this concentration, and as a result the destruction of associational emotion in poetry and prose. She knows that beauty, music, decoration, the result of emotion should never be the cause, even the events should not be the cause of emotion nor should they be the material of poetry and prose. They should consist of an exact reproduction of either an outer or an inner reality.

It was this conception of exactitude that made the close understanding between Gertrude Stein and Juan Gris.

Juan Gris conceived exactitude but in him exactitude had a mystical basis. As a mystic it was necessary for him to be exact. In Gertrude Stein the necessity was intellectual, a pure passion for exactitude.

Because of this passion for exact description of inner reality (as in the 'continuous present' of *The Making of Americans*, for example) and of outer reality (as in the still-lifes of *Tender Buttons*), Gertrude Stein ceased to collect the work of what the rest of the world thought of as the avant-garde. She was not at all interested, for example, in abstract painting, as in the work of Kandinsky or the De Stijl group. In fact, she believed, as she wrote in a letter of 1937: 'The minute painting gets abstract it gets pornographic.' By this apparant paradox, I believe she meant that as soon as painting moves away from 'exact description' of reality it becomes both offensive and the work of artists who have prostituted their talents (in the original Greek meaning of the word 'pornographic' – 'pertaining to prostitutes') and denied the true goals of art.

Nor was she interested in the work of the Surrealists, whom she thought offered only a tricky, sophisticated view of appearances, and achieved their effects by mere complication of a basically banal concept of reality. In *Picasso*, written in 1937, she defended this view:

> The surrealists still see things as every one sees them, they complicate them in a different way but the vision is that of every one else, in short the complication is the complication of the twentieth century but the vision is that of the nineteenth century. ... Complications are always easy but another vision than that of all the world is very rare. That is why geniuses are rare, to complicate things in a new way that is easy, but to see the things in a new way that is really difficult, everything prevents one, habits, schools, daily life, reason, necessities of daily life, indolence everything prevents one, in fact there are very few geniuses in the world.

Gertrude Stein did not really like her painters to come in groups, she did not like movements and she did not believe in common artistic causes. There were individual geniuses and there were their followers. So, for her, 'the surréalistes are the vulgarisation of Picabia as Delaunay and his followers the futurists were a vulgarisation of Picasso'. Picabia, it may be said, was at the time she wrote this (1932) a special friend, and a special interest of Gertrude's. She liked him because he was Spanish – and she had by then, what with Gris and Picasso, developed the idea that twentieth-century painters must be Spanish, or, as she explained, have the qualities of wildness, exaggeration, cruelty, superstition, mysticism and 'no sense of time'. For that reason, she had been interested in Miró and Dali, but not enough to buy their paintings. Her idea that modern painting was Spanish had much to do with her delight in having been proved right about

Picasso. Others of her ideas about painting had also to do with this early triumph. One was that '. . . most people that do anything in painting are not very tall and broad, there may be exceptions but generally speaking you have to be small'. However, in the twenties she began to think that being Russian was almost as good as being Spanish, and she was soon demonstrating this by buying the work of Pavel Tchelitchew.

Gertrude had met Tchelitchew through Jane Heap and Margaret Anderson, the founders of the *Little Review*, which had published several of her pieces. He was one of a group with Christian Bérard, Kristians Tonny, and Genia Berman who exhibited together in 1926 and called themselves the Neo-Romantics, and who were then having some vogue in Paris. They painted portraits and landscapes in a lyrical, tender and fantastic manner, very different from the austere and violent productions of the Surrealists. Although Tchelitchew was himself wild (Alice called him 'absolutely cannibal – he devoured everything – men women children – flats – furniture – everything except the original Russian ballet which he caressed'), he and his group exhibited a soft, decorative and, as Gertrude thought, pastoral quality in their work. In this they appeared to share an interest evident in Gertrude's own current work. Since the first of her annual summer stays in the countryside around Belley in the Ain district in 1923, Gertrude had been much absorbed with the concept of landscape. In 1927 she was working on a 'pastoral novel' called after a church in Lucey, near Belley, *Lucy Church Amiably*, and, according to the subtitle, 'A Novel of romantic beauty and nature and which Looks Like an Engraving'.

It was characteristic of Gertrude to be interested in painting which she thought was developing along lines similar to those of her own writing. Such had been the case with the Cubists. Now she began to collect the work of Tchelitchew and his friends. Although she later dismissed his efforts and his motives as childish: ('He was painting, so he said, color that was no color, he was painting blue pictures and he was painting three heads in one. Picasso had been drawing three heads in one. Soon the russian was painting three figures in one,' she wrote in 1932 in *The Autobiography*), she ardently collected his work in the late twenties, and developed a rationalisation for its significance. By 1936 in *Everybody's Autobiography*, although she had conceded four years earlier that 'Painting after its great period has come to be a minor art', a minor interest in a minor artist was defended by a major theory:

Why are Russians important in the same way as Spaniards, she asked herself.

And then it came to me it is perfectly simple, the Russian and the Spaniard are Oriental, and there is the same mixing. Scratch a Russian and you find a Tartar. Scratch a Spaniard and you find a Saracen.

And all this is very important with what I have been saying about the peaceful penetration into European culture or rather the tendency for this generation that is for the twentieth century to be no longer European because perhaps Europe is finished.

And how, one asks, suspicions aroused, does Gertrude Stein fit into all this? Quite simply: to be Jewish is also to be Oriental: 'Einstein was the creative philosophic mind of the century and I have been the creative literary mind of the century also with the Oriental mixing with the European.'

But however far her racial theories took her with regard to her own position in cultural history, it did not last long as a basis of art patronage. Eventually the work of the Russian, together with that of Tonny, Bérard and Berman found its way into what Alice called the salon des refusés at 27 rue de Fleurus, and the artists disappeared from her life. Tchelitchew departed in a particularly bizarre manner, as a letter which Alice wrote in 1951, describes: 'Then one day we asked Edith [Sitwell] to lunch and Pavlik Tchelitchew came in and shortly after lunch they left together and we never saw either of them again for years. They had a very violent affair – Edith is perhaps still in love with him. They have written to each other every day for years and years and they promised to give the other's letters sealed of course to Yale University Library not to be opened until 2000.'

Of the painters in whose work Gertrude had been interested in the late twenties, only the work of Francis Rose, a young English Neo-Romantic (also a disciple of Picabia and with some Spanish ancestry) continued to interest her. Although she did not meet Rose himself until 1930, after which they became good friends, she had been collecting his work regularly in the late twenties. His paintings were hung in the company of the Picassos and Grises that dominated the rue de Fleurus flat. Not even the sarcasm of Picasso would make her remove them. As Virgil Thomson tells the story, Picasso noticing one of Rose's Neo-Romantic landscapes, asked how much it had cost. 'To her reply that she had paid 300 francs ($10) he muttered, half-smiling, "For that price one can get something quite good." '

If the twenties could provide for Gertrude no really important paintings or artistic causes, for the rest of Paris life went on as if they had. Someone was always the last word in the new or the beautiful or the outrageous. It was a decade when, as Virgil Thomson wrote, 'money, caviar, and diamonds; intelligence, amiability, and good looks; talent, imagination and wit; ambition, success and charm were available everywhere'. Fashionable and scandalous parties were duly reported in the leading Paris journals and in these Gertrude took part: the opium parties of the English poetess Mary Butts, where one met the Surrealists; orgies given by the painter Pascin, where one could meet artists' models and drunken American writers; literary evenings at the home of Nathalie Barney, the Ohio-born 'Amazone' of Rémy de Gourmont's *Lettres à l'amazone*, famous for such celebrities as Radclyffe Hall, the man-tailored authoress of the recently published *Well of Loneliness*; and costume parties at the elegant homes of Nancy Cunard or the Duchesse de Clermont-Tonnerre, according to Alice the real model for Proust's Duchesse de Guermantes.

The Duchesse de Clermont-Tonnerre was a particular friend of Gertrude's. In 1927 she appeared before Gertrude with her hair cut very close to her head, a style which Gertrude thought particularly fetching. Soon thereafter, Gertrude had Alice cut her hair in the same way. When Sherwood Anderson, then on a visit to Paris, came to call on the ladies, he was stunned by the new look .What do you think, asked Alice. 'I like it,' said Sherwood, 'it makes her look like a monk.' Picasso was less pleased. He felt she had violated an obligation to remain in resemblance to his 1906 portrait.

Gertrude also gave parties in the twenties, for the Sitwells, for the Van Vechtens, for Sherwood Anderson and his new wife, and for the several blacks that Carl Van Vechten – a great frequenter and patron of twenties Harlem – had been sending to see her in Paris. Blacks were then very fashionable in Paris, thanks particularly to the performances of Josephine Baker, then appearing in such costumes as a hip-skirt made of bananas, in the highly erotic *Revue Nègre*, which had come to Paris from America in 1925. Among Carl's friends who visited and were hosted by Gertrude at that time were the singer Paul Robeson and his wife Essie. Gertrude liked Robeson, but she rebuked him for singing negro spirituals: 'They do not belong to you any more than anything else, so why claim them she said.'

The sight of Gertrude, as well as her autocratic pronouncements must have been alarming to the unprotected young Americans whom Carl Van Vechten thought it his duty to introduce to Gertrude. A rather more sophisticated American, Bravig Imbs, speaks of her prima donna behaviour in society and of the deference she was accorded by other people, who treated her 'as though she might catch on fire from the sacred flame at any minute'. Bravig Imbs also gives a good description of her appearance in the late twenties, which somehow never detracted from her regal presence:

> There was never anything equivocal about Gertrude's hats; they were either excessively mannish, Napoleonic and severe, or of a dowdy, blousy, flower-bedecked femininity which was disconcerting to behold. The same tendency was marked in her dress. She could be very handsome, indeed, in austere brown monastic gowns – there was one made out of some Egyptian cloth that I liked very much, falling straight from the shoulder to foot and giving her the height she needed, for she was rather small in stature. But Gertrude also had a penchant for brightly coloured cloths, bearing patterns of tiny flowers, and for blouses, both of which should have been forbidden, because they made her look dumpy and old.
>
> Alice on the contrary, never made an error in dress, and always looked exceedingly smart. She had adopted the Frenchwoman's restraint, and seldom wore anything but greys and black.

Gertrude and Alice made an odd and striking couple in the late twenties, but to be seen in their society was *de rigeur* for anyone who wished to claim serious 'arrival' in Paris. Besides, there were many who genuinely wanted to know Gertrude Stein, and among these was the young American composer Virgil Thomson, who was soon to become important to Gertrude's writing and future 'gloire'.

Thomson had come to Paris just after the war to study with the famous Nadia Boulanger at the American School of Music at Versailles. He had also come to be at the international centre of modern music, to be near his idols Satie and Stravinsky, and to meet if he could the famous composers of recent years: Ravel, Fauré, Saint-Saëns, and the younger ones like Schoenberg and Les Six: Durey, Auric, Taillefer, Honegger, Milhaud, and Poulenc, all of whom were then experimenting radically in Paris. In this celebrated society, Thomson was soon to establish himself, and like Aaron Copland and George Antheil – whose musical score for Léger's film 'Ballet Méchanique' had been performed at Shakespeare and Company in 1925 – to create for himself a reputation as one of several promising American composers.

George Antheil was, soon after his triumph at Sylvia Beach's bookshop, much in vogue when in the winter of 1925–6 Gertrude asked to meet him. He arrived at the rue de Fleurus shortly thereafter, bringing with him Virgil Thomson, who had read *Tender Buttons* and *Geography and Plays* at Harvard and was anxious to meet the author. The meeting, as Virgil remembers, was only a partial success: 'Alice Toklas did not on first view care for me, and neither of the ladies found reason for seeing George [who was rather vain and truculent] again.' 'But,' Virgil adds, 'Gertrude and I got on like Harvard men.'

Virgil believed that Gertrude's work could, as she claimed, 'be compared to the great poetry of the past'. Gertrude, on the other hand, did not like music; she felt it was 'for adolescents' and a mark of barbarity in nations. In 1939 she wrote patriotically in *Paris France*: 'After all really civilised countries do not continuously make music, and that is the reason that France and England are the most civilised countries. They are not everlastingly making music.' But Virgil's music she liked, it was pleasant at least, and it often accompanied her text. More than this, she liked Virgil himself. 'From the fall of 1926,' Virgil wrote, 'in fact, till her death in July of 1946 we were forever loving being together, whether talking and walking, writing to each other, or at work.'

Not long after their first meeting, Virgil began to write music for some of Gertrude's shorter pieces. He set her poem 'Susie Asado' to music for voice and piano, and performed it to her with success. He had chosen Gertrude's work, partly because it was a challenge to intelligibility and partly because its very obscurity made it musically adaptable. As he wrote of her work in his autobiography: 'With meanings already abstracted, or absent, or so multiplied that choice among them was impossible, there was no temptation toward tonal illustration, say, of birdie babbling by the brook or heavy heavy hangs my heart.' So might he have set to music random speech or mathematical calculations. But there was also something decidedly musical in the rhythms of her prose, Virgil felt, much of which 'lies closer to musical timings than to speech timings. The rigamarole ending of *Capital Capitals*, for instance, I have always felt to have small relation to Spenser, Shakespeare, Milton, or Keats; but I do recognise in its peroration-by-repetition the insistences of a Beethoven finale.'

Early in 1927 Gertrude agreed to write for Virgil an opera libretto. What he wanted was something in the format of 'classic Italian opera' with some historical subject. Gertrude suggested the life of George Washington, but this Virgil rejected on the grounds that its performance in eighteenth-century costume would make everyone look alike. Eventually they agreed to base the work on the lives of saints.

Gertrude's interest in saints was hardly a religious one. Indeed, she rejected Christianity as a fairytale and felt that the advantage of her own religion was that 'when a Jew dies he is dead'. But she was an avid reader of saints' lives, nonetheless, and had a long time ago been particularly moved by Avila and its saint, Theresa, when she had gone with Alice to Spain in the summer of 1912. That summer in Avila she had worked on the last part of *Tender Buttons*, having been struck she said by 'a desire to express the rhythm of the visible world'. That work was for her a real achievement of an expression of 'outer reality', the result of a new way of seeing. Saints were also seers in this way. Their vision, like hers, and, as she said, like the mystic vision of Juan Gris, penetrated through the preconceived reality of the rest of the world to the true reality of things. Saints were therefore interesting because they were like Cubists. And like Cubists (for Gertrude only Spaniards were Cubists) the Saints she chose were Spanish: Theresa, St Ignatius Loyola, St Chavez. Though these were all historical figures, as seers of this other reality and above all, as Spaniards, they were among the few people who were really modern, like her, 'twentieth century'.

In *Picasso*, written in 1938, Gertrude expressed this conviction about Spain:

Spaniards know that there is no agreement, neither the landscape with the houses, neither the round with the cube, neither the great number with the small number, it was natural that a Spaniard [Picasso] should express this in the painting of the twentieth century, the century where nothing is in agreement, neither the round with the cube, neither the landscape with the houses, neither the large quantity with the small quantity. America and Spain [also Gertrude Stein and Picasso and the saints] have this thing in common, that is why Spain [Columbus] discovered America and America [Gertrude] Spain [Picasso and saints], in fact it is for this reason that both of them have found their moment in the twentieth century.

Gertrude was also interested – and particularly since her recent success in England – in the idea of legend and sudden fame, how by simply existing in a certain way, almost as a 'personality' as she was, a person can become famous, like a saint. In 1936 in *Everybody's Autobiography* she wrote about this quality of magical being: 'A saint a real saint never does anything, a martyr does something but a really good saint does nothing, and so I wanted to have Four Saints who did nothing and I wrote Four Saints In Three Acts and they did nothing and that was everything.' This is not very different from Gertrude's own way of working and her justification of simply being: 'It takes a lot of time to be a genius, you have to sit around so much doing nothing.'

At the time of writing 'Four Saints In Three Acts', Gertrude was also interested in the concept of landscape. Since 1922 when she and Alice had spent most of the year in St Rémy, Gertrude had thought about landscape and composition. 'Lend a Hand', a piece she wrote that year was, she said, her 'first conception of landscape as a play'. Now she was writing a play as landscape. She wrote to Virgil that she would make the libretto 'pastoral. In hills and gardens'. For Gertrude, landscape was, like a saint, 'a natural phenomenon, a thing existent in itself'. The opera was to present the saints as figures who by their simple existence were magical, and they would be figures in a landscape, itself by simply existing, magical. In a later lecture she wrote, 'In *Four Saints* I made the Saints the landscape. All the saints that I made and I made a number of them because after all a great many pieces of things are in a landscape all these saints together made my landscape.' The saints in Gertrude's opera would simply be presented: 'as a landscape they were just there, and a play is just there.'

Gertrude's work for 'Four Saints' also inspired her to write a long novel, a romantic, lyrical paean on the countryside around Belley, where she had spent every summer since that first one in 1923. *Lucy Church Amiably* was written out of doors, and its prose was, according to Virgil, set to the tune of Belley's 'streams and waterfalls'. Here is a typical 'engraved' passage: 'Very little daisies and very little bluettes and an artificial bird and a very white anemone which is allowed and then after it is very well placed by an unexpected invitation to carry a basket by an unexpected invitation to carry a basket back and forth back and forth and a river there is this difference between a river here and a river there.'

Gertrude's method of working on her novel, indicates with just what precision she used the term 'landscape' about this work. As in her earlier portraits, or the 'still lifes' in *Tender Buttons*, she meant to draw a close analogy between the way she wrote and the way painters painted. Virgil's description of Gertrude's open-air compositions in his autobiography indicates to what extent the analogy may be made:

The scene took place in a field, its enactors being Gertrude, Alice, and a cow. Alice, by means of a stick, would drive the cow around the field. Then at a sign from Gertrude, the cow would be stopped; and Gertrude would write in her copybook. After a bit she would pick up her folding stool and progress to another spot, whereupon Alice would again start the cow moving around the field till Gertrude signaled she was ready to write again.

That winter Virgil set 'Four Saints' to music, and Gertrude was pleased by the results. Although he was criticised by some for setting 'backward looking music [Virgil was also much influenced by the Neo-Romantics] to forward looking text', the work received a good deal of praise when it was performed privately in Paris. Encouraged by this reaction, Virgil spent some months in the winter of 1928–9 promoting the opera in New York. There in February 1929 he performed some of the work to a select group of friends, including Carl Van Vechten and Mabel Dodge. As Carl wrote back to Gertrude, 'Mabel liked it so much that she said it should be done, it would finish opera just as Picasso had finished old painting.'

Although Virgil failed to find a backer for 'Four Saints' in America, 'Capital Capitals', Gertrude's 1923 work, a 'conversation' among the four capitals of Provence (Aix, Arles, Avignon, and Les Baux), was performed in New York in February 1929. Virgil sent Gertrude his report:

Capitals swell success. N.Y. talks of nothing else since three days. Audience roared with laughter during and bravos afterwards. Critics charmingly confused. Some thought it a good joke, some a bad joke and one or so got quite angry. . . .

. . . The poets were all disgusted with the words and the composers thought the music too low for anything. But the audience's way of taking it proved to me the possibility of having a regular boob success with the opera, at least it might run long enough to pay its expenses and it might just might (and without surprising me at all) make a little money.

Gertrude was, of course, thrilled. As she wrote back to Virgil, 'gloire' might be just around the corner: '. . . perhaps we will get on the radio and the gramophone yet and have royalties and buy a prize Bedlington terrier and a telephone and pay for my new Ford car, perhaps, but anyway, I am most awfully pleased.'

That year, 1929, Gertrude got neither a Bedlington terrier, nor a telephone, nor money to pay for the new Ford. But she did get something that she and Alice had always wanted.

Ever since the summer of 1923 when, looking for a place to stop between Paris and the Picassos' home in Antibes, Alice had found the Hotel Pernollet at Belley in the *Guide des gourmets*, Alice and Gertrude had spent their summers with the Pernollet family, eating well and inexpensively, and enjoying the countryside of the Ain region in the Alpes Maritimes. Although it was surrounded by high mountains and spectacular views, Belley itself was in open country, which Gertrude found a good deal preferable to the insecurities of the mountainside. Furthermore, Belley was where the Romantic poet Lamartine had gone to school and where Brillat-Savarin, the eighteenth-century philosopher-gourmet, had been born. As a summer retreat it was ideal, both dramatically beautiful and prosaically comfortable, with the promise of both aesthetic and culinary delights. Belley was also gradually becoming an important part of Gertrude's highly personal sense of the past. It was here that she and Alice had corrected the proofs of *The Making of Americans* for Robert McAlmon's Contact Editions in 1925, here that she worked on her opera and her long romantic novel *Lucy Church Amiably*, here with the help of Alice, she had been composing landscapes; and now, if possible, it would be here that she would find a permanent country home.

With this in mind, in the spring of 1929 Gertrude and Alice took a series of motoring trips in the surrounding region. They had their new Ford, and now a new dog – a large white poodle, which Alice had wanted ever since reading Henry James's *The Princess Casamassima*. As a puppy, the previous year, the poodle had seemed a little saccharine, with blue eyes and a pink nose; Alice called him Basket because he looked as though 'he should carry a basket of flowers in his mouth'. But as he grew older, Basket became more himself and more part of the family – a masculine, slightly lewd-looking poodle, whose character interested Gertrude (she said Basket had made her into a doggy person) and whose behaviour even influenced her work: 'She says that listening to the rhythm of his water drinking made her recognise the difference between sentences and paragraphs, that paragraphs are emotional and that sentences are not.' Basket was also a clever dog, and Gertrude could teach him tricks. With a handkerchief held out in front of him as a

Paul Cézanne, *Portrait of Madame Cézanne, c.* 1877.

The Twenties and the Thirties

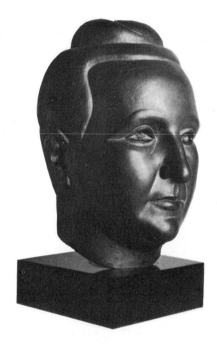

ABOVE Portrait head of Gertrude Stein by Jacques Lipchitz, 1920.

BELOW Sylvia Beach with James Joyce, in her bookshop Shakespeare & Company.

ABOVE F. Scott Fitzgerald with his wife
and daughter.

OPPOSITE Ezra Pound, 1923.   ABOVE Ernest Hemingway in the 1920s.

LEFT Ford Madox Ford.
BELOW LEFT Sherwood Anderson.
BELOW The Sitwells, photographed
by Cecil Beaton.

ABOVE Gertrude and Alice in the Twenties.
ABOVE RIGHT Gertrude Stein and Alice B. Toklas in 'Godiva'.
RIGHT Gertrude Stein and Alice B. Toklas with Pavel Tchelitchew.

LEFT Leo Stein and
Nina Auzias.
BELOW LEFT Paul Robeson.
BELOW The Duchesse de
Clermont-Tonnerre.

ABOVE Francis Rose.
LEFT Portrait of Alice B. Toklas by
Francis Rose, 1932.
BELOW LEFT Francis Rose, *Homage to
Gertrude Stein*; water-colour study for
a picture never painted.

LEFT *Four Saints* on Broadway;
a photograph sent in 1934 by Carl Van Vechten.

ABOVE Gertrude Stein with Virgil Thomson.

OPPOSITE RIGHT The photograph which inspired
Rose's study.

Portrait of Gertrud~
by Tal Coat.

cape to a bull, she would instruct him: 'Be fierce play Hemingway.' Together with the Ford, the recent haircut, the deep laugh, and the picture collection, Basket was to become an important part of the Gertrude Stein legend.

While Gertrude, Alice and Basket, making a highly photographable and frequently photographed family group, were driving in the Ford, they spotted a house across a valley which they thought was just what they wanted. It was a small and elegant seventeenth-century manor in Bilignin just outside Belley, and there was no reason to suppose it would be given to them just for the asking. Gertrude Stein, however, quite characteristically insisted on finding out about the house, and Alice was sent to the nearest farmer to make enquiries. The house, Alice was told, belonged to a child whose parents were dead, and on her behalf it had been let to an army lieutenant stationed at Belley. It might just conceivably be available.

But the lieutenant had no intention of giving up the lease. Undeterred, Gertrude adopted an extremely clever plan. She would have the lieutenant promoted to captain and as there was already a captain in Belley, the second one would surely have to move. Gertrude got a friend, a former war office clerk, to make some enquiries. His news was not good. The thing could not be done because this particular lieutenant would never qualify for his examinations to become captain; nor was it worthwhile for the army to promote him, since he was near retirement and the pension for a captain was more than that for a lieutenant. There are French troops in Morocco, said Gertrude's friend, why not get him sent there. This seemed excessive to Gertrude. Two months later, however, when they were told that the lieutenant had indeed been transferred to Morocco, they asked no questions. That spring, having only seen the house from across a valley, they signed the lease on their new house in Bilignin.

They were not disappointed. Inside was the furniture of the descendants of Brillat-Savarin himself. Outside was a lovely semi-formal garden, with gravel walks and flower beds. There were little balconies and shutters, and a spectacular view of the countryside. It was a perfect home for a woman of letters.

But though Gertrude had now all the appurtenances of a successful career, her goal of wider recognition still eluded her. *The Making of Americans* had been appreciatively received in certain critical quarters in America, but not many people had actually read the book, and as Gertrude felt, 'everybody ought to be reading at it or it . . .'. She knew that, as Sherwood Anderson had recently written to her, 'anyone who follows writing sees your influence everywhere', but the more tangible proofs of success were yet to come. With this in view, she and Alice began to think seriously of publishing their own edition of the yet unpublished works of Gertrude Stein. It was to be financed by the sale of Picasso's *Girl with a Fan*, and it was to be called the Plain Edition.

Alice conferred with Maurice Darrantière, who had printed *The Making of Americans* and, it must be said, James Joyce's *Ulysses*, and who was then using a hand-press to print limited, special editions. For Alice's less de luxe needs, he suggested Monotype, and inexpensive paper, and that the books be bound in paper. Alice herself would distribute the books. From friends in America she acquired a list of booksellers, and when their orders began coming in, she began to prepare for press the first of the books which would appear under the Plain Edition imprint, *Lucy Church Amiably*.

At the same time, plans were afoot to rescue the neglected *The Making of Americans*. Georges Hugnet, a friend of Virgil Thomson, who with Virgil had translated some of Gertrude's Portraits for the 1927 volume *If I Told Him*, illustrated by Picasso and her Neo-Romantic painter friends, had been working on the French translation of portions of *The Making of Americans*. In 1929 these appeared as *Morceaux choisis de la fabrication des américains*, under Hugnet's own imprint, Editions de la Montagne, and illustrated with a portrait of Gertrude by Christian Bérard.

The second volume of the Plain Edition, which appeared in 1931, was a direct result of Gertrude's work with Hugnet. In 1930 she had returned the compliment of his translation, by offering to do an English version of Hugnet's poem *Enfances*. What started as a translation soon became, not surprisingly, something altogether different – a Steinian étude inspired somewhat vaguely by the original. Unfortunately for Hugnet, he treated Gertrude's version as a translation. When the subscription notice for the book appeared, Hugnet's name was printed in letters twice the size of Gertrude's. Her poem he called simply a *traduction*. A certain deference to genius was, as Gertrude thought, lacking. As the work was intended as an important debut for the twenty-five-year-old poet, he was naturally concerned that readers should know that they had not collaborated on the poetry, that Gertrude's poem was but a 'translation' of his own. But Gertrude was furious. She had her translation printed separately by Alice in an edition of one hundred copies. Its new title was a clear and uncharitable statement to Hugnet: *Before the Flowers of Friendship Faded Friendship Faded*.

The Making of Americans was finally translated into French in full by Gertrude's friend Bernard Faÿ, Professor of American Studies at the Collège de France and by Baronne Seillère, to be published by Librarie Stock in 1932. But it was Hugnet's work which made Gertrude's novel most accessible to Frenchmen, who had for years known of her reputation without knowing her work. Although it hardly broke over Paris like the French edition of *Ulysses*, it did make some little splash. As Gertrude was delighted to repeat, the critic Marcel Brion had, in the pages of *Echange*, compared her prose to the music of Bach. 'I knew it was a wonderful book in english,' she said in *The Autobiography*, 'but it is even, well, I cannot say almost really more wonderful but just as wonderful in french.'

But if she thought the French public might soon know something of her work, she was dismally aware that her American public remained fairly unenlightened. Robert Coates, then working for the *New Yorker*, wrote to Gertrude in 1930 to describe the situation: 'You must know, if you read any American publications at all,' he wrote, 'how your name is bandied about. I should think it would infuriate you sometimes – it certainly does me – to see your name used by critics who obviously have never read a line of yours as a tag for anything from 3 A.M. at the Select Bar to Communism.'

During the next two years, however, two events were to push Gertrude Stein close to the brink of the 'gloire' she had longed for since 1900. The first was the publication in

1931 of Edmund Wilson's *Axel's Castle*. It dealt at length with the work of Gertrude Stein, totally without parody or innuendo; and it dealt with her work in the company of such, by now established, writers as Proust, Joyce and Eliot. Although it was hardly a statement of allegiance to Gertrude's artistic aims, it was the first full and serious discussion of her work by a major critic.

The second event, far more spectacular in its results, was the writing in 1932, after long entreaty from publishers, of *The Autobiography of Alice B. Toklas.*

8

Remarks
Are Not Literature

GERTRUDE STEIN'S FRIENDS had for a long time been pressing her to write some kind of account of her life and times. Such a book, they said, would make fascinating reading. Though she had few reservations about blowing her own trumpet, it was not the sort of writing she was interested in. But if Alice would do it, she thought, she would not mind. Alice agreed to think about it. But, when, late in the autumn of 1932, it was clear that Alice was not going to abandon her gardening and cooking activities at Bilignin for writing, Gertrude decided she would do the book herself. She would write it as though it came from Alice's hand. She would tell her tale in the voice of Alice Toklas, 'as simply,' she said, 'as Defoe did the autobiography of Robinson Crusoe'.

The Autobiography of Alice B. Toklas, with its surprise ending which reveals, without changing the voice of the speaker, the true identity of the author, was a literary joke that owed its inspiration to Gertrude's love of detective novels (she claimed to read one a day). But it also enabled her to undertake a triumphant feat of mimicry in the recreation of the voice of its purported authoress. 'The essence of genius is to be able to listen,' Gertrude had often said, and after almost twenty-five years of listening to the speech of her friend, she was able to reproduce accurately the clipped pace, the casual, almost throw-away treatment of anecdote, the love of paradox ('I like a view but I like to sit with my back to it'), delicate irony ('I led in my childhood and youth the gently bred existence of my class and kind'), and the cloaked, sometimes inadequately cloaked, malice of Alice's speech.

The book was totally unlike anything Gertrude had written before. The clarity of the narrative was startling. After all those years of dense obscurity and infuriating word play, *The Autobiography* was as extraordinary when it appeared as the emperor without his clothes. Why, it was demanded, if Gertrude could write like this, clearly, with great wit, and speed, had she previously dragged her readers through the obstacle course of her 'continuous present', her unrecognisable Portraits and still-lifes, her unearthly 'land-scapes', her tantalising and desperately frustrating meditations and 'elucidations'? Did this book not herald the dawning of rational speech from the Sybil of Montparnasse, the beaching on the shores of sanity of this hulk of modernism; the return, in fact, of the prodigal?

There were many who thought it did. William Bradley, the Paris literary agent who had never before been able to see commercial possibility in any work of Miss Stein's, now received the manuscript with an eagerness prompted by the distant sound of clinking coins. In a phrase which he would never have believed it possible to use about any work of Gertrude Stein's, he told her that the second part of the manuscript had now arrived, and 'wild horses couldn't keep me from reading it at once'.

In no time, Bradley had sold the book to Alfred Harcourt of Harcourt, Brace, New York. Better than that, he fulfilled Gertrude's lifelong ambition by selling serialisation rights to the most regal of literary magazines, *The Atlantic Monthly*. Ellery Sedgwick, the head of *Atlantic*, with whom Gertrude had often pleaded to publish her work, wrote enthusiastically in February 1933: 'There has been a lot of pother about this book of yours, but what a delightful book it is, and how glad I am to publish four installments of it! During our long correspondence, I think you felt my constant hope that the time would come when the real Miss Stein would pierce the smoke-screen with which she has always so mischievously surrounded herself. . . . Hail Gertrude Stein about to arrive!' But this was mixed praise indeed. The 'real Miss Stein' was sheer imitation of Alice's way of talking and writing – as any reading of Alice's own memoir *What is Remembered*, Alice's cookbooks, or her published letters will reveal. The so-called smokescreen was Gertrude herself – in deadly (of course, some thought too deadly) earnest.

But Ellery Sedgwick was right in one respect: the book was a delight. It told the history of 'the old crowd' and the 'heroic age of cubism'; it told of the World War I adventures of the two spinsters, of the life of the 'lost generation' in the Paris of the twenties. It told the story through anecdote and aphorism, with marvellous humour and quickness, mixing domestic detail with the very stuff of legend. More than this, it created the persona of Gertrude herself: the centre of the art world for three decades, the best friend of the great, feared and recognised by all as a genius. There was none of the becoming modesty of ordinary autobiography in the book. In Alice's words, Gertrude told how she was a child prodigy, writing a Shakespearian drama at the age of eight, how she was the favourite student of the great William James, how she almost single-handedly discovered modern art, and how with 'Melanctha' took 'the first step away from the nineteenth century and into the twentieth century in literature'; how she was adored by the dough-boys; how she advised Picasso and created Hemingway; how 'she realises that in english literature in her time she is the only one. She has always known it and now she says it'. It painted a convincing picture – far from the decadent ogre of modernism – of the lovable eccentric, an innocent in the midst of scandalous Montmartre, wearing fantastic clothes, driving dangerously an old Ford, walking a large white poodle, talking to French workmen and dismissing the famous, playing clever tricks on celebrated artists, getting away by sheer charm with social murder.

But it *was* convincing. It was gripping and it was a *succès de foudre*. Mr Answell, an editor at *The Atlantic Monthly*, wrote to tell her the extraordinary effect *The Auto-*

biography had had on him. He had begun to read, he said, in a bad temper, first thing in the morning. 'I read the first page, and right there you had me. I was instantly fascinated and went on reading, turning page after page automatically not knowing that I turned them, so completely absorbed had I become in your story.' By the end of the day, he said, 'I had forgotten time, forgotten my lunch, forgotten a dozen things I had meant to do that day, so entirely had I been caught by the spell of your words.' Then, he adds, in a prophetic sweep, 'If you could do this to an editor, of all people the least susceptible to the magic of print, what, I wonder, will be the effect of your story on the general public?'

Like thunder. The American public fell in love with the character of Gertrude Stein, like Victorian readers with Little Nell. Carl Van Vechten wrote ecstatically when the book appeared in September 1933, '. . . it is a joy to know you and to shake your hand across the sea and I think you'd better come over and take the tribute due you and be photographed.' The book was a sensational best-seller, and as Max Ewing wrote to her, '. . . you are more discussed in Hollywood these days than Greta Garbo'.

The phenomenal success of the book brought with it the kind of 'gloire' that Gertrude had always wanted. And it brought money as well: '. . . First I bought myself a new eight cylinder Ford car, and the most expensive coat made to order by Hermes and fitted by the man who makes coats for race horses for Basket and two collars studded for Basket. I had never made any money before in my life and I was most excited.' It was a rare pleasure and, as she wrote in *Everybody's Autobiography*, 'there is no doubt about it there is no pleasure like it, the sudden splendid spending of money and we spent it.'

As she was the talk of America, Gertrude was soon to be the talk of Paris as well. When the French edition of *The Autobiography*, translated by Bernard Faÿ, appeared in 1934, she became an overnight celebrity. Her appearance at French literary salons and high-society dinner parties suddenly became highly desirable. At the age of sixty Gertrude was now enjoying the life of a debutante. As she wrote in *Everybody's Autobiography*:

> Everybody invited me to meet somebody, and I went. I always will go anywhere once and I rather liked doing what I had never done before, going everywhere. It was pleasant being a lion, and meeting the people who make it pleasant for you to be a lion.
>
> So we went on accepting invitations and going out to see the people . . . and we had engagements a week ahead for every day and sometimes twice a day always before that they used to come as they came but now it was all arranged to come. We did not yet use a tiny engagement book and look at it in a nearsighted way the way all the young men used to do as soon as they were successful but we might have. Being successful is all the same and we liked it.

The stir that *The Autobiography* created for Gertrude in Paris did not emit only the bubbles of general delight. It also produced from certain quarters a deeply drawn and bitter vapour of resentment. The characteristic voice of Alice, together with the genius persona of Gertrude, lent themselves very well to malicious and slighting description of some of those with whom she had shared the centre stage of her glory. In February 1935, *Transition*, the revue which had done much to advance Gertrude's reputation in the late twenties, collected a number of responses from those who felt they had been mistreated in the book. These were published as a special supplement to the magazine, entitled 'Testimony Against Gertrude Stein'. As her former friend and editor, Eugene Jolas wrote in his Foreword:

> These documents invalidate the claim of the Toklas-Stein memorial that Miss Stein was in any way concerned with the shaping of the epoch she attempts to describe. There is a unanimity of opinion that she had no understanding of what really was happening around her, that the mutation of ideas beneath the surface of the more obvious contacts and clashes of personalities during that period escaped her entirely. Her participation in the genesis and development of such movements as Fauvism, Cubism, Surrealism, Transition [sic] etc. was never ideologically intimate and, as M. Matisse states, she has presented the epoch 'without taste and without relation to reality'.

So much was more or less true. Gertrude had fallen almost by accident into.the great events which took place in Paris, and took up the ideology of art movements only when they suited her own literary interests. Her great success in this had, of course, been Cubism; but from that platform she had claimed to understand and in some cases direct the further activities of the avant-garde. Nor can it be said that her book was in any way an objectively – or, as she would quote William James, 'abjectly' – true account of what had taken place in Paris between 1903 and 1932. Such truth she did not believe existed. History was not fact, it was merely 'something you remember', and she felt no obligation to strain to 'remember right'. Even the picture of one's own history was bound to be, in this sense, untrue. In *Everybody's Autobiography* she wrote about this aspect of recreation:

> And identity is funny being yourself is funny as you are never yourself to yourself except as you remember yourself and then of course you do not believe yourself. That is really the trouble with an autobiography you do not really believe yourself why should you, you know so well so very well that it is not yourself, it could not be yourself because you cannot remember right and if you do remember right it does not sound right and of course it does not sound right because it is not right. You are of course never yourself.

If *The Autobiography* was, as her critics claimed, mere legendising, it was because legend was more potent, more 'true' than history: 'And so autobiography is written which is in a way a way to say that publicity is right, they are as the public sees them.'

Jolas and his swarm of contributors could hardly be expected to act as midwives to the birth of this legend, nor to nurse it at their own expense. Instead, they voiced their fury: the *Autobiography of Alice B. Toklas*, in its hollow, tinsel bohemianism and egocentric deformations, may very well become one day the symbol of the decadence that hovers over contemporary literature.' There followed a list of specific complaints.

Matisse, who had certainly been slighted in the account, and whose wife's beauty had been compared to that of a horse, led the attack. He denied Gertrude's part in the heroic purchase of the *Femme au chapeau* in 1905, and said that that had been done by Sally Stein, whom he called 'the really intelligent, sensitive member of the family' (she had helped to found the Matisse classes and had continued to support the artist for many years after Leo and Gertrude had lost interest). He movingly defended his wife's beauty; cited the inaccuracy of several allegations and time-sequences in the book; denied Gertrude's assertion that Picasso had invented Cubism without Braque, and charged that she 'understood nothing'. Furthermore, he challenged her statement that she had been a constant friend to Juan Gris. His quarrel with her, he claimed, had dated from her abandoning Gris during World War I, and he had not wished to see her since.

Maria Jolas was furious with Gertrude's account of her dealings with *Transition*, in which she claimed that Elliot Paul had been the editor and responsible for the appearance of her work in the magazine. After Paul left, Gertrude had written, *Transition* had published nothing else of hers. Shortly thereafter, she wrote, more than implying causality, '*Transition* died'. Now Maria vigorously denied that Paul had had much to do with the selection of material for the magazine, which had been the brainchild and care of herself and her husband, Eugene. They had initially wanted Gertrude's contribution, Maria said, because she 'seemed to be experimenting courageously'. With a phrase that sticks, Maria now accused her would-be protégée of 'Barnumesque publicity' and rank ingratitude: 'What we should have foreseen however, was that she would eventually tolerate no relationship that did not bring with it adulation. This was undoubtedly lacking in our otherwise entirely correct and cordial attitude towards her, so when the moment came to play the mad queen in public, our heads had to come off with the others, despite the very real service we had rendered her.'

Tristan Tzara, although he was hardly mentioned in the book except as 'like a pleasant and not very exciting cousin', willingly joined the attack. As a long-time Surrealist, signer of many manifestoes, and professional declaimer of false gods, he once again hired out his pen for a bout of spleen. Unconvincingly shrill that his name should be mentioned even once in a book which he called 'a considerable display of sordid anecdotes destined to make us believe that Miss Gertrude Stein is in reality a genius', Tzara whirled like a mad little dervish into a fury against the 'lowest literary prostitution', stemming from a 'clinical case of megalomania'. Its authors, he said, were 'two maiden ladies greedy for fame and publicity'. 'I therefore have the right to ask on what grounds my name is mixed up with a story about which the least we might say is that the superficial and burlesque character of the persons quoted is such as to discredit certain humanly important enterprises which Miss Stein, who understands nothing, contacted in the final analysis only thanks to the weight of her pocket-book.'

Braque, however, had a real grievance. In her account of the early days of Cubism,

Gertrude had implied that Braque was merely a facile imitator of her friend Picasso. She had linked him with Derain, Apollinaire, and André Salmon as one of a ludicrous band who trailed after the great man, 'the little bull-fighter followed by his squadron of four', 'Napoleon followed by his four enormous grenadiers'. She had ascribed to Picasso, or put into his mouth, disparaging remarks about Braque, as, for example, that he was one of 'les incompréhensibles que tout le monde peut comprendre'. By other accounts, Braque had invented Cubism with Picasso. They were certainly together most of the early days of the discoveries, turning out pictures which, Braque now said, were so similar they are hard to assign to either accurately. He denounced her for seeing Cubism 'simply in terms of personalities'. How else could it have been, he said, when her French was so bad that she was hardly party to the goings-on. 'For one who poses as an authority on the epoch,' he said, 'it is safe to say that she never went beyond the stage of the tourist.' Nor was she held in the high regard she claimed by the painters she did know. 'We in Paris always heard that Miss Stein was a writer, but I don't think any of us had ever read her work until *Transition* began to make her known in France.' Then, he implies, we had our doubts. 'Now that we have seen her book, nous sommes *fixés*.'

André Salmon had similar cause for complaint. At the time, it is true, Gertrude and Alice had been pleased enough to be included in the activities of a crowd of artists involved in serious pursuits and whose lives were far more exciting than anything they had known in America. While it is more than likely that at first Gertrude had been merely tolerated, as a potential source of income for artists – until she became known and respected as an intelligent friend and writer – in the book she implies that she had always been a royal participant in the golden era of Montmartre – an era which in dramatic terms culminated in the Rousseau banquet. Forgetting how frail her footing had been in this early bohemian social climb, Gertrude had written dismissively of those whom she was then greatly pleased to know. André Salmon, for example, an important member of the group, she dismissed as not 'particularly interesting'. She made him, as she made most of the others, a comic figure in her account of the Rousseau banquet, a scandalous drinker and show-off. She and Alice, on the other hand, she depicted as the prime audience on that occasion, coldly watching minor players in a low farce.

Salmon attacked the shallowness and inaccuracy of the account, and her condescension to the now-famous: 'Miss Stein often mentions people whom she never knew very well, and so irresponsibly, in fact, that the reader is astounded.' 'What incomprehension of an epoch!', he writes, and what a betrayal: 'I am all the more astounded for I had thought, along with all our friends, that she really understood things. It is evident that she understood nothing, except in a superficial way.'

Gertrude's account of them all had been semi-fictional. That is, she had made into winsome comedy a very complex combination of events, personalities and motivations, taking the amusing peaks of truth and ignoring the large bulk of facts below. As she had caricatured herself in the book, so she caricatured the artists and the art movements themselves. To make an historical account readable it is necessary to isolate the significant at the expense of the 'abjectly' true general picture (to do the reverse would result in, for Gertrude, a serious work like *The Making of Americans,* in which every element was 'as important as any other' element in the narrative), and in this Gertrude had been successful. But the success of the book had depended on casting into low relief elements which did not suit her narrative. Some of these elements had been friends, who were now justifiably shocked at the disloyalty of an account they saw as an attempt to turn a fast buck by cashing in on the glory of *their* life's work, to acquire a certain gilt by association.

André Salmon had claimed that Gertrude 'went too far' in her account of the early days. Other former friends felt the same. While serious artists like Matisse shuddered at the cheapness and triviality of her description of their work, many others felt morally compromised with their present wives or family. Marie Laurencin complained to Gertrude that it was wrong to depict the pasts of writers and artists since they always lived in the present, without heed to the possibilities of future reporting of those lives. Besides, as Gertrude paraphrased Marie's statements later: '. . . if one had a son one had no past and so nobody could dare to describe anything. . . . The men could not say this thing because as they said it it would have sounded foolish to them but that is the way they did feel. . . .' Indeed, Marie was right. Olga Picasso had been very upset by Gertrude's account of Picasso's affair with Fernande. After she had listened to Gertrude reading out passages of the book to Picasso, Olga had flounced out of the room.

Hemingway, whom Gertrude had called 'fragile' and 'yellow', had compared with Derain in that he looked 'like a modern and he smells of the museums', had compared unfavourably with Fitzgerald, who she said 'will be read when many of his well known contemporaries are forgotten', and whom she had called the creation of herself and Sherwood Anderson ('and they were both a little proud and a little ashamed of the work of their minds'), now raged privately. He bided his time, however, until he could take his vengeance on Gertrude in *A Moveable Feast.* In the meantime, he sent her a copy of his recent book, *Death in the Afternoon,* with the circular inscription: 'A Bitch Is A Bitch Is A Bitch Is A Bitch. From her pal Ernest Hemingway.'

But of all the book's victims, the greatest was Leo, whom she left out almost entirely from her account of the early days in Paris, and to whom she referred always as 'Gertrude Stein's brother'. Leo did not bother to write to her now. He had tried to effect a reconciliation in 1919 on his return from America, but she had refused to answer his letter. In 1920, when by chance she had seen him in a Paris street, she condescended to nod in recognition. Then she went home and wrote 'She Bowed to Her Brother'. By now she had almost eradicated his existence from her memory and was able to deny to friends that she had any brother but Michael. *The Autobiography* shows her very near to the final exorcism of Leo from her sense of the past, and the distortions of fact which necessarily accompanied such exorcism understandably enraged him. '. . . God what a liar she is!' he wrote to Mabel Weeks in December 1933. 'Some of her chronology is too wonderful. . . . Practically everything that she says of our activities before 1911 is false in both fact and implication, but one of her radical complexes . . . made it necessary practically to eliminate me.' In another letter, to Ettie Stettheimer, In January 1934, he wrote: 'I wonder how near this comes to being an average autobiography for authenticity? Nothing of the pre-war period is accurately true, very little of the whole is accurately true, and very little of it is even approximately true.'

Besides being inaccurate, Leo found the book embarrassingly crass. A later letter to Mabel Weeks showed him amazed by the simple-mindedness of his sister: 'Imagine the stupidity of anyone sixty years of age who makes that remark about the qualities of sentences and paragraphs from the rhythm of her dog's drinking. I doubt whether there is a single comment or general observation in the book that is not stupid.' But *The Autobiography*, which Leo characterised as 'that farago of rather clever anecdote, stupid brag and general bosh' very much hurt him. For a long while he meditated on their different fortunes, her successes and his lifelong failure. By October 1934, when he wrote to his friend Albert Barnes, he had resolved the problem: 'Gertrude and I are just the contrary,' he said. 'She's basically stupid and I'm basically intelligent.' It was only Gertrude's 'massive self-admiration and in part, self-assurance' which had, he felt, enabled her to 'build something rather effective' of her life and work.

Both Gertrude's critics and her enthusiastic fans were right about *The Autobiography*. It had taken a gross insensitivity to 'reality' to create the character of Gertrude Stein in *The Autobiography of Alice B. Toklas*. The book had bulldozed its way through facts and sensibilities and had arrived triumphant on the other side of the destruction. But the book had, like any good fiction, its own truth, and it was this that was recognised by those thousands of readers who admired it.

And thousands did admire it. All that summer and winter of 1933 and 1934 Gertrude enjoyed the adulation of the French and American public. Her private life had been radically changed by the success of the book; she was no longer a semi-obscure writer, but a celebrity: '. . . a real celebrity who can decide who they want to meet and say so and they come or not come as you want them. I never imagined it would happen to me to be a celebrity like that but it did and when it did I liked it. . . .' But the change was as disturbing as it was pleasant. It was profoundly upsetting to think that the character she had created in *The Autobiography* could have an impact which her real self had not. It worried her with questions about who she was and whether a 'real' Gertrude even existed. 'The moment you or anybody else knows what you are you are not it, you are what you or anybody else knows you are.' The reality of the Stein image had, as she recognised, an independent truth: 'And so autobiography is written which is in a way a way to say publicity is right, they are as the public sees them.' But publicity itself was disturbing. It created for Gertrude, for the first time, a full awareness of an audience. 'I write for myself and strangers,' she had written in *The Making of Americans*. Now the strangers were in some way influencing that self: 'Inside and outside and identity is a great bother,' she wrote in *Everybody's Autobiography*. 'And how once you know that the buyer [audience] is there can you go on knowing that the buyer is not there. Of course when he is not there there is no bother.' Never before had the audience been so evidently there. The winter of 1933-4 Gertrude stopped writing altogether. The impact of *The Autobiography* had made her too frightened to put pen to paper.

'Buyer' was the word Gertrude used about this new audience. The word was appropriate to another result of the book's success: 'Before one is successful that is before any one is ready to pay money for anything you do then you are certain that every word you have written is as important as any other word and you keep everything you have written with great care. And then it happens sometimes sooner sometimes later that it has money value I had mine very much later and it is upsetting because when nothing had any commercial value everything was important. . . .' Something of the absolute quality of Gertrude's writing was jeopardised. Since some work had more value than other, it was impossible for this fact not to intrude upon the writing itself.

The writing, which had been a totally unself-conscious act of comprehension and description of reality, now became utterly self-conscious. The result was that Gertrude stopped writing altogether and worried about identity: '. . . somehow if my writing was worth money then it was not what it had been, if it had always been worth money then it would have been used to being that thing but if anything changes then there is no identity and if it completely changes then there is no sense in its being what it had been.' The success of the clear exposition of *The Autobiography* threw Gertrude back into worries about her own 'real work', and she wondered whether it was possible to be both a genius and a popular success. But the longer she was upset, the longer she was unable to write, and this also threw her into musings on identity: 'And if you stop writing if you are a genius and you have stopped writing are you still one. . . .'

She had made one attempt to deal with these problems of identity in a story that took as its basis two bizarre deaths which occurred in Bilignin in 1933, both apparent, though improbable, suicides. Inspired by her favourite detective reading, she wrote about existence and non-existence and called it 'Blood on the Dining-Room Floor'. Again that year she worried out these themes in a book called *Four In America*. For her exploration of the relationship between publicity and identity, and audience and creativity, she chose four people who were both 'geniuses' and well-known public figures. She gave them roles they had not played in history in order to discover whether the identity of genius was absolute or whether it depended on doing something, some productivity as proof of being that genius. For her analysis of the relation of role played to individual identity she chose Henry James, George Washington, Ulysses S. Grant, and Wilbur Wright, two men of thought and two men of action. She meditated on the possibility of Henry James having been a general, Washington a novelist, Grant a religious leader, and Wilbur Wright a painter, in order to 'find out just what it is that what happens has to do with what is'. The book is hardly a lucid meditation. But the section on James, for example, makes exciting and strenuous reading as Gertrude thinks out loud about 'the question of an audience', the differences between the knower and the thing known, and between knowing and communicating that knowledge. It was, in a way, her defence of her 'difficult' style, in the face of the popularity of the easy, false style of *The Autobiography*. At one point she declares, 'Clarity is of no importance because nobody listens'.

'I am not I any longer when I see', she says, 'that is, when I am conscious of the outside world, or audience. This sentence is at the bottom of all creative activity. It is just the exact opposite of I am because my little dog knows me.' That last had been a favourite phrase of hers; it insisted on the relation of existence or identity to recognition by something outside – the dog or audience. Now she worked out the argument that identity for the genius did not depend on an audience; nor did it depend on whether or not he fulfilled his role, as an artist or general. *Four In America* was an attempt to answer negatively the question of whether one was a genius only while one produced the work of genius. As she wrote five years later with more resoluteness in *Picasso*:

> It is always astonishing that Shakespeare never put his hand to his pen once he ceased to write and one knows other cases, things happen that destroy everything which forced the person to exist and the identity which was dependent upon the things that were done, does it still exist, yes or no.
>
> Rather yes, a genius is a genius, even when he does not work.

As with the 'continuous present', Gertrude's conviction that being a genius was an absolute thing, independent of popular success or even of audience comprehension had a profound psychological appeal. Genius could not be subjected to mortality or change. 'What is the use of being a little boy if you are to grow up to be a man.' Identity had to be changeless, absolute; being a genius was inviolable.

Four In America, difficult though it is, is part of an important body of work in which Gertrude Stein philophises on questions that concerned her directly, and passages in it have a tremendous force and brilliance. It was also an important work in that it not only defended her position as a 'difficult', if not mostly inaccessible writer, but it allowed her to ignore the implications of the success of *The Autobiography*, implications which had threatened to stop her short and awkwardly and demand a reappraisal of her life's work. Having settled the doubts about her work, having assured herself that the outside, 'publicity' and 'audience', could not tamper with the inside, with the reality and absoluteness of her genius, Gertrude Stein was free to enjoy the, to her mind, unearned spoils of *The Autobiography*'s success and to throw herself with ease into the role-playing that was now demanded of her.

Meanwhile, in the winter of 1932–3, just after the publication of *The Autobiography*, Virgil Thomson had been in New York, trying once more to find sponsors for their opera 'Four Saints in Three Acts'. By chance, the directors of the Wadsworth Atheneum in Hartford, Connecticut, were planning to open a new wing of their gallery early in 1934. They had prepared to mount a retrospective exhibition of the paintings of Picasso (the first Picasso retrospective in America) to coincide with the opening celebrations. After attending two of Thomson's semi-private concerts of the work in New York, they agreed to stage the opera as well. Dedicated to modern art, they believed they could do no better than subsidise this 1927 work of Virgil Thomson and the renowned Gertrude Stein. With such promises, Virgil returned to Paris early in 1933 to negotiate royalties and sign a contract with Gertrude and her agent.

The previous autumn when he was in New York, Virgil had accompanied Carl Van Vechten and his wife on a night out in Harlem. Although Virgil was unconquered by the charms of high-society slumming, he did return home greatly impressed by the night-club singing he had heard, and he began to think of using Negroes for the opera. The next morning, as he wrote in his autobiography, 'I was sure, remembering how proudly the Negroes enunciate and how the whites just hate to move their lips.' Enunciation would be crucial for any opera of Gertrude Stein's. Incoherence would deprive the opera not only of the peculiar force of its imagery, but also of its special humour: 'If a magpie in the sky on the sky can not cry if the pigeon on the grass alas can alas and to pass the pigeon on the grass alas and the magpie in the sky on the sky and to try and to try alas on the grass alas the pigeon on the grass alas the pigeon on the grass the pigeon on the grass and alas.'

Although an all-black cast had been recently seen on stage in Marc Connelly's Broadway success 'Green Pastures' of 1930, and in Paris in the celebrated *Revue Nègre* in the mid-twenties, these shows had used blacks to portray blacks. Virgil's use of only black singers and actors was the first occasion that Negroes were used simply instead of whites. As such it was a novel idea.

In the summer of 1933 Virgil had interrupted his dealings with Gertrude Stein's agent in Paris to make a trip to London. There at a party he met Frederick Ashton, a young man just beginning his career as a choreographer at the dance theatre of Sadler's Wells. Inexperienced as he was, Ashton impressed Virgil as someone who might be able to stage the opera. He now offered the Englishman a second-class ticket to New York and expenses without salary for the work of getting 'Four Saints' on stage, and Ashton accepted. Alexander Smallens, a fashionable American conductor, had already promised to conduct the opera. Lacking only a director for the work, Thomson sailed back to New York in October 1933, in the company of Arnold Schoenberg, an early refugee from Nazi anti-semitism, to begin work in earnest on 'Four Saints in Three Acts'.

Within weeks of his return to New York, Virgil Thomson had hired the basement of Saint Philip's Episcopal Church in Harlem to audition the cast and chorus of the opera. His choice of Negro singers was a success. Not only were they able to deliver Gertrude Stein's words with perfect clarity, they also entered easily into the spirit of the music and delighted in the text. According to Virgil, they were soon speaking to each other in quotes from the opera.

By the middle of the winter, Virgil had got the young playwright John Houseman to direct the work, and Florine Stettheimer, a fashionable theatre decorator and society hostess, had already begun to design the costumes and sets. In December 1933, he sent Gertrude a progress report:

The cast of the opera is hired and rehearsals begun. I have a chorus of 32 and six soloists, very, very fine ones indeed. Miss Stettheimer's sets are of a beauty incredible, with trees made out of feathers and a sea-wall at Barcelona made out of shells and for the procession a baldachino of black chiffon and bunches of black ostrich plumes just like a Spanish funeral. . . .

Everything about the opera is shaping up so beautifully, even the raising of money

(It's going to cost $10,000), that the press is champing at the bit and the New York ladies already ordering dresses and engaging hotel rooms. . . .

That very week Ashton was arriving from London to do the staging, as Virgil explained, 'not only for the dance-numbers, but for the whole show, so that all the movements will be regulated to the music, measure by measure, and all our complicated stage-action made into controllable spectacle'. For this, too, Virgil felt, black actors would be superior to whites, who, as he wrote, 'always tend to look arch in the presence of song', and who 'do not walk well and who stand around like lumps'. Virgil and Ashton now worked out a simple and effective staging, a constant flowing rhythm which, together with the celebrated sets, was to make 'Four Saints' one of the most successful spectacles in America.

As with Picasso, Satie and Cocteau's *Parade*, which had been not so much a ballet as a colourful presentation of music, movement and images, 'Four Saints' would be something other than opera, something closer to what Gertrude meant by 'landscape', an event which does not tell a story or *do* anything – but which merely presents itself and *is*, as 'bright filled space'.

That 'Four Saints' achieved success as a spectacle was due in large part to the skill and inspiration of young Ashton, but the man himself was to prove difficult. Although the cast were charmed by his English manners, his graceful and dandyish looks (he might have been a successful 'juvenile' lead in a Broadway musical), they were also flustered and alarmed by his outbreaks of impatience and despondency. After a while Virgil saw to it that young Freddy was kept away from rehearsals. By this time, however, rumours of what was going on in Harlem began to reach the ears of the New York press, and it was not long before the rest of New York were eagerly awaiting the opening night in Hartford. Towards the end of the rehearsals, Henry Moses, an important Broadway producer, arrived and offered to back the show for a New York run, following its scheduled week in Hartford. When the cast moved to Connecticut for final rehearsals, Henry McBride, an art critic and old friend of Gertrude's, was sent out to report their progress to the readers of the *New York Sun*.

On the week before its official opening Hartford itself began to fill with people who had been lucky enough to get tickets and the Newhaven Railroad had to lay on extra parlour cars for its New York to Hartford run. There was nothing to compete that season with the combined attractions of the opening of the new Wadsworth Atheneum wing, the Picasso retrospective, and most of all, the opera of Virgil Thomson and Gertrude Stein.

On the night of 8 February 1934, the audience in the Avery Memorial Hall heard the now-famous opera. Loyal as ever, Carl Van Vechten wrote to Gertrude that same night:

Four Saints, in our vivid theatrical parlance, is a knockout and a wow. . . . People not only wore evening clothes, they wore sables and tiaras. . . . I haven't seen a crowd more excited since Sacre du Printemps. The difference was that they were pleasurably excited. The Negroes are divine, like El Grecos, more Spanish, more Saints, more opera singers in the dignity and *simplicity* and extraordinary plastic line than *any* white singers could ever be. And they enunciated the text so clearly you could understand every word. Frederick Ashton's rhythmic staging was inspired and so were Florine's costumes and sets. Imagine a crinkled sky-blue cellophane background, set in white lace borders, like a valentine against which were placed the rich and royal costumes of the saints in red velvets, etc. and the dark Spanish skins. . . .

After a phenomenally successful six performances in Hartford, the cast and company and directors were put on salary, and 'Four Saints' moved to New York. Outside the Broadway theatre, the name of Gertrude Stein was in lights, and every one who could get them had tickets for the grand première on 20 February. In the first night audience, among the high-society and the New York art crowd could be seen such musical celebrities as George Gershwin and Arturo Toscanini. The latter was to return for another performance, when Gertrude's publisher Alfred Harcourt spotted him, 'completely absorbed in the performance and applaud[ing] vigourously'. At that first night there were, too, many of Gertrude's friends, among them Henry McBride, who wrote to her: '. . . we were totally unprepared for the unearthly beauty that the first curtain disclosed and which mounted and mounted as the thing went on and finally left all the hard-boiled and worldly connoisseurs in tears at the end.'

And there were, of course, the critics. Although most of them wrote long and loving reviews, there were those who attacked Virgil's 'backward looking music'. Nonetheless, the opera was by all accounts a sensation. As Virgil recorded, 'For six months and more the show was named at least once every week in every New York paper and in some paper somewhere in the United States every day. There were constant editorials, cartoons, and jokes about it [Macy's department store advertised its autumn collection as Four Suits in Three Acts]; all the music and drama critics in the East reviewed it.' Clifton Fadiman had given Gertrude the title 'The Mama of Dada', and as such she was now famous to everyone. As her friend Paul Bowles wrote to her, her opera was in general demand: 'People walking on Broadway and sitting in Automats talk of "the Saints Play" and usually sound doubtful as to whether it would be worth while trying to get tickets for it.'

By this time, of course, thousands were clamouring for the appearance of Gertrude Stein. Her agent, William Bradley, had already introduced her to a man who organised lecture tours in the States, but Gertrude had not liked him. Now with strong pressure on him from New York, and knowing that a long visit to the country would do a great deal to promote her books, Bradley once again implored her to go. Gertrude said she would *if* he found a publisher for all her many, many unpublished pieces. To this Bradley had to refuse. It would, he said, be impossible; but all the same, he informed her, the lecture trip was now arranged. Furious, Gertrude now unconditionally refused. Don't you want to be rich?, he implored. '. . . Certainly I said I do want to get rich but I never want to do what there is to do to get rich.'

Her friends begged her to go. Carl Van Vechten arrived at Bilignin and took ninety publicity photographs of her and Alice. He had already sent her a photograph of her name in lights on Broadway, and now pumped her with news of her American triumph. But to his insisting on her visit, she still said no: 'It was really getting very exciting that we could not go,' she wrote in *Everybody's Autobiography*, 'it excited us and it was an exciting thing to tell.'

Bernard Faÿ, the recent translator of both *The Making of Americans* and *The Autobiography* and an experienced lecturer in America, told her that it would be a simple matter to arrange a lecture tour as she liked it rather than as it suited a tour-operator. He reminded her, too, of her success that winter when she had stood in for him to lecture at the American Women's Club in Paris, a success largely due to her charm and wit during the question-and-answer session that followed the rather inaccessible lecture. Others wrote that she had not been to America for thirty years and that she ought to have a new look at it. But she countered them all: 'As I say I am a person of no initiation, I usually stay where I am. Why not as long as there are plenty of people about and there are pretty much always plenty of people about why not.' 'After all,' as she later wrote in *Everybody's Autobiography*, 'I am American all right. Being there does not make me more there.'

Eventually, of course, Gertrude Stein was persuaded. 'I often wonder,' she had written in *The Autobiography*, '. . . if any of the doughboys who knew Gertrude Stein so well in those days ever connected her with the Gertrude Stein of the newspapers.' William Rogers, known in 1918 by Alice and Gertrude as the Kiddie, *had* connected her. After the success of 'Four Saints' in Hartford, he had written to her answering the challenge of *The Autobiography*. Now a reporter on a Connecticut newspaper, Rogers wrote to her about her great popularity in America. Delighted by his enthusiasm, Gertrude agreed to see him late that spring at Bilignin. There, William Rogers finally persuaded her to go to the States. He would fix everything, he said, just as she wanted it. Charmed by his simple good nature, and stirred by memories of her popularity with the Americans in 1918–19, Gertrude chose to believe him. In the end it was the Kiddie, and not any of her famous friends from the New York or French literary scene, who took away her promise to come to America that autumn.

While Rogers made the arrangements for her tour in America, Gertrude began to write the lectures that she would deliver. Although she found writing lectures distasteful: 'I do not like it. I like to read with my eyes not with my ears,' she took seriously the task of putting down her ideas on art and literature for her future audience. The six lectures that Gertrude wrote were: 'What is English Literature', 'Pictures', 'Plays', 'The Gradual Making of *The Making of Americans*', 'Portraits and Repetition' and 'Poetry and Grammar'. In these she tried to set out her theories of aesthetics and to explain the intentions and the significance of her own work. It was an enormous task. 'It always did bother me that the American public were more interested in me than in my work,' she later wrote. Now, with these lectures, she was to go to America, not as the famous raconteuse of *The Autobiography*, but as the difficult and elusive writer of *The Making of Americans*, the Portraits, *Tender Buttons* and *Lucy Church Amiably*. With great courage she set out to tell fully and simply and as clearly as she could just what it was that she had been working at during the last thirty years. Rather than *The Autobiography*, *Lectures in America* was the real attempt of Gertrude Stein to come out of obscurity. But it was difficult and unnerving to come so clean to this 'audience' of strangers. As she wrote that summer to William Rogers, 'I get quite a bit of stage fright while doing them but if one must one must . . .'. Nor was she quite convinced they would be as clear as she wanted: 'The lectures are good,' she wrote, '. . . but they are for a pretty intelligent audience and though they are clear very clear they are not too easy.'

They were certainly not easy. But there were passages of enormous brilliance and clarity. Perhaps the most appealing was 'Poetry and Grammar', in which Gertrude tried to define the difference between poetry and prose, and to explain the functions of different parts of speech, and of punctuation.

Of poetry, she wrote: 'Poetry is I say essentially a vocabulary [that is a list of nouns] just as prose is essentially not.' 'Poetry is doing nothing but using losing refusing and pleasing and betraying and caressing nouns.' Nouns, or names, are at the heart of poetry, verbs are at the heart of prose; and loving and insisting and repeating the names are the natural result of the emotion which makes good poetry: '. . . You can love a name and if you love a name then saying that name any number of times only makes you love it more, more violently more persistently more tormentedly.' 'When I said.

A rose is a rose is a rose is a rose. . . . I made poetry and what did I do I caressed completely caressed and addressed a noun.'

Ardour and repetition are not all. Poetry is also getting inside of nouns or objects, finding their reality and calling them by their appropriate and peculiar names. For this reason the references in her poetry might seem obscure. In fact they are closer, with a mystic closeness, to the thing described than in ordinary poetry: 'As I say a noun is a name of a thing [a conveniently given name], and therefore slowly if you feel what is [really] inside that thing you do not call it by the name by which it is known. Everybody knows that by the way they do when they are in love and a writer should always have that intensity of emotion about whatever is the object about which he writes.' Poetry was 'really loving the name of anything and that is not prose'.

As she had important things to say about the functions of nouns and verbs and other parts of speech, Gertrude had thoughts about punctuation. As in the discussion of nouns, she related her general analyses to her own work. Her own peculiarities of punctuation (she used only periods and, very rarely, commas), she now justified.

The question-mark she felt was unnecessary and 'positively revolting', as were exclamation marks. Although she herself, she said, never used an apostrophe, she could understand the emotional appeal of the possessive case and its symbol: 'I do see that for many that for some the possessive case apostrophe has a gentle tender insinuation that makes it very difficult to decide to do without it.' Periods were all right: they had 'a life of their own'. They could be used almost anywhere in a sentence and be happy. But commas, she wrote, 'are servile'. They 'are dependent upon use and convenience and they are put there just for practical purpose', that is, they have no aesthetic and no independent function—and they make life too easy for the reader and writer. That her refusal to make use of them was more than mere whim, she now showed with startling effect: 'A comma by helping you along holding your coat for you and putting on your shoes keeps you from living your life as actively as you should lead it and to me . . . the use of them was positively degrading.'

Having written lectures which she knew to be good and important, Gertrude Stein now waited and prepared for a tour which was becoming increasingly desirable to her as an act of aesthetic revelation. The last victory over enforced obscurity seemed to Gertrude to have been won when in July that year she received a letter from Bennett Cerf of Random House in New York. If she would do another autobiography for him, he promised, he would undertake to publish all her works at the rate of one volume a year. Furthermore, he would act, without reward, as distributor in the States of all the unsold copies of the four works in the Plain Edition.

Increasingly excited about the coming tour, that summer Gertrude had herself a leather lecture case made at Bilignin, together with an entirely new wardrobe of clothes for herself and Alice 'and a great many new shoes'. She was no longer scared: '. . . everything was getting ready, I was not worried any more, worrying is an occupation part of the time but it cannot be an occupation all the time.'

With letters asking her to speak at schools and colleges all over America and a lot of fan mail from strangers who had seen 'Four Saints' or had read *The Autobiography*, she and Alice Toklas said goodbye to their dogs Basket and Pépé, took last-minute advice from their friends, and boarded the ss *Champlain* on 17 October 1934. As Gertrude later wrote in *Everybody's Autobiography*, '. . . I used to say that I would not go to America until I was a real lion and a real celebrity at that time of course I did not really think I was going to be one. But now we were coming and I was going to be one.'

9

La Gloire

AFTER SEVEN DAYS OF BEING LIONISED on the SS *Champlain*, Gertrude and Alice arrived inside New York harbour on 24 October. The sight of the Statue of Liberty greatly moved Gertrude, but the famous New York skyline seemed less dramatic than she had expected: '. . . it did not look very high,' she wrote later, 'and I was disappointed.' Nevertheless, Gertrude was buoyant with expectation. She knew that 'People had always been nice to me because I am pleasing but now this was going to be a different thing'. But she was little prepared for the sight that greeted her as the ship waited for its clearance to dock.

A whole boat-load of reporters and photographers, headed by her recent friend William Rogers, speeded out to the New York harbour to trap and question the celebrity. Although they were polite – they asked about her crossing (fine), her literary influences (Shakespeare, Trollope and Flaubert), her feelings for Hemingway (affectionate), the role of Alice Toklas (someone 'who makes life comfortable for me') – it was not long before questions were asked which revealed that the reporters had come, as they confessed to Rogers, 'loaded for bear'. 'Why don't you write the way you talk?' one asked. 'Why don't you read the way I write?' was the reply. To the question why had she come to America, Gertrude replied stoutly: 'to tell very plainly and simply and directly, as is my fashion, what literature is.' Then after she had broadcast to New York from the ship's radio, and had agreed to do a short reading from 'Four Saints' for a Pathé News film, the press left, totally charmed and confused and eager to write their copy.

The headlines in the New York press were effusive:

GERTY GERTY STEIN STEIN
IS BACK HOME HOME BACK
GERTRUDE STEIN BARGES IN
WITH A STEIN SONG TO STEIN
GERTRUDE STEIN, STEIN
IS BACK, BACK, AND IT'S
STILL ALL BLACK, BLACK

Her picture was on the front page of every New York newspaper, but an easy snideness came through in the text. With heavy irony they referred to Gertrude as the 'Sybil of Montparnasse', described in detail her figure and her clothing (heavy tweeds and golf shoes, an ornamental vest and a sort of wool shooting hat), and described Alice as serpent-like, Gertrude's 'queer, birdlike shadow'.

As Gertrude observed later during her tour, it was useless to expect much of reporters; they had their stories already written in their heads, and were only interested in catching quotes that could fit in with these. They never really heard what was said. Photographers, on the other hand, were always able to listen and they usually understood. Of reporters Gertrude wrote in *Everybody's Autobiography*:

> I always knew that of course they would say what it was the habit for newspapers to say I said and yet I did like talking to them. Once ... I was talking there were two or three of them and a photographer with them and I said you know its funny but the photographer is the one of the lot of you who looks as if he were intelligent and was listening now why is that, you do I said to the photographer you do understand what I am talking about don't you. Of course I do he said you see I can listen to what you say because I don't have to remember what you are saying, they can't listen because they have got to remember.

Yet despite the fact she was often mocked, Gertrude found being quoted a consolation in itself. 'All the same' she said, 'my sentences do get under their skin.'

In the crowd waiting for her in New York harbour were Carl Van Vechten and his wife, and her new publisher Bennett Cerf, and, of course, more members of the press. She found that the harbour 'did not look real', and for a moment she was intimidated by her surroundings: 'We knew where we were it was alright but it was strange really strange.' Eventually they were taken off to the Algonquin Hotel – named after a tribe of New York State Indians – which specialised in literary celebrities. In the four-room suite they had been given, they found telegrams and flowers and more reporters. She gave a long interview to Jo Alsop, who told her 'that I talked so clearly why did I not write clearly'. 'I do write clearly,' she insisted once more.

In the hotel she had her first taste of American food. She ought to have been prepared for its strangeness, she said, by her experiences with Americans in Europe: 'In France you talk about food but then you talk about food in any country. When the doughboys came to France they called it the eats and they did not like it.' Gertrude called the American food 'moist', and she did like it: '... most of the time I was in America I ate honey dew melon every morning and every evening and I ate oysters and I ate hot bread that is corn muffins, they were moist and I ate green apple pie and butter scotch pie and pumpkin pie not so good but twice superlative lemon pies ...'.

Late that evening Gertrude and Alice set out for a brief walk around the city. Gertrude had always been interested in how things that perform the same functions can be different and she was now fascinated by the shapes of the trucks, the buses, the rhythm of the pedestrians in the streets. She found New York breathtakingly beautiful, especially its lights, which were better, she said, than Paris, even though Paris is *la ville lumière*. But certain things were alarming. As they walked from their hotel to Times Square, they saw the electric sign on the top of the New York Times building, which flashed news bulletins in moving letters all around the sides of the building. In this case, the moving lights informed New York that Miss Gertrude Stein was here. To venture unexpectedly on her own name flashing in Times Square, Gertrude found 'upsetting'. Alice, too, felt a little threatened on that first night: '. . . she said my knees are shaking and I said what is it and she said I just happened to see it, the sides of the building. She just happened to see it, and if you do just happen to see one of those buildings well her knees had not shaken since the first bomb in nineteen-fifteen had fallen in Paris so the sky scrapers are something.'

Gertrude Stein stayed in New York for a month. From the city she made various trips to New England, Pennsylvania and up-state New York and in the meantime she decided to give a pre-lecture try-out for an audience of two hundred that had been especially arranged for her by Carl Van Vechten. But before this took place, she received a call from Mr Potter of Columbia University, where she had planned to give her first official performance. Mr Potter in his previous arrangements with Gertrude had assured her that she would be lecturing to no more than a few hundred students, and she had agreed on that basis to deliver four lectures at Columbia. Now, however, he explained, that thanks to the tremendous publicity preceding her arrival, the first audience would number over a thousand. The idea of such a crowd terrified Gertrude. She informed Potter that since her lectures would be difficult, she could certainly not expect to hold the attention of an audience that size. Unless the number were cut by half, she absolutely refused to take part.

In the circumstances, Potter could only accede to her demands, but the initial shock of his announcement had shaken her. She had expected to be a little nervous for this first try-out lecture, and for this reason she had insisted that there be no introductions from the platform: 'Besides it was silly everybody knew who I was if not why did they come and why should I sit and get nervous while somebody else was talking.' But on the eve of the lecture, Gertrude Stein had constriction of the throat. Her voice simply would not come.

As it happened she had made friends on the ss *Champlain* with a prominent throat specialist from New Jersey. He had impressed her by the fact that he had with him on board a copy of *The Autobiography*. She gave him her autograph and he, in turn, promised to be of assistance if she needed any favour in America. Within her first week in America she did need one. When she telephoned him, he reassured her, drove from New Jersey to New York, treated her throat, and stayed to listen to her first, successful, lecture. As Gertrude wrote in *Everybody's Autobiography*: '. . . his voice was already soothing but having him come and feel my pulse was everything and he was there at the first lecture and so was my voice and we have never seen him again but we do not forget him.' After that, she said, she was never frightened again.

In New York Gertrude was fêted at numerous dinner parties. Bennett Cerf introduced her to the *New Yorker* crowd, among them Alexander Woollcott – a literary lion and dandy who greatly impressed her. 'Miss Stein,' he said, 'you have not been in New York long enough to know that I am never contradicted.' Later Woollcott came to Paris to write about Basket for his book on poodles. The Van Vechtens gave numerous parties for Gertrude, among them an all Negro one. Gertrude enjoyed the typically Van Vechten evening, but she objected to the nicety of having to use the liberal term 'coloured': '. . . its name is Negro if it is a Negro,' she said, 'and Jew if it is a Jew and both of them are nice strong solid names and so let us keep them.'

The parties, however, interested Gertrude less than her walks through the city streets. For Gertrude it was like being in Bilignin though here it was complete strangers who came up to greet her. Everywhere she was stopped and welcomed to New York. One elderly Negro came up to her and introduced himself, 'I was the first music teacher of Mr. Mathews who sang Saint Ignatius and I wanted to say how do you do to you.' 'And I was very touched,' Gertrude wrote. All sorts of people who only recognised her face and knew for some reason she was a celebrity also came up to shake hands and politely bid her welcome – taxi-drivers, policemen, children, elderly couples, waiters and businessmen. And complete strangers were always offering to be of service. This, she noted, made a difference from Europeans: 'all the men in America are such nice men, they always do everything, they do.'

The reception that Gertrude everywhere received seemed to her extraordinary. It seemed equally extraordinary to the publisher of *The Autobiography*, Alfred Harcourt. During a meeting at his office in New York, he pressed Gertrude for an explanation. '. . . Remember,' she told him, 'this extraordinary welcome that I am having does not come from the books of mine that they do understand like the Autobiography but the books of mine that they did not understand, and he called his partner and said listen to what she says, and perhaps she is right.'

By this time, Gertrude was delighting in being in New York. She especially liked the drugstores: '. . . I was always going in to buy a detective novel just to watch the people sitting on stools. . . . The people sitting on stools and eating in the drug store all looked and acted as if they lived in a small country town.' It was extraordinary, too, she thought, that in a store that sold medicines and health aids, only the eating sections should be clean. Gertrude also liked the 'nut stores', tiny shops that sold only different kinds of nuts; but she was disappointed in the five and ten cents stores, such as Woolworths: '. . . there was nothing that I wanted and what was there was not for ten cents.'

By this time, too, she liked the buildings and the tall, cloudless skies of New York. She felt one of the differences between America and Europe was that America had no sky, 'just air', 'and that makes religion and wandering and architecture'. Even Alice was beginning to like the skyscrapers. As she told Gertrude, 'it is not the way they go into the air but the way they come out of the ground' that makes them special; 'European buildings sit on the ground but American ones come out of the ground.'

Alfred Harcourt had invited Gertrude and Alice to join him in New Haven, Connecticutt, for one of the biggest college football games of the season, the Yale/Dartmouth match. On 4 November, they and Harcourt were three in a crowd of eighty thousand. Gertrude liked the conventions of the game, the squatting of the players 'like indians', the lack of real movement, as each side blocked the other. She liked football because nothing happened -- it was a spectacle, a 'landscape', and a ritual, like dancing, war, bull-fighting and theatre. About the particular game she was less enthusiastic: 'we did see them playing football,' she wrote later in *Everybody's Autobiography*, 'not very well it must be said not very well.'

Back in New York after the weekend, Gertrude decided to accept an invitation to fly to Chicago to see a performance of 'Four Saints', which had recently moved from Broadway for a ten-day stint in Illinois. Despite her terror of flying, Carl Van Vechten convinced her she should go, and she had managed to get a free passage for him as well. The size and look of the airplane frightened her. Nothing else, she felt, had really changed in America – the trains, for instance, were pretty well what they had been: 'They use words like air-conditioned but it smells just about the same.' But once inside the plane, and moving, and comforted by Carl, Gertrude began to enjoy her flight. As she wrote later, 'It was nice. I know of nothing more pleasing more soothing more beguiling than the slow hum of the mounting.' After the first trip, she was hooked on flying: '. . . whenever we could we did it. They are now beginning to suppress the noise and that is a pity, it will be too bad if they can have a conversation. . . .'

But the sight from the air was more interesting to her: 'It was then in a kind of way that I really began to know what the ground looked like. Quarter sections make a picture and going over America like that made anyone know why the post-cubist painting was what it was. The wandering line of Masson was there and this mixed line of Picasso coming and coming again and following itself into a beginning was there, the simple solution of Braque was there and I suppose Léger might be there but I did not see it not over there.' As usual, new revelations led back to herself; and this experience of flying '. . . made it right that I had always been with cubism and everything that followed after'.

Seeing her opera in Chicago was less exciting. She could barely recognise her own work in this elaborate production: 'I was less excited about it than I had expected to be. It was my opera but it was so far away.' At a party afterwards, Gertrude got to know the singers. She liked Saint Theresa especially, but they were all friendly, and 'they all did they all said all the words were such natural words to say'.

Back in New York, Gertrude and Alice continued to bask in the 'gloire'. Their lecture schedule enabled them to see many of the places that Gertrude had not seen since she was a child. Her birthplace, at Allegheny, now absorbed by Pittsburgh, hardly interested her since she had not seen it for sixty years. But in Bryn Mawr, Pennsylvania, they were given the old room of Helen Carey Thomas, the notorious dean of Bryn Mawr College who had inspired Gertrude's 1904–5 tale of decadence, *Fernhurst*. Here, she thought, nothing had changed; she even recognised the same art reproductions that had hung in student rooms during her own college days. On the other hand, at Cambridge, where they went to lecture at Radcliffe and the Harvard Signet Club, Gertrude '. . . recognised nothing. Considering that I had spent four years there it was sufficiently astonishing that nothing was there that I remembered nothing at all.'

The lectures took her to Vassar College, Princeton, and to Brooklyn where she met the poet Marianne Moore, once an editor of *Dial*, who had praised *The Making of Americans* in 1926. She lectured at schools and colleges all over New England, and in all her lectures she met with success and adulation. The students responded easily to her. Carl Van Vechten quotes a typical reaction from an Amherst student: 'I was dead against her and I just went to see what she looked like and then she took the door of my mind right off its hinges and now its wide open.'

Gertrude's phenomenal success with her audiences owed much, as she said, to her reputation as an enigma, an eccentric and obscure writer. Her appearance, her clothes and her style seemed fantastic, it is true; but Americans had seen exotics before. That by itself cannot have accounted for the impact she had, month after month of her tour, nor for the hundreds of testimonials to her intelligence, and to the influence of her ideas which followed. 'She has the clearest intelligence I have ever encountered,' Louis Bromfield declared, and many were surprised to agree. But it was not so much the existence of that intelligence which excited her audiences, as her ability to communicate the act of intelligence itself.

In the lecture halls where she spoke, a strange intimacy was created as the audience was taken up and held in the rhythms of her thinking. It was a gradual process because Gertrude's words were difficult to understand. She used, as always, extremely simple words, but so simple that the audience had to strain to listen until the context which gave meaning to those words was made clear. Sometimes what she said would become nearly totally clear, and when that happened it released an energy in her listeners, which was manifested in the after-lecture discussions that frequently went on all night. But always, the earnestness of Gertrude's efforts to make something difficult clear, her awareness of the audience's straining, created a partnership between her and them. Linked together in a hard effort at understanding, Gertrude and the audience were sometimes moving as one. Not willing to leave the customary space between speaker and spoken to, Gertrude made constant asides in her lectures which acted as an elbow-propping or an earnest assurance to her partners that they could follow:

'Oh yes you do see. You do see that.'
'Yes you do feel what I mean.'
'Do you see my point, but of course yes you do.'
'Oh yes you all do understand. You understand this.'
'That makes something clear to you does it not.'

And flirtatiously:

'I hope you like what I say.'

And half-retreating:

'I wonder if you know what I mean. I do not quite know whether I do myself.'
'Do you understand. Do any or all of you understand. Anyway that is the way it is.'
'Do you do you do you really understand. And does it make any difference to you if you do understand. It makes an awful lot of difference to me. It is very exciting to have this be.'

And more defensively:

'I hope you all quite see what I mean. Anyway I suppose inevitably I will go on doing it.'

And sometimes, despairingly:

'What is the use unless everybody knows what I want to say and what is the use if everybody does want to know what I want to say.'

The lectures were, for Gertrude, a deeply personal appeal, and she made her audiences feel it. Her earnestness, her vulnerability, and the humility of the Sybil in making that appeal touched the students and won them over to her side. Whatever they might think of its results, it was difficult for them not to be impressed by the heroism of her life's work as she described it:

When I was up against the difficulty of putting down the complete conception that I had of an individual, the complete rhythm of a personality that I had gradually acquired by listening seeing feeling and experience, I was faced by the trouble that I had acquired all this knowledge gradually but when I had it I had it completely at one time. Now that may never have been a trouble to you but it was a terrible trouble to me. And a great deal of *The Making of Americans* was a struggle to do this thing, to make a whole present of something that it had taken a great deal of time to find out, but it was a whole there then within me and as such it had to be said.

That then and ever since has been a great deal of my work and it is that which has made me try so many ways to tell my story. . . .

In the portraits that I did in that period of which I have just been speaking the later period considerably after the war the strictness of not letting remembering mix itself with looking and listening and talking which began with *The Making of Americans* and went on all through *Tender Buttons* and what came immediately after, all the period of *Geography and Plays* this strictness perhaps weakened a little weakened a little because and that in a way was an astonishment to me, I found that I was for a little while very much taken with the beauty of the sounds as they came from me as I made them. . . .

. . . This melody for a little while after rather got the better of me and it was at that time that I wrote these portraits of which I have just spoken, . . . quantities of portraits. Portraits after my concentrated efforts at Saint Rémy to really completely and exactly find the word for the air and sky and light and existence down there was relatively a simple thing and I as you may say held these portraits in my hand and they came easily and beautifully and truly. But as I say I did begin to think that I was rather drunk with what I had done. And I am always one to prefer being sober. I must be sober. It is so much more exciting to be sober, to be exact and concentrated and sober.

So then I say I began again. . . .

I began again not to let the looking be predominating not to have the listening and talking be predominating but to once more denude all this of anything in order to get back to the essence of the thing contained within itself. That led to some very different writing . . . but it also led to some portraits that I do think did do what I was then hoping would be done that is at least by me, would be done in this way if it were to be done by me.

Gertrude also told her audiences once and for all why it was that her words had to be obscure: 'And the thing that excited me so very much at that time and still does is that the words or words that make what I looked at be itself were always words that to me very exactly related themselves to that thing the thing at which I was looking, but as often as not had as I say nothing whatever to do with what any words would do that described that thing.'

In her discussion of punctuation, she spoke against the indulgence of wishing to have reading made simple. It forcefully applied to her own writing: 'When it gets really difficult you want to disentangle rather than to cut the knot, at least so anybody feels who is working with any thread, so anybody feels who is working with any tool so anybody feels who is writing any sentence or reading it after it has been written.'

Finally, she told her audiences why, difficult to understand though it was, what she was doing had to be done:

The business of Art as I tried to explain in *Composition As Explanation* is to live in the actual present, that is the complete actual present, and to completely express that complete actual present. . . .

I have of course always been struggling with this thing, to say what you nor I nor nobody knows, but what is really what you and I and everybody knows, and as I say everybody hears stories but the thing that makes each one what he is is not that.

Gertrude never knew whether what she said was understood by her enthusiastic audiences. She hoped so, and she said often that she hoped so. But she believed, as she had written in *Four In America*, that the force of her intelligence would eventually come through to convince people that she did know what she was trying to do:'. . . if you have vitality enough of knowing enough of what you mean, somebody and sometime and sometimes a great many will have to realise that you know what you mean and so they will agree that you mean what you know, what you know you mean, which is as near as anybody can come to understanding any one.'

Whether or not this understanding of her work was forthcoming on her American tour, her effort to make her audiences understand had by itself a profound effect. Bernard Faÿ, then in New Orleans, wrote to Gertrude at the end of November:

I feel that what is going on now in America – what this trip of yours is doing is tremendously important in the mental life of America. What you bring them, nobody has brought them since Walt Whitman. . . . And they know it, they feel it. You know I have watched them very closely since 1919 – and seen them get excited over all kinds of things: the new Ford cars, Mr. Hoover, Al Smith, air-travel, the Queen of Rumania, speak-easies, etc; but I have never seen them act as they do now with you. – It is something deeper and more personal. What your work and yourself stir up in them had not been stirred up for decades. It is a fine and fascinating sight for a historian, who is in love with America and who loves you. . . .

At the end of November, Gertrude and Alice left their rooms in New York and flew out to Chicago to stay ten days at the Drake Hotel. Here she admired the skyscrapers and the fact that the skyscrapers had been first made in Chicago, where there had always been 'plenty of land to build on', rather than in New York, an island where expansion had to be upward rather than outward. 'Choice,' she said, 'is more pleasing than anything necessary.' But the cultural life of the city she found inferior to that of New York. With Bobsy Goodspeed, head of the Chicago Arts Association, for whom Gertrude had written an introduction for her Francis Rose exhibition catalogue, Gertrude and Alice attended the Chicago opera. After seeing performances of *Lohengrin* and *Salome*, Gertrude was disappointed: '. . . it seemed as if Europe [the art movements of the last quarter century] had not been, it was just the same as it had been' when she was last in America.

Thanks to Bobsy Goodspeed, Gertrude made a friend who was to remain one of her closest admirers and intellectual companions for the remainder of her life, the novelist Thornton Wilder, widely acclaimed for his 1927 *Bridge of San Luis Rey*. Of Gertrude, Wilder later said, 'she was *the* great influence on my life. . . . It was from her that I learned to write drily and objectively.' It was after years of instruction from Gertrude that he was to write his two masterpieces, the plays 'Our Town' and 'The Skin of Our Teeth'. Thornton also contributed significantly to Gertrude's work. Together during the next few years in France, they engaged in long discussions on art and philosophy, the results of which were the important meditations of the late thirties. Alice, on the other hand, was less comfortable with the novelist. As she wrote in a letter of 1948, 'Thornton has such a seeing eye and then what he doesnt see he has felt and the combination has always made me a little afraid of him.'

In Chicago Gertrude gave her lecture 'Poetry and Grammar' at a session organised by the President of the University of Chicago, Robert Hutchins. It was here, after a student's question as to the meaning of 'a rose is a rose is a rose is a rose', that she gave her famous reply. Over the last hundred years, she said, words had come to lose their meanings, words in poetry were now 'just worn out literary words'. The poet today, she said, had a very difficult job, he 'must work in the excitingness of pure beauty; he has got to get back that intensity into the language'. 'Now you have seen hundreds of poems about roses and you know in your bones that the rose is not there. . . . Now listen! I'm no fool. I know that in daily life we don't go around saying "is a . . . . is . . . is". Yes, I'm no fool; but I think that in that line the rose is red for the first time in English poetry for a hundred years.'

Gertrude saw Robert Hutchins on several occasions. At one dinner party, he and his colleague Mortimer Adler, now head of Encyclopaedia Britannica, were talking about their newly-instituted (and soon notorious) History of Ideas course for the University of Chicago. What sort of ideas, asked Gertrude. They replied with a long list of great philosophies that had changed the world. Gertrude noticed that none of the ideas had originated in the English language and that all the ideas concerned the state and society. Annoyed by the orthodoxy of their approach, Gertrude attacked:

Government is the least interesting thing in human life . . . creation and the expression of that creation is a damn sight more interesting . . . and I began to get excited yes I know naturally you are teachers and teaching is your occupation and naturally what they call ideas are very easy to teach and so you are convinced that they are the only ideas but the real ideas are not the relation of human being as groups but a human being to himself inside him . . . after all the minute that there are a lot of them they do not do it for themselves but somebody does it for them and that is a damn sight less interesting.

Then she turned on Adler and told him that anyone could see by looking at him 'that he was a man who would be singularly incompatible to ideas that one created within oneself . . .'. Within minutes, the dinner party was in shambles, everyone was arguing violently and loudly. Suddenly they were interrupted by the announcement that the police were at the door. Seeing the instant pallor on her adversaries' faces, Gertrude and Alice began to laugh. 'Fanny Butcher had arranged that Alice and I should go off that evening in the homicidal squad car and they had come and there they were waiting. We all said good night and we went off with the policemen.' Just before they left, Hutchins had recovered himself to throw out a challenge – if Gertrude thought she could do better why didn't she take over their class next week.

The upshot, of course, was that Gertrude did do better. Hutchins, who had been present during the discussion, on the subject of epic poetry, came up when it was over to congratulate her. I must admit, he said, they do talk to you more freely and more enthusiastically than they talk to us. Of course, Gertrude said,

. . . you see why they talk to me is that I am like them I do not know the answer, you you say you do not know but you do know if you did not know the answer you could not spend your life in teaching but I really do not know, I really do not, I do not even know whether there is a question let alone having an answer for a question. To me when a thing is really interesting it is when there is no question and no answer

. . . that is the reason that anything for which there is a solution is not interesting, that is the trouble with governments and Utopias and teaching, the things not that can be learnt but that can be taught are not interesting.

Hutchins then arranged that Gertrude should return later in the year to conduct two weeks of classes and seminars at the university.

In the meantime, Alice and Gertrude had gone with the policemen for their night-tour of the city. In the homicide car, they visited a Negro slum, where showing off to the two celebrities, the policemen harassed and cross-questioned a family of poor blacks. After this, they were taken to look at a dance marathon – one of those bizarre inventions of the Depression – where couples were fed and sheltered as long as they were able to go on dancing. It was a cruel spectator sport: the couples staggered around the floor, one partner sleeping on the other until only one couple remained. This particular marathon had been going some six weeks. When asked by the cheerful organiser if they wanted to be photographed with one of the exhausted pairs, Gertrude hastily refused. It was not a part of American life she liked at all.

Back in the squad car, the sergeant apologised for the dullness of the evening. It was the fault of the rain, he said: '. . . when it rained nobody moved around and if nobody moved around there could not be any homicide unless it was a family affair . . . and that was not interesting.' But as they drove home in the early hours of the morning, news came over the car radio that twenty-five miles away Baby Face Nelson had just been caught.

Early in December, Gertrude and Alice left Chicago, promising to return for the seminars, and set off West: for Wisconsin, Minnesota, Ohio, Indiana, and Michigan. She was treated as a celebrity, trailed by reporters, given souvenirs. In Wisconsin she met Frank Lloyd Wright, in Minnesota she saw Sherwood Anderson and his family; and wherever she went she was introduced to local celebrities and fêted at elaborate dinner parties. Eventually, Gertrude began to refuse these invitations, much to the irritation of would-be hostesses. But as Gertrude said, she preferred '. . . not being entertained because I like a quiet life and do not like to go out to dinner and above all not to a reception certainly not when I am not to know any one, so the social life I preferred in travelling was the life with reporters and I did enjoy them.'

On one occasion Gertrude was able to be of service to a reporter. At a party in St Paul, Minnesota, she told her hostess how much she had enjoyed a paper's report of her lecture. It had been hostile, but it was clever, she said, and had grappled with what she had said 'like a wrestling match'. But, said her hostess, we were all furious with the writer; everyone's complained to the paper, and they've agreed to fire him. But it's one of the best-written pieces I've read, said Gertrude, and she sent a messenger to tell the paper's editor. When he returned, the messenger informed Gertrude that the writer had had 'tears in his eyes and he said you had saved his life'. As Gertrude said later, 'In America everybody is [a celebrity] but some are more than others. I was more than others.'

That Gertrude was to be treated like royalty was never doubted by the Americans that entertained her or who listened to her lectures. Although she had mostly good things to say about the country, she was also capable of telling the blunt truth as she saw it. When taken through a museum of American painting by a proud curator, she never hesitated in telling him that in America, 'there was architecture there was writing but there was no painting'. She preferred, she said, to stare out of the American museum windows at American landscape.

That was not mere provocation. American landscape, Gertrude thought, was an important contributor to American ideas. The vast, empty spaces made America like Spain:

> ... there is something of the same thing, after all there can only be religion where there is a desert country. That is natural enough. Deserts do not make painters but they make charm and religion, because where there is nothing to do and nothing to see anybody can not know that the time is passing and so naturally there is religion but there is no painting because there is no pleasure in looking. There can be architecture and religion there cannot be painting and looking of course there can be writing anywhere even when writing is talking or singing.

So she wrote in *Everybody's Autobiography*, in one of several attempts to link Picasso's home country with her own. In *The Autobiography*, she had written, 'Americans ... are like spaniards, they are abstract and cruel. They are not brutal they are cruel. They have no close contact with the earth such as most europeans have. Their materialism is not the materialism of existence, of possession, it is the materialism of action and abstraction.'

Gertrude credited to the vast areas of the American landscape, American alienation from the earth, American mysticism, and the American sense of reality: 'In America they want to make everything something anybody can see by looking. That is very interesting, that is the reason that there are no fences in between no walls to hide anything no curtains to cover anything and the cinema that can make anything be anything anybody can see by looking.' But most importantly, American landscape because of its scale and emptiness, made for the Americans (and for Gertrude it was the same as for painters 'ever since Cézanne') their sense of space and rhythm, and of the present: '... a space of time is a natural thing for an American to always have inside them as something in which they are continuously moving'. As she wrote in her lecture 'The Gradual Making of *The Making of Americans*',

> Think of anything, of cowboys, of movies, of detective stories, of anybody who goes anywhere or stays at home and is an American and you will realize that it is something strictly American to conceive a space that is filled with moving, a space of time that is filled always with moving and my first real effort to express this thing which is an American thing began in writing *The Making of Americans*.

The things Gertrude recognised in America were its mystic and unmystified sense of reality, its directness, its sense of time, its regular rhythm of living, and its size. Her near-contemporary, the American collector John Quinn, had written: 'I hate the puritanism of this country, its banality, its crudeness, the insanity of its idea of speed, its lack of taste, and the mechanization of life that is almost universal here. The damned country is too big.' These qualities Gertrude also saw in America, but these were the qualities in America that she admired. Perhaps for this reason, she had named her heroine's American birthplace Gossols in *The Making of Americans*. In 1906 Picasso had returned from a summer in Gosol, Spain, with the first paintings from which he evolved the style of Cubism. Gertrude had taken the sensations which were to develop into the 'continuous present' from America, just as from Spain Picasso had taken the sensations which were to develop into Cubism.

Returning East that December, Gertrude and Alice went once more to Ohio and Pennsylvania and Baltimore, where they visited Gertrude's eighty-year-old aunt Fanny, and uncle Ephraim Keyser. In Baltimore, too, they saw Scott and Zelda Fitzgerald, with whom they spent Christmas Eve. On 29 December, Scott wrote, in rather mixed metaphor, to thank Gertrude for her visit: 'You were the same fine fire to everyone who sat upon your hearth – for it was your hearth, because you carry home with you wherever you are – a home before which we have always warmed ourselves.' Scott also thanked Gertrude for having shown an interest in Zelda's painting. She lacked confidence in her own work, he said. For himself, he thanked her for her intelligent conversation: '. . . everyone felt their Christmas eve was well spent in the company of your handsome face and wise mind – and sentences "that never leak".'

From Baltimore, Gertrude and Alice went to Washington, where Gertrude was invited to a private tea by Mrs Roosevelt; then to Virginia for the new year and the beginning of their tour of Civil War battlefields. 'After all,' wrote Gertrude, 'there will never be anything more interesting in America than that Civil War never.'

After returning once more to New York to pick up winter clothes, Gertrude and Alice went on their extensive lecture tour of New England schools and universities. She was surprised by how many of them there were: 'I did not know that New England had become like Switzerland, where there were [nothing but] schools and colleges and hotels and houses.' There were, too, a surprising number of private schools, which she found strange. In California, when she was a child, she said, nobody ever went to private school unless 'you were defective in some way or came from South America or something'. It was alarming to her to think that in this way America was becoming more like class-oriented Europe. But she enjoyed her visits to the schools. The younger her audiences, the more readily they responded to what she said. She was particularly impressed by Choate, the elegant private preparatory school for boys. They printed the text of her lecture in their school magazine, together with their own work. And '. . . it is striking how well they are writing,' she remarked, 'It is a bother.'

The usual reaction to her lectures in New England was enthusiastic, but on one occasion at least, according to William Rogers, with whom she stayed in Springfield, the audience had been profoundly shocked: 'I don't care to say whether I'm greater than

Shakespeare,' Gertrude told them, 'and he's dead and can't say whether he's greater than I am. Time will tell.'

From New England Gertrude and Alice went South once again. Having never been further than Baltimore, Gertrude was eager to see the great Southern states: North Carolina, South Carolina, Louisiana, Alabama, Tennessee, Kentucky, Georgia and Missouri. She visited Edgar Allan Poe's house, and met the author of *Porgy and Bess*, Du Bose Heyward. She saw Sherwood Anderson again, in New Orleans, and met Marc Connelly, author of *Green Pastures*. She visited the birthplace of her hero, Ulysses S. Grant, in Missouri; went on tours of cotton and tobacco plantations; talked to black jazz musicians in Louisiana, and saw the Mississippi river, smaller, she said, than Mark Twain had led her to expect. By this time it was March, and Gertrude and Alice were due back in Chicago for two weeks' teaching at the university.

In Chicago, they stayed in Thornton Wilder's apartment, and hired a car to drive to and from the university. As William Rogers wrote, Gertrude's driving was eccentric: '. . . she regarded a corner as something to cut, and another car as something to pass, and she could scare the daylights out of all concerned.' But the Chicago authorities had been warned, and Gertrude was never stopped.

Gertrude gave four lectures at the university, which were later published, with an Introduction by Wilder, by Chicago University, under the title *Narration*. She had composed them, she said, after her trip through New England, where she had been impressed by the use of direct and simple language on billboards and in newspapers and advertisements. Now in the lectures and seminars, she discussed the American language. Having inherited the language from England, she said, 'the American had then decided that any word which was a word which was there if you put enough pressure upon them if you arranged and concentrated and took away all excrescences from them you could make these same words do what you needed to do with them.' This discovery, and the sense of freedom to use the words as they liked, have given to Americans the ability to make '. . . of these words words that move as Americans move with them move always move and in every and any direction'. They 'indicate and feel moving existing inside them'.

Having successfully delivered her lectures and conducted her ten seminars, Gertrude and Alice headed once again westwards, this time to Texas. In Galveston a woman of eighty came up to tell her how much her writing had always meant to her. At Miss Hockaday's School for Girls, the schoolmistresses noticed with amazement how easily their pupils understood what Gertrude told them. Old people and young people understood her easily, Gertrude concluded. It was only the ones in the middle that had trouble.

As Gertrude and Alice flew over the Badlands from Texas to Oklahoma, they were surprised to see the oil wells moving so slowly. Gertrude thought they symbolised the rhythms of Americans. 'I do think,' she wrote, 'Americans are slow minded, it seems quick but they are slow minded yes they are.' Just like herself, she said, impulsive but slow.

Gertrude and Alice were heading gradually towards California. It was a visit that she expected to be exciting. Not only would she see her old home, but she was once again to be treated as a celebrity whom other celebrities would be invited to meet. In March she had received a letter from her friend, the actress Gertrude Atherton in San Francisco:

I have asked the most interesting and distinguished persons in San Francisco and environs – at least all that would be likely to interest you, and it promises to be the most notable cocktail party that has been given for years. Not one regret have we received! They fairly sputter over the telephone when asked. Already we are up to seventy-five, and hope to stop there, for if there are too many few will get a chance to talk to you.

Gertrude was also fêted in Los Angeles, and taken up by the movie moguls, who invited her to lunch and a tour of the studios. The cinema did not really interest her – except as a phenomenon on which to hang aesthetic theory. It was photography, and like photography uninteresting: 'Painting looks like something and photography does not,' she later wrote. Besides, she had once been to the cinema to see Charlie Chaplin. After that she vowed never to go again. Nothing else, she said, could ever be as good.

At Beverly Hills, outside Hollywood, Gertrude had a chance to meet Charlie Chaplin at a dinner party where she was invited to choose the guests – others were Dashiell Hammitt, Lillian Hellmann, and Anita Loos. 'Of course I liked Charlie Chaplin,' she wrote in *Everybody's Autobiography*, 'he is a gentle person like any Spanish gipsy bullfighter he is very like my favourite one Gallo. . . .' Chaplin agreed with Gertrude that movies were uninteresting now, ever since the talkies had come in. Before that, he said, films were creative; they could be speeded up or slowed down. Now, action had to be 'naturalistic', it had to match the speed of the words that accompanied it. They were like newspapers, 'just a daily habit'.

With Dashiell Hammitt, whom Gertrude believed to be one of the great American writers, she discussed the aspect of crime novels that interested her. Detective novels were, she said, the only modern form of writing. They had none of the psychological nonsense which belongs to the nineteenth and not the twentieth century. There was no interest in character and, oddly enough, no real interest in plot. As she wrote later in 'What Are Masterpieces': 'It is very curious but the detective story which is you might say the only really modern novel form that has come into existence gets rid of human nature by having the man dead to begin with the hero is dead to begin with and so you have so to speak got rid of the event before the book begins.' Unlike newspapers, which deal – banally, thought Gertrude – with events, in detective novels the interest is not in the crime but in the detection. They are interior works made for thinking and watching thoughts in the making. In fact, rather like her own writing.

In California Gertrude went with Alice through the San Joaquin valley to see where Alice's pioneer grandfather had been born, through the Yosemite forest to see the wild animals and Indians, to Monterey where she stared for a long time at the Pacific Ocean, before dismissing it: '. . . the coast looked like all the ordinary nineteenth-century school of California painting, just like it there was no use looking at it. . . .' Gertrude's visit to her old home in East Oakland made her uncomfortable. The places she remembered had not changed, but they had no place in her memory or her sense of herself, and 'That's what makes your identity not a thing that exists but something you do or do not remember'.

And Gertrude continued her lecturing. On one occasion she lectured at a convent school for girls where, once again, the teachers were surprised how easily the children understood what Gertrude told them. Gertrude enjoyed the experience, but she was not surprised: 'Convents and monasteries make people gay,' she said, 'and it was a pleasant afternoon.' One of Gertrude's last lectures was at Berkeley at the University of California. At the lunch which followed, she was once more asked by the students why she did not write as she spoke: 'if they had invited Keats for lunch,' she asked them, 'and they asked him an ordinary question would they expect him to answer with the Ode to the Nightingale.'

At the end of April Gertrude and Alice flew back to Chicago by way of Nebraska, and then on to New York. Once more Gertrude was struck, as she flew over America, by 'the physical beauty of the country', and by its size. As she said in an earlier interview with the *New York Herald Tribune*, the size of America was wonderful:

> There is nothing that I have seen or heard in Europe that has been to me so romantic as when in Oakland California when I was young we went to the railroad station just to get an ordinary local and the man said in a loud voice not to us but to a great many others this way for all points East. It is still for me a romance to be starting for all points East or West or South or North and each one of them a different city and a different state and all of them America.

By the time Gertrude returned to New York, she had lectured at some thirty universities. She had given dozens of interviews, been photographed, filmed and recorded, and had been front-page news every day. Her lectures had been published in both Chicago and New York. The thing had been an undoubted triumph. Now once more, Bennett Cerf repeated his promise to publish a volume of her manuscripts each year. Thornton Wilder had promised to visit them that summer in Bilignin, and so had Carl Van Vechten, who now called Gertrude 'Baby Woojums', Alice 'Mama Woojums', and himself 'Papa Woojums'. After collecting their numerous presents and fan letters, writing thank-you letters, and saying especial goodbyes to the staff of the Alonquin Hotel, on 4 May 1935, Gertrude and Alice 'happily very happily went on to the Champlain'. Seven days later they were once more in Paris, at 27 Rue de Fleurus.

10

Altogether Too Much Fathering Going On

Not surprisingly, when Gertrude arrived back from her trip to America, Paris seemed to have changed since she had left. For a start, everything 'looked little and littler than it looked' before; the cities seemed, in their modern parts, uglier than the modern American cities. Gertrude, too, had changed. As she told an Associated Press reporter who interviewed her in Paris, her reunion with America had altered her feelings about herself and about the country in which she was born: 'Yes I am married,' she told him. 'I mean I am married to America, it is so beautiful. I am going back to America sometime, someday not too long. I am already homesick for America. I never knew it was so beautiful. It was like a bachelor who goes along fine for 25 years and then decides to get married. That is the way I feel, I mean about America.'

That summer, reunited with their dogs Pépé and Basket, Gertrude and Alice went once more to Bilignin. Gertrude was happy to be back, and the villagers welcomed her with a surprise party, but somehow she was unable to resume life as it had been before her visit to the States. As she wrote her thank-you letters, planted the American corn she had received from the Rogers, read the American fan mail that continued to come from both students and writers (among them, the young Henry Miller who, in an unlikely tribute, sent her a copy of *Tropic of Cancer* for advice and comment), she was thinking of her recent experiences. When Thornton Wilder arrived that summer, she spent long days discussing with him both the nature of America, and the nature of fame and genius – both ideas that arose from her meditations on her recent triumph in the States. Late that summer she committed these meditations to words, in a book which was to appear with Wilder's Introduction as *The Geographical History of America or the Relation of Human Nature to the Human Mind*.

In this rambling and clever meditation, Gertrude attempts to define by a series of questions and half-answers the difference between human nature: remembering, experience, feeling; and human mind: thinking, as they relate to concepts such as death, change, war, poetry, time, creativity, excitement, play, recognition and identity, audience, romance, money, superstitions. As usual, there is no tightly structured philosophical argument in Gertrude's meditation. Instead she sets forth propositions such as:

'A play'

I say two dogs, but say a dog and a dog.

The human mind. The human mind does play. Of course the human mind does play.

Human nature. No human nature does not play, it might desire something but it does not play.

And:

Whether or whether not the human mind could exist if there had been no human speech this I do not know but this I do know that the human mind is not the same thing as human speech. Has anything to do with the other is writing a different thing, oh yes and this is so exciting so satisfying so tender that it makes everything everything writing has nothing to do with the human speech and with human nature and therefore it has something to do with the human mind.

Throughout the meditation, there are conclusions reached, such as: 'No one need have any doubt that there is no relation between human nature and the human mind,' and 'Human nature is not natural it is what anybody does and what anybody does is not natural and therefore it is not interesting.' These are mixed with encouragements to herself: 'You will find that all this is true when I get through'; 'It is natural that again a woman should be one to do the literary thinking of this epoch'; 'I tell you it is true that I do the literary thinking for you.' There are asides to Alice: 'Bless a wife who has made this clear'; and to friends: 'Listen Jo Alsop while I make this clear.' And a good deal of word play: 'What you cannot eat you can'; and more philosophically:

Become Because.

Beware of be.

Be is not what no one can be what no one can see and certainly not what no one can say.

Anybody can say be.

Be is for biography.

And for autobiography

Detective story number I. About how there is a human mind.

And how to detect it.

Detective story number I.

The great thing to detect in a detective story is whether you have written as you have heard it said. If you do write as you have heard it said then you have to change it.

Through it all, there is confidence that what she is doing is valuable. In the importance of meditation: 'Now is just the time to think about what is or is not interesting because nothing else is interesting.' In the importance of rambling as a method: 'I do not know where I am going but I am on my way and then suddenly well not perhaps suddenly but perhaps yes I do know where I am going and I do not like it like that.' And in the simplicity of the philosophy: 'That is what I mean to be I mean to be the one who can and does have as ordinary ideas as these.'   As Thornton Wilder wrote to her when he had read her manuscript that October, the work was 'as big as an alp yet as homely as a walk in the village'. It made him, he said, 'crazy about America', enough to leave his study of philosophy in Vienna to return there permanently. It had, like most of Gertrude's philosophical works, a progressive excitement which comes from Gertrude's manner of revealing her thought process, as it moves from proposition to proposition, side-tracked by linguistic jokes or domestic interruption, moving from sing-song irrelevance to blindingly sharp insight, and all of it expressed in her special voice, the most human of human intelligences.

As incidents from her recent trip to America appear in various forms throughout *The Geographical History*, so do certain ideas which were then current in France, namely the prospects of war and political change. Though she was largely engaged with thoughts about America, Gertrude could not help noticing the changes taking place in France. Everywhere people spoke of the coming revolution. That summer five hundred French army troops were stationed in Bilignin, and twenty-eight of them were billetted in her own barn. Try as she might to ignore the fact that 'something was up', something strange and potentially dangerous, it was becoming oppressively clear to Gertrude that the old life was disappearing.

For a start, Gertrude's brother Michael and his wife Sally were no longer living at Les Terrasses, their house in the Paris suburb of Garches, which the then-unknown architect Le Corbusier had built for them in 1927. After some thirty years living in France, Michael had suddenly announced his desire to go home. '. . . You dont understand,' he said to Gertrude, '. . . I want to say in English to the man who brings the letters and does the gardening I want to say things to them and have them say it to me in American.' Michael's longings for America were by now understandable to Gertrude, but with his leaving, one of the last important elements of her old life was gone. In the event, she never saw him again. In 1938 he died in San Francisco. Thanks both to age and the effects of *The Autobiography*, Gertrude was now more and more cut off from the 'old crowd'. Even Picasso had changed.

In 1934 Picasso had parted with his wife Olga. But the influence of the woman whom his friends had called 'a real little lady' was, according to Gertrude, still evident. Picasso was now something of a dandy, in attitude as well as dress. In the mid-thirties, thanks largely to the influence of Cocteau, Picasso was under the spell of the then-fashionable Surrealists. Gertrude, who had never thought much of the work of this group – believing them to be obsessively concerned with an uninteresting misinterpretation of Freud – deplored the association. Even more did she deplore the fact that Picasso had now decided to give up painting and devote himself to writing poetry. Not only did Gertrude find this desire a piece of pretentiousness in her friend, she also considered it an intrusion into her chosen field. Poetry, she felt, was not something just anyone could write, as she explained in *Everybody's Autobiography*:

When I first heard that he was writing poetry I had a·funny feeling. It was Henry Kahnweiler the dealer who first told me about it. What kind of poetry is it I said, why just poetry he said you know poetry like everybody writes. Oh I said.

Well . . . I had a funny feeling one does you know. Things belong to you and writing belongs to me, there is no doubt about it writing belonged to me.

The idea that Picasso could write good verse Gertrude found impossible: 'You know perfectly well the miracle never does happen the one that cannot do a thing does not do it but it always gives you a funny feeling.'

Prompted by this funny feeling and, to be sure, a hope for disaster, Gertrude, together with Alice and Thornton Wilder, accepted Picasso's invitation to his evening poetry recital. At the reading Gertrude was able to sit next to Picasso; she put on her glasses and read the pages as he turned them over and recited. It did not take her long to reassure herself that her friend was not a poet, but it would clearly be necessary to say something pleasing to him. Not wishing to lie outright, Gertrude peered hard at the words on paper, and finding, as always, something beautiful in the painter's handwriting, was able to tell him when he asked: 'Que c'est beau'. Thornton agreed, 'very interesting', he said. Pressed a bit harder by Picasso, Gertrude managed to divert the discussion to an appraisal of handwriting and the differences between the French and Spanish languages. Then, making their exit as gracefully as they could, Gertrude and her friends discussed Picasso's achievement. Thornton said Picasso's poetry was 'the school of Cocteau'. 'For heaven's sake do not tell him,' Gertrude said. 'And then I said but after all why should it not be he never felt anything in words and he never read anything unless it was written by a friend.' And not always then – Picasso was hardly familiar, for example, with Gertrude's work. But he had read Max Jacob and Apollinaire, and quite clearly, Jean Cocteau.

According to *Everybody's Autobiography* Picasso appeared at the rue de Fleurus several days later to get Gertrude's further opinions of his work. Again, she evaded his questions, and read him her recent American lecture, 'Painting'. Impatient with this, Picasso told her, '. . . I will never paint again very likely not I like the life of a literary man, I go to cafés and I think and I make poetry and I like it. It is most interesting I said and for a little time we did not see each other again.' That 'little time' was, according to Alice, 'several years'. Picasso was clearly wounded by Gertrude's indifference to his writing.

As Gertrude tells the story in *Everybody's Autobiography*, some time after the last meeting Picasso rang her and invited himself and his friend Salvador Dali to dinner. On the night arranged, only the Dalis arrived. Dali read to Gertrude his poem about Picasso. But Gertrude interrupted him and told him: '. . . I was bored with the hopelessness of painters and poetry. That in a way was the trouble with the painters they did not know what poetry was.' When Dali said it was Picasso's poems that had made him understand Picasso s paintings, Gertrude attacked him and attacked Picasso's 'poetry'. It was after that, because Dali had been sent by Picasso to find out what Gertrude really thought, that Gertrude and Picasso stopped seeing one another. Their quarrel lasted for a period of some months, until Picasso saw Gertrude from the doorway of Paul Rosen-

The Later Years

Gertrude Stein at Bilignin.

OPPOSITE Gertrude Stein at Bilignin,
with Alice B. Toklas and Bernard Faÿ;
photograph by Cecil Beaton.

ABOVE With Basket at Bilignin.

LEFT On board the ss *Champlain* on arrival in New York, 24 October 1934.
BELOW LEFT Gertrude with Fania Van Vechten in New York.
BELOW A scene from *Four Saints*.

ABOVE With GIS at Culoz during
the Second World War.
RIGHT Gertrude Stein greeting the
American troops on their entry into Paris –
from the window of 27 rue de Fleurus.

OPPOSITE Gertrude and Alice, photographed
by Cecil Beaton.

The collector among her pictures; photograph by Cecil Beaton.

berg's gallery and beckoned her to come inside. Why did you tell Dali what you would not tell me, Picasso demanded. '. . . Why I said because you see one discusses things with dull people but not with sensible ones. . . .' 'What he said Dali cannot understand anything, of course he can't I said you know that as well as I do, he looked a little sheepish yes I guess that is true, he said and then he got excited but you said that painters can't write poetry, well they can't I said, look at you. . . .'

There is much more of this in *Everybody's Autobiography* until we reach the climax of the story, where Gertrude is once more present at the making of art history:

Well he said getting truculent, you yourself always said I was an extraordinary person well then an extraordinary person can do anything, ah I said catching him by the lapels of his coat and shaking him, you are extraordinary within your limits but your limits are extraordinarily there and I said shaking him hard, you know it, you know it, you know it as well as I know it, it is alright you are doing this to get rid of everything that has been too much for you alright alright go on doing it but don't go on trying to make me tell you it is poetry and I shook him again, well he said supposing I do know it, what will I do, what will you do said I and I kissed him, you will go on until you are more cheerful or less dismal and then you will, yes he said, and then you will paint a very beautiful picture and then more of them, and I kissed him again, yes said he.

And there is, of course, an audience for this very stuff of legend: 'Rosenberg went out with me, oh thank you thank you, he said, he must paint again oh thank you thank you said he.'

Whether or not Gertrude ever had this film-classic moment as the woman whose love enabled a disillusioned genius to return to his brushes, there is no corroboration. But the story is typical of the way in which she often saw herself after her American triumph. Picasso was at her command. She could dismiss Dali, Breton and the other Surrealists. She was even at this time given to playing humiliating party tricks on her distinguished guests, as when she made Picasso stand up next to Picabia, whom he disliked, in order to demonstrate that they were wearing the same shoes and ties. The fact that they were the same height and build added to her enjoyment, but not so much as the fact that though they hated each other, they agreed to her requests.

In reality, Gertrude had little or no influence over her former friend Picasso. In the thirties she hardly saw him, and when she did there was likely to be a certain reserve – from Picasso because of her attacks on his friends in *The Autobiography*, from her because he was so evidently able to do without her support. Of her clique of one-time painter friends, there remained in the thirties only Picabia, Alvaro Guevara, and Francis Rose, a fashionable painter of decorative works, but someone who clearly adored her.

While Gertrude's power over and involvement with modern painters declined almost to a memory (although in 1937 she was chosen to sit on the painting selection committee of the Exposition Mondiale), her fame and influence as a writer continued to grow. In the summer of 1935 she had been visited by Sir Robert and Lady Diana Abdy, old friends who were eager for her to renew her position in England. By now totally assured of her powers as a lecturer, she agreed at once to their proposal that she give lectures once again in Oxford and Cambridge. The following January, 1936, Gertrude and Alice crossed the Channel to deliver the gospel to a new generation of Englishmen, this time in the form of the lecture 'What Are Masterpieces and Why Are There So Few of Them?'

The Abdys had arranged for Gertrude and Alice to stay with Gerald Berners at Faringdon House in Berkshire, a rather eccentric home notable, as Daisy Fellowes told Gertrude, as 'the only house in England where the corridors are warm'. Lord Berners was also eccentric, and Gertrude and he got on well, each seeing what was genuine in the other's peculiarities. Berners was, besides, an important figure in the English musical world, and he was interested in the work of Gertrude's that had been set to music. Together they made plans for setting to music Gertrude's 'They Must. Be Wedded. To Their Wife', soon to become the ballet, 'A Wedding Bouquet'.

From Berkshire Gertrude set out with Alice for her second conquest of Oxford. The place seemed to have changed during the previous ten years. The once-exclusive university seemed much larger. '. . . Of course,' she wrote in *Everybody's Autobiography*, 'there always had been a great many Hindus and a great many pale yellow-haired men and many small men . . . but there did seem to be a good many more of them.' There were also a good many Americans. While the reaction to Gertrude's prepared lecture – a short sequel to the meditations on time, identity and genius in *The Geographical History* – was the usual mixture of admiration and incomprehension, the reaction to her lecture on the differences between America, France, and England, delivered at the Oxford French Club, was tumultuously enthusiastic. Several American and Canadian students approached her after the discussion to thank her for her patriotic words, for 'talking up to them' and 'making them take it'. For them, as for Americans at home, Gertrude represented the triumph of the New World over the Old; she was America's sweetheart and the nation's finest spokesman. At Cambridge, too, she was taken up almost exclusively by the American community there. So much so that she was puzzled on one occasion to find an Englishman among the group of young men sitting at her feet: 'I said to him what part of England do you come from, Southampton he said oh I said that is the reason and they all burst out laughing.'

Following a brief stay in Cornwall with the Abdys, Gertrude and Alice returned to Paris to listen in gloom to the increasingly dominant talk of war and revolution. Although she was upset by the Civil War in Spain, she tried not to think about it. She reassured herself by repeating that Europe was too small to have another war, and that in France revolution was merely a 'matter of habit' and therefore not to be taken seriously. She wrote, however, a series of articles on money for the *Saturday Evening Post*, in which she observed that the great economic ills of the day had resulted from too much organisation, and too much corporate thinking, the separation of government from simple realities: 'Everybody now just has to make up their mind. Is money money or isn't money money. Everybody who earns it and spends it every day in order to live knows that money is money, anybody who votes it to be gathered in as taxes knows money is not money. That is what makes everybody go crazy.'

And she worked on the autobiography that she had promised Bennett Cerf. *Everybody's Autobiography* is among the very best of Gertrude's writing. The voice that dominates the work is very different from that of the bumptious, autocratic, charming buffoon who speaks in *The Autobiography of Alice B. Toklas.* Although anecdotes are delivered with similar point and humour, they tend to ramble at leisure, side-stepping to deliver general observation: 'It is funny the two things most men are proudest of is the thing that any man can do and doing does in the same way, that is being drunk and being the father of their son'; to announce the interruptions of daily life: 'If a bird or birds fly into the room is it good luck or bad luck we will say it is good luck; to indulge in word-play which renews the pleasure of writing: 'I weep I cry I glorify but that has nothing to do with that.

'He weeps he cries he glorifies'; to make familiar claims about her place in the history of literature: 'I know that I am the most important writer writing to-day'; and to deliver important aesthetic pronouncements: 'Artists do not experiment. Experiment is what scientists do. . . . An artist puts down what he knows and at every moment it is what he knows at that moment. If he is trying things out to see how they go he is a bad artist.'

These are offered together with marvellous descriptions of her early life, of her trip to America, of her own writing, and with serious meditations on the nature of genius, time and memory, personality and history, much of which has already been quoted here. Together with *Wars I Have Seen* which appeared in 1944, *Everybody's Autobiography* speaks with the true and original voice of Gertrude Stein, without apparent art ('I am telling it now so simply that perhaps it is not anything') or bravado ('And then after all I can remember that I am one of the masters of English prose and that there are not many of them and when I get low in my mind that revives me . . .'). Occupied with this important work, Gertrude strengthened her sense of herself in the face of the threats of the outside world, and continued to receive friends and admirers at her country retreat in Bilignin.

In the spring of 1937 Lord Berners arrived at Bilignin to accompany Gertrude to the opening of their 'Wedding Bouquet' in London. On the trip, Gertrude cheered up enormously. 'London and Paris have changed characters,' she wrote later that year to William Rogers, 'it is London that is gay and Paris that is somber. . . .' Removed from her life in Paris, Gertrude enjoyed the holiday atmosphere of London. She met Frederick Ashton, who also choreographed 'A Wedding Bouquet', and declared him 'a genius'. She was fêted at numerous parties, and photographed at several sessions by Cecil Beaton. Gertrude was, Beaton said, 'the best sitter any photographer could ever hope to have', thanks to 'the magnanimity [that] shone through her trusting brown eyes'.

In England, Gertrude was relieved to find that the only political talk centred around Mrs Simpson and the abdication. It was a typically English worry, she thought, and showed a healthy preoccupation with tradition. Tradition was everywhere in England: it even crossed barriers; in farming, for example, she detected the tradition of public schools: 'In the country I went over to a village called Littleworth and passed a field full of calves, being English calves they are ... separated from the cows and the bulls, in France the calves are always with the cows not often with the bulls but often with oxen.'

Of the ballet itself, Gertrude had little hope. Ever since seeing the performance of 'Four Saints' in Chicago she had known better than to expect to recognise her original writing in its stage form. She knew that the members of the so-called avant-garde who produced her work for the theatre were really rather timid: 'As yet they have not done any of mine without music to help them,' she wrote that year, 'They could though and it would be interesting but no one has yet.' On the other hand, she felt 'there is no use going to see a thing if you have not written it no use at all'. She enjoyed hearing her own words, and taking her stage-bows and knowing 'it was a great success'. And 'of course' she liked 'la gloire': 'And then we went somewhere and we met everyone and I always do like to be a lion, I like it again and again, it is a peaceful thing to be one succeeding.'

The peace of succeeding was, in the event, to be short-lived. Back in Paris after her brief triumph in England, Gertrude was soon made aware once more of the general anxiety of the times. While she continued to worry out the questions of identity and entity, the inside and the outside life of writers, the problems of genius, publicity and time in both her autobiography and in her poetry and meditations it was clear that world events were pulling her thoughts elsewhere. Confused and alarmed by the prospect of radical changes in her future life, Gertrude fell upon glib reassurances and specious argument to tell herself all was well.

Gertrude's reaction to the economic and political situation in the late thirties was characteristic of her nature and habit of mind at that period. Events came to her in the form of intrusion upon her work, threats against her security and mental calm, as baubles to entice her play of mind, triggers for abstract meditation. She saw the general panic largely as a nuisance which could be dealt with by her brand of common sense. Although, when on their return to France in 1935, talk of revolution had spurred Alice to send all Gertrude's unpublished manuscripts to Carl Van Vechten for safe keeping, Gertrude was content to dismiss the likelihood of revolution with a bored prediction: 'After every great war there is a time of spending and having everything and then there is nothing and everybody talks about revolution and France having the habit of revolution is pretty sure to have one. After all revolutions are a matter of habit.'

The trouble with the present world, according to Gertrude, was twofold: it was getting too crowded and it was getting too modern; people were losing their natural habits of living. This had happened in France, she thought, when the French had learned to spend money in a manner which was unnatural for them:

Nobody in France no matter how poor or how rich ever thought of living on current earning, they always lived on last year's earnings and that made the French live their unworried living, the only thing that ever troubled them was the possibility of war or the possibility of changing the régime, that is a revolution, but otherwise there was nothing to worry them except family quarrels and family quarrels are exciting but not really worrisome, so Frenchwomen never had worry lines in their faces. And now they had because they were spending this year's earnings.

Not only had the French lost the habit of saving, they had also lost the habit of work. This much she knew from her own difficulties in getting servants: 'It is curious very curious . . . that when there is a great deal of unemployment and misery you can never find anybody to work for you.' 'But that is natural enough', she decided, 'because if everybody is unemployed everybody loses the habit of work, and work like revolutions is a habit it just naturally is.'

Together with this loss of the old way of living, was the evil of overcrowding. In the thirties Gertrude began to think that only in a country like England (despite its population Gertrude considered it small), could you find 'constitutional republican government' because England was tidy and civilised. In larger countries – like Spain, France and America – where, according to Gertrude, there were too many people, the masses were susceptible to dictatorships. Mass organisation had made them lazy. Ordinary people, so Gertrude thought, were interested only in 'normal daily living', and they preferred to leave politics to politicians like Mussolini, Franco and Roosevelt, who would do their thinking for them. Once people accepted the rule and authority of such people – fathers, as Gertrude called them – they were bound to lose their freedom: '. . . feudal days were the days of fathers and now once more these days are the days of fathers.'

In 1936 she wrote in *Everybody's Autobiography*:

There is too much fathering going on just now and there is no doubt about it fathers are depressing. Everybody now-a-days is a father, there is father Mussolini and father Hitler and father Roosevelt and father Stalin and father Trotzky and father Blum and father Franco is just commencing now and there are ever so many more ready to be one. Fathers are depressing. England is the only country now that has not got one and so they are more cheerful there than anywhere. It is a long time now that they have not had any fathering and so their cheerfulness is increasing.

The metaphor has the force of real feeling; and it directly conveys Gertrude's unhappiness and sense of subjection to outside events. As she concluded, 'The periods of the world's history that have always been such dismal ones are the ones where fathers were looming and filling up everything.'

Gertrude saw the history of the world since the eighteenth century as one in which individual freedom had come to be eroded by the demands of economics. As she wrote in one of her articles on money for *The Saturday Evening Post*:

The beginning of the eighteenth century, after everything had been completely under feudal and religious domination, was full of a desire for individual liberty and they went at it until they thought they had it, which ended up with first the English and then the American and then the French revolution, so there they were and everybody was free and then that went on to Lincoln. Then they began inventing machinery and at the same time they found virgin lands that could be worked with machinery and so they began organization, they began factory organization and laborers organization, and the more they began organization the more everybody wanted to be organized and the more they were organized the more everybody liked the slavery of being in organization.

Organised politics, Gertrude wrote in *Everybody's Autobiography*, made events uninteresting for ordinary people. So much she had seen on her visit to the States, when she watched people reading newspapers on their evening train journey from work: 'They kind of read the newspaper but it was not really very interesting but when they got to the part about the quintuplets and how the doctor took care of them then they folded their paper so that they only had that spot and then they settled down to solidly reading. It was interesting to me that that was the only thing in the paper that was really real to them.'

Neither were the French really interested in politics: '. . . . the men in politics are like the women in dressing, sometimes the skirts are long and sometimes they are short. . . .' More than this, the French have an actual aversion to government: '. . . Frenchmen do not really think they have anything to do with anything that governs, they live their own life and they fight for that country and beside that they have no responsibility. Their life is secret that is it belongs to themselves and up till now that is what has made French elegance and French style, . . .' It was '. . . one of the curious things about a European democracy', Gertrude wrote, that the people '. . . do not feel that they have any more to do or to say about what is going to happen than when it was a kingdom . . . after all they do not know who decides these things all they know is that there is a decision'.

Gertrude's own politics were simply based on a dislike of being disturbed and a general dislike of father figures. She disliked Trotsky as much as Franco, and Roosevelt as much as either, and she referred to liberals like Blum as 'people with unhappy childhoods'. It was a position that irritated her friends. When William Rogers sent her a packet of American corn seeds and warned her not to give any of the corn to her fascist neighbours in Bilignin, Gertrude returned the gift with a request: 'please send us unpolitical corn.' Why shouldn't she give her friends the corn, she asked, 'why not if the fascists like it and we liked the fascists . . .'. To Rogers's serious attempt to argue with her against fascism, for example that under fascism her own and other writers' freedom of speech would suffer, she replied: 'As to their not letting me write, well most of them do let you write and I guess it would have taken me just about as long to be published anywhere as anywhere.'

William Rogers called Gertrude a 'rentier'. She possessed, he wrote in *When This You See*, 'a rentier mentality in matters of taxes, jobs and government'; but Gertrude believed her principles to be those of an eighteenth-century 'individualist': 'I cannot write too much upon how necessary it is to be completely conservative that is particularly traditional in order to be free,' she wrote in 1939 in *Paris France*. By then Gertrude was sixty-five years old and for her the world had moved on too quickly. She quite clearly wished for history to go backwards, for the pleasure and peace of things as they were.

It was one of the results of a life spent in pursuit of an art whose purpose was to 'live in the actual present' that one should be unable to be convinced of the future consequences of present choices. Ironically, 'living in the present' had made her reactionary. Now, along with her Bilignin neighbours, elderly aristocrats like the Baronne Pierlot, François and Robert d'Aiguy, and like Bernard Faÿ, Gertrude became a royalist and a supporter of Pétain.

Gertrude's devotion to her writing, to the demands of genius, made her position incomprehensible to her friends. She was attacked as a reactionary by readers of her articles in *The Saturday Evening Post* and by those who were offended by passages in *Everybody's Autobiography* such as this one: 'All the time that I am writing the Spanish revolution obtrudes itself. Not because it is a revolution but because I know it all so well the places they are mentioning and the things there they are destroying.' The deaths of great numbers of people did not affect her because she was incapable of thinking of people in large numbers. But it enabled her to make seemingly callous statements: '. . . anybody can know that the earth is covered all over with people . . . there are an awful lot of them anyway and in a way I really am only interested in what a genius can say the rest is just there anyway.' Gertrude's position was that of Saint Theresa in 'Four Saints' who answers the question, 'If it were possible to kill five thousand chinamen by pressing a button would it be done' with the reply, 'Saint Theresa not interested'. Death and suffering were not the concerns of the living or of artists. They were not interesting, and '. . . I could not see why there being so many more of them made it any more interesting'.

Gertrude believed in art, but she also believed in the rightness of 'daily living', like, she said, everyone else. She did not feel superior to ordinary people as a writer, she just did not feel that she or any other ordinary people should be bothered with questions of revolution, death and war. As she wrote in a long reply to William Rogers, taking political decisions was not something one ought to be concerned with:

> You see what in Europe everybody is hollering about is whether communism is not worse than fascism and here everybody thinks you have to be either red or white and I am not so sure they are not right and certainly white is bad but not so bad as red. After all the people don't mean anything, there are about 5 in every European village that holler, sometimes the majority red and sometimes the majority white, and the remaining 10 are just scared and say yes to whatever they think is the stronger, now you cannot call that a government by the people, I must say my sympathy is largely with the 10 who are scared it would be nice if they could be let alone but can they, I can be scared myself so I know how they feel.

Gertrude's profound desire not to be disturbed by political events in the thirties was strangely at odds with her reaction to those upheavals which did take place in her life during the last years of the peace in Europe. In 1938 the lease on her flat at 27 rue de Fleurus had expired. Far from complaining to her friends about the injustice of eviction, she accepted the abrupt change gracefully. As she wrote to Rogers in February the move was almost a necessity: 'We were tired of the present which' also was the past because no servant would stand the kitchen, there was no air in the house, the garage they had built next door made it uncomfortable. . . .' She was seemingly unaffected by the end of an important element in the Stein legend – the studio and flat where she had lived and worked for some thirty-five years.

Later that year, another important element of the legend was to end, with the death of Basket, famous to thousands, and photographed and painted almost as often as his owner. Picasso offered Gertrude an Afghan hound as a replacement. But as she replaced her Fords with other models, which would be the same but different, she now acquired Basket II. In a letter to Rogers she wrote, '. . . Baby Basket has lovely eyes so we feel he is basket's baby and we feel so much better.'

Gertrude's resistance to change evolved in the last years of peace into a cheerful acceptance of change when it was inevitable. Gertrude always understood change as a principle of art, and now she came to recognise it as a positive principle of life. In 1938 in her tribute to Picasso in the book she wrote of that name, she makes the declaration: '[Picasso] understands what is contemporary when the contemporaries do not yet know it, but he is contemporary and as the twentieth century is a century which sees the earth as no one has ever seen it, the earth has a splendor that it never has had, and as everything destroys itself in the twentieth century and nothing continues, so then the twentieth century has a splendor which is its own. . . .'

As she wrote in 1939 of Basket, there was a certain promise of continuity in the willing submission to what has to be: 'certainly', she wrote, 'le roi est mort vive le roi is a normal attitude of mind.'

II

A Small Hard Reality

IN APRIL 1939, Gertrude had written to Rogers her last word on the subject of the coming war:

I do not believe that there is one human being on the continent of Europe who wants a general European war, not even members of the armies and navies of any European country and since they not one of them want a European war the chances are there will not be one, of course accidents can happen and chips on shoulders can be knocked off but when nobody wants a thing generally speaking if they have anything to do with it they avoid it, this conviction left me calm in September and has left me calm ever since. . . .

In this state of mind Gertrude began to write her tribute to the sanity of the French people and to voice her great affection for the land of her adoption. *Paris France* was written in 1939 as an act of gratitude: 'Paris was the place that suited those of us that were to create the twentieth century art and literature, naturally enough. . . . England had the disadvantage of believing in progress, and progress has really nothing to do with civilisation, but France could be civilised without having progress on her mind, she could believe in civilisation in and for itself, and so she was the natural background for this period.' It was also written as a vindication of her own 'French' indifference to politics: '. . . french people do not believe that anything is important except daily living and the ground that gives it to them and defending themselves from the enemy. Government has no importance except insofar as it does that.' 'I remember so well,' she wrote, 'it was during the 1914 war and they were all french and they were talking about women voting and one of the women who was listening said, oh dear I have to stand in line for so many things coal and sugar and candles and meat and now to vote, oh dear.' '. . . Tradition and their private life and the soil which always produces something, that is what counts.'

All the current talk of war was, Gertrude felt, merely a form of divertisement for the French: 'But after all it might only be a fire drill, it might only be make believe, any frenchman knows that you really ought not to know the difference between danger and no danger.' Furthermore, the idea that the French could be attacked by the Germans did not accord at all with any of her theories: 'The characteristic art product of a country is the pulse of the country, France did produce better hats and fashions than ever these last two years and is therefore very alive and Germany's music and musicians have been dead and gone these last two years and so Germany is dead well we will see, it is so, of course as all these things are necessarily true.'

When therefore, in September 1939, France declared war on Germany, Gertrude was profoundly horrified. She was sitting with a group of friends in the garden at Bilignin when news of the war reached them. 'They all were upset but hopeful,' Gertrude wrote in an article in 1940, 'but I was terribly frightened; I had been so sure there was not going to be war and here it was, it was war, and I made quite a scene. I said, "They shouldn't! They shouldn't!" and they were very sweet, and I apologized and said I was sorry but it was awful, and they comforted me – they, the French, who had so much at stake, and I had nothing at stake comparatively.'

That month Gertrude and Alice returned to Paris for forty-eight hours to arrange Gertrude's manuscripts and pictures and to collect winter clothing for their first long stay in Bilignin. There, together with other refugees from the capital, Gertrude passed her first winter in the country since her childhood. This itself made it an adventure: '. . . I did enjoy it; there was snow and moonlight and I had to saw wood.' As she described this winter in 'The Winner Loses: A Picture of Occupied France', which she wrote for the *Atlantic Monthly* in 1940, it was something of a children's treat for Gertrude and Alice, one in which they could play Robinson Crusoe. That the war going on was a real war, they managed to ignore: '. . . we had plenty of society and we talked about the war, but not too much, and we had hired a radio wireless and we listened to it, but not too much, and the winter was all too soon over.'

That winter and the following spring, 1940, Gertrude lived a pleasant life, accommodated herself to shortages of meat and petrol, read books prophesying the fall of Germany and carried on with her real interests, writing about the problems of identity and the effects of publicity in *Ida A Novel*. It was not until May 1940 that the war became real to her, when the German army arrived in the local town of Belley:

> We were in the biggest store in Belley, a sort of bazaar, when all of a sudden the proprietor called out 'Go to the back of the shop!' Well, naturally we didn't, and we heard a rumbling noise and there two enemy machine-gun tanks came rushing through the street, with the German cross painted on them. Oh my, it did make us feel most uncommonly queer. 'Let's go home' we said, and we did not do any more shopping; we went back to Bilignin.

Written like a Beatrix Potter adventure, this account of the coming of the Germans expresses only one side of Gertrude's feelings in those first months of the war. It is true that her profound innocence protected her from the realization of what it might mean to be an alien Jew in occupied France; but another side of Gertrude responded fully to the muted panic of the times. In *Mrs Reynolds*, a novel she began in 1940, Gertrude successfully expressed the feelings of a middle-aged woman in occupied France. Using a near-allegorical form, Gertrude depicts the life of her heroine, whose sister-in-law is called Hope, and her relation to an ominous figure in the village, whom she calls Angel Harper. Together with Joseph Lane (Stalin), who is not in the village but who is spoken of by the villagers, Harper (or Hitler) sinisterly appears and disappears in their lives. 'The hoot-owl was hooting terrifically up the valley. Nobody knew just when or how Angel Harper was born. Not that it made any difference. It did not.'

Generally anxious, Mrs Reynolds (the name has possibly something to do with the painter; Gertrude considered herself both an eighteenth-century 'individualist' and someone for whom eighteenth-century pastoral was a significant aesthetic; she was also, of course, a portraitist), like Gertrude Stein, spent much of the time thinking about food: 'Mrs Reynolds stayed at home and breathed out a sigh.'

'She thought about butter and sugar and oil and coffee, she thought about meat and ham and hunger. She was never hungry but she always ate. She thought about noodles and cream. She was often thoughtful.'

Or like Mrs Reynolds's sister-in-law Hope, Gertrude would dream shadowy, uncertain dreams about Hitler: 'Hope dreamed one night that very much later Angel Harper the dictator, said everything was all over, and she dreamed that she said to him and what are you going to do, and he said they will not go, they are all to be drowned but they will not go, and she dreamed she said to him and what will you do, and he said to her tell me what to do and she said to him you have invented so much invent a way to disappear that is to say to die and he said why, and she said why not die, and he said yes, I will die, and then she woke up.'

Or else Gertrude just ignored Hitler: 'Angel Harper looked just the same as he used to but Mr Reynolds' brother and his wife Hope did not see him. They were alive all right but they did not see him.'

She worried about the black market: 'Mrs Reynolds the wife of Mr Reynolds stayed at home and breathed out a sigh. She liked to prophesy. She said, purchase bye and bye will not be a matter of money but a matter of personality. If you are popular you can buy if you are not popular you can die.'

She took pride in her strength: 'Not easily can older people not walk. Really older people walk more easily than younger people.'

She was comforted by her lover, who could transform (here expressed by the pun on Angel) the terrors of the time: 'Mr Reynolds turned in his sleep, what is it you wanted me to do, he said. Nothing but be my angel said Mrs Reynolds. Mr Reynolds was still asleep. That is easy he said.'

As Gertrude wrote in her Epilogue to the novel, the book described 'a perfectly ordinary couple living an ordinary life and having ordinary conversations and really not suffering personally from everything that is happening but over them, all over them is the shadow of two men, and then the shadow of one of the two men gets bigger and blows away and there is no other.' 'There is nothing historical about this book,' she added, 'except the state of mind.'

By whatever means Gertrude coped with her fears in 1940, events often moved faster than she could deal with. In June 1940 when Italy entered the war, Gertrude began to be badly frightened. In Bilignin, they would be 'right in everybody's path; any enemy that wanted to go anywhere might easily come here'. Besides that, the Italians, according to Gertrude, were far worse than the Germans. In the late thirties she had impressed a new acquaintance, Eric Sevareid, with her strange views: 'Hitler will never really go to war,' he reports her as saying in his book *Not So Wild A Dream*. 'He is not the dangerous one. You see, he is the German romanticist. He wants the illusion of victory and power, the glory and glamour of it, but he could not stand the blood and fighting involved in getting it. No, Mussolini – there's the dangerous man, for he is an Italian realist. He won't stop at anything.'

Whether in June 1940 Gertrude still held these views is not clear, but when Mussolini's army entered the war, she and Alice panicked. Having ignored the warnings issued by the authorities since December 1939 that American citizens should leave the country, they now telephoned the American consul in Lyon, who told them to leave at once. That night Gertrude and Alice began to pack; they found a home for Basket II and spent a sleepless night preparing for their journey of escape. By the next morning, however, Gertrude had begun to see things in a different light. Although the *préfet* at Bourg now joined the consul at Lyon in urging them to leave, Gertrude decided to ignore their advice: 'They all said "Leave", and I said to Alice Toklas, "Well, I don't know – it would be awfully uncomfortable and I am fussy about my food. Let's not leave." So we came back, and the village was happy and we were happy and that was all right, and I said I would not hear any more news – Alice Toklas could listen to the wireless, but as for me I was going to cut box hedges and forget the war.'

Unfortunately for Gertrude, Alice *did* listen to the wireless, and two days later she was insisting to Gertrude that they must go. Gertrude gave in to Alice's pressure and the two women set out in the Ford on the Lyon road. En route they met a friend of theirs, a doctor from the village. He did not think it at all necessary for them to leave, he said. In the last war, he told them, all those who left lost their property, and those who stayed were safe. ' "Everybody knows you here," ' he said, according to Gertrude's account. ' "Everybody likes you; we all would help you in every way. Why risk yourself among strangers?" '

' "Thank you," we said, "That is all we need. We stay." ' And so they stayed.

Gertrude Stein remained in a state of quiet anxiety during the first year of war. As she described her feelings to William Rogers in a letter of 1940: '. . . we go along peacefully and then sometimes about 10 o'clock in the evening I get scared about everything and then I complete[ly] upset Alice and she goes to bed scared and I walk in the garden and I come in and I work and I am all peaceful and luckily Alice can sleep and that is the worst moment, during the day we are busy and that is the way it is.'

Gertrude did not listen to the radio, not only because of the war news but also because of the amount of martial music that was broadcast. As she wrote to Rogers, '. . . there is a deplorable amount of music going on in the world, if they would suppress most of it perhaps the world would be more peaceful . . .'. But she did not give way to her fears. Though all her friends in America implored her to return, and though the prospect of another lecture tour was offered, she continued to believe that the war was only a 'phony war'. Instead she threw herself into the simple life of the villagers in Bilignin. In August 1940 Pétain had signed the Armistice, the Germans had come and gone, and the completely 'daily living' had survived unharmed. '. . . Everybody is very busy accommodating themselves to everything,' she wrote in the article which was to appear in the *Atlantic Monthly* that November, '. . . and I must say the French are really happy in combining and contriving and intriguing and succeeding and above all in saving.' The end of the article, which soon appeared before amazed friends in America, was full of hope for the future:

> I have been talking to the young people and asking them how they like it and they said they are very pleased. They say now they can begin to feel they have their future to create, that they were tired of the weak vices they were all indulging in . . . they want France to be self-sufficing, and they think it will be and they all think French people were getting soft, and French people should not be soft. Well, anyway they are looking forward. . . . In short, they feel alive and like it. . . .

Gertrude Stein and Alice Toklas spent their days chopping wood, making jam, visiting their neighbours, writing to friends in America – occasionally to ask for such things as darning-thread, soap, and cigarettes, all in short supply in France. Otherwise, the two elderly ladies found they could cope easily with the shortages. ('As Alice does know how to make everything be something,' wrote Gertrude, 'we get along fine.') When there was no soap they washed their clothes in wood-ash, when there was no petrol they ran their car on alcohol, when there was no coal they walked miles each day in search of fallen branches to burn. And when money ran short, they simply sold what they had. And so, as Gertrude wrote later, they 'ate Cézanne'.

News of the progress of the war did not depress them, although, as Gertrude wrote, in order not to be depressed, a constant effort and vigilance had to be maintained: 'You just go on talking to yourself in war-time. You talk to yourself about caterpillars but you never talk to yourself about spiders or lizards, you talk to yourself about dogs and cats and rabbits but not about bats or mice or moths.'

What grief she suffered in the first year of war came from personal news, of Zelda Fitzgerald's insanity and of Scott Fitzgerald's death in Hollywood in 1941, and of the sudden death in March 1941 of Sherwood Anderson, on board ship at the start of a long-awaited trip to South America. It was not until December 1941 and the bombing of Pearl Harbour that Gertrude seems to have been personally and wholeheartedly involved in the war. Her letter to Rogers expresses a new and uncharacteristic fierceness: 'The first days of the attack of the Japs was pretty awful, Alice and I were pretty done up, it does not seem that it would be worse than an attack on France but I do suppose that one's native land is more one's native land than any other native land. . . . We . . .

sort of could not get over it until I began to say in a refrain, they will solemnly go to and
fro and every day they will solemnly bomb Tokio, and I began to feel better.'

Gertrude's new bloodthirst applied rather strictly to the perpetrators of the horror in
America. With regard to France, Gertrude remained sanguine. The department of the
Ain, where she lived, was not occupied by the Germans, nor had any of the locals
suffered as yet at the hands of the Nazis. One of her closest friends, Bernard Faÿ, had
been treated especially well by them – and was appointed head of the Bibliothèque
Nationale, and Francis Rose had, she knew, been amorously involved with the Nazi
leaders. According to Rose's memoir he even extracted a promise from Goering to watch
over Gertrude Stein and Alice in France. About collaborators, Gertrude had then no
strong feelings. Nor had she turned against Pétain, whose speeches she offered to translate for the *Atlantic Monthly* (they were not receptive to the proposal). As she wrote in
Wars I Have Seen, the journal of her war life she began in 1943, her feelings about
Pétain's Armistice were mixed:

> . . . we were all glad in a way and completely sad in a way and we had so many
> opinions. I did not like his way of saying I Philippe Petain, that bothered me and we
> were in the unoccupied area and that was a comfort. Many months later somebody
> wrote to me and said that in America everybody said there was no difference between
> the occupied and the unoccupied zone but we who lived in the unoccupied zone we
> knew there was a difference all right. . . . Petain was right to stay in France and he
> was right to make the armistice and little by little I understood it.

Wars I Have Seen, which Gertrude began at the instigation of William Rogers as a
way to earn some badly needed money, is among the very best of her books, and arguably
the best of her biographies. It tells the story of her 'daily living' and her thoughts from
the spring of 1943 to the autumn of 1944 and the liberation of American France. For
two years Gertrude kept the journal, in her large illegible handwriting, not to be typed
out by Alice so that it might remain safe from the possibility of German confiscation
and its consequences. *Wars I Have Seen* began as an account of her early life and the
influence of wars – chiefly the Civil War and the Boer War – on her childhood and
adolescence, and describes her own growing up in terms of the developments of modern
history. She also offers her theories of modernism, and recounts how both she and the
times were struggling to 'kill off the nineteenth century'. From that point she discusses
the present war as a final death-throe of the last century. The unshakable nineteenth-
century belief in progress and permanence was dispelled in her view by this war.
Wartime life in Bilignin and Belley, says Gertrude, is more like life in the Middle Ages,
or as she had it elsewhere in the book, like adolescence, where nothing is sure and life
has no logical sequences, no beginning, middle or end.

> . . . Everybody knows that there will be no progress anybody knows that there will
> be no progress everybody knows everybody knows that there will be no progress but
> there will be insecurity and there will be courage and fear, and hope and death and

sickness and health, and strength and terror, and they will go on and nobody will want to give anybody what is not theirs to give nor theirs to take no nobody at all, and the nineteenth century is dead stone dead on this month of November in 1943.

What had happened to Gertrude in the first years of the war to convince her she was living as people had lived in the Middle Ages was partly a question of returning to a simpler way of life: farming by means of hand-threshing, transport by horses instead of cars, using wooden soles on shoes because rubber was scarce. But it had more to do with the day-to-day, hand-to-mouth existence, in which it was impossible to plan for a future and it was a necessity to live only in the present moment. In such a situation people ate what they found to eat and if they did not find it they did not have it. Any day they could find themselves without spouse or children because of an action by an absolute, and seemingly whimsical, outside authority. In this enforced living in the present moment, one not only did not think of the future, one often did not think at all. Early in 1943, in one of her last war letters to reach the outside world, Gertrude wrote to Rogers: 'Just at present we are all very quiet waiting for what comes next, but there is one thing one has learnt and that is to empty your mind of all thinking about things you cannot manage, in fact . . . you kind of learn not to think and not to plan but like the busy bee to be very busy, and to busy yourself with that.'

In 1943, Gertrude Stein was entirely cut off from the kind of life she had known before. There were now no letters to be had or sent to and from America – or indeed, to and from Paris or any of the other occupied French territories. Travelling was limited to the erratic trains that came to Belley and near-by towns such as Aix-les-Bains and Chambéry. If a return trip was cancelled it meant for Gertrude and Alice an overnight wait at these stations, or a long walk home. Nothing – not eating, sleeping, working, nor at times existing – could be planned for or guaranteed. Neither could home. In February 1943 the lease on Gertrude's house in Bilignin expired. Unaware of the great danger of calling attention to herself and her enemy status (Americans in France were by then being sent to concentration camps – among them the consul at Lyon who had earlier advised her to leave the country), Gertrude hired herself a lawyer to dispute the eviction.

In the end, Gertrude lost her case against the landlord at Bilignin. She was offered another house, a modern building with well-kept lawns at the near-by village of Culoz. But Culoz itself was closer to a railway station that was important to the Germans. Her position there would be far more dangerous. Therefore, before Gertrude could move in to the new house, the *sous-préfet* contacted the lawyer: '. . . tell those ladies,' he said, 'that they must leave at once for Switzerland, to-morrow if possible otherwise they will be put in a concentration camp.' Then, as Gertrude continues the story, the *sous-préfet* arranged 'by fraud' for safe-passage to the Swiss frontier, and she and Alice agreed to escape. But Gertrude 'felt funny' about it:

> . . . Alice Toklas and I sat down to supper. We both felt funny and then I said. No, I am not going we are not going, it is better to go regularly to wherever we are sent than to go irregularly where nobody can help us if we are in trouble, no I said, they

are always trying to get us to leave France but here we are and here we stay. . . .
I said to-morrow we are going to move to Culoz, with our large comfortable new
house with two good servants and a nice big park with trees, and we all went home,
and we did move the next day. It took us some weeks to get over it but we finally did.

Gertrude's courage in this case was simply and characteristically a childish wilfulness.
She just did not want to be moved. She did not want to accept the war and the cruelties
of the war as they were. She dismissed both German racism and European anti-semitism
as silly and unfounded, and since it was silly, it could not, she felt, be dangerous. But
her innocence during the war was that of a child who always finds being happy more
natural than being unhappy. *Wars I Have Seen* is an extraordinary account of Gertrude's
day-to-day cheerfulness during a long and exhausing war. At the age of seventy she was
not only a survivor, but one who took profound joy in all the challenges to that survival.
As a document of the artist's ability to make a pleasure of hell's despite, *Wars I Have
Seen* is unique, and uniquely moving.

Gertrude's safety at Culoz was in fact largely due to the courage of the mayor and his
Swiss wife, who kept Gertrude and Alice's names off their official records. According to
Eric Sevareid's account, the mayor had said to Gertrude: 'you are obviously too old for
life in a concentration camp. You would not survive it, so why should I tell them.' But
she was also protected by the villagers themselves, all of whom knew exactly who she
was and might easily have denounced her. Instead, she was protected by them, sheltered,
and often fed, because she cared for them, too, and quickly became just one among many
villagers working hard for survival. Like them, Gertrude walked twelve kilometres a day
to buy bread, like them searched the woods for nuts and mushrooms, like them traded
on the black market. With them she shared gossip, war rumours, prophesies, good news
and grief; advised their sons to go to the mountains with the maquis or to accept
deportation to the labour camps in Germany. Although her age brought her certain
privileges, she was treated, to her delight, simply as one of them.

Not that Culoz was an unusually friendly or coherent village. On the contrary, as
Gertrude noted in her journal:

. . . now in June 1943 something very strange is happening, every day the feeling is
strengthening that one or another has been or will be a traitor to something and
what do they do they send them a little wooden coffin sometimes with a letter inside
sometimes with a rope inside to tell them to hang themselves, and sometimes it is
sent by post or by railroad and sometimes it is hung up in a tree and sometimes hung
up in front of the front door. . . .

. . . And every neighbour is denouncing every neighbour, for black traffic, for theft
for this and for that, and there are so many being put in prison, poor Madame
Berard said it was so sad to see her husband going off between two policemen just as
if he was a criminal and to know that some of their neighbours were pleased to see it.
To be sure he had been killing meat and did he sell it or not – or only serve it in

quantity in his restaurant and her boy has to go to Germany because he is twenty-one even though he is a great mathematician and is to be a great man at the university of Lyon and the family were always gentle and kindly and obliging and never charged too much even when they might have and indeed it was all true they never did.

That was one side of wartime living, and it was depressing. But for Gertrude there was another.

There was the rediscovered joy of taking trains and the pleasures of belonging:

. . . and now there being only walking bicycling and trains we take trains and all the old delight in trains comes back. The making of so many acquaintances. There being so many people in a compartment and in the corridors, there being so many things happening, there being eating and drinking and very strange eating and drinking these days in a train, everybody carrying something and some quite openly eating what they are not supposed to be having and others not eating anything at all at least it might just as well not be anything, and in a station having a long conversation with a very nice refugee she in one train and I in another one, and telling each other all about what we were and where we came from.

There was pioneering:

There are so many things that happened, we are burning peat, one used to read about that being done in Ireland, and here there are a great many marshes and there is peat and although it smells a little and smokes a good deal it is not bad to burn not at all, and as the windows in Grenoble and Annecy are all broken by explosions they all have paper windows, and as I say it really is like pioneering, we are all on the roads all the time going here and going there to find things to eat, in the country of course you do find plenty and at least there is so much that you can even refuse to buy more of it, of which we are all inordinately proud, up to date we all have bought anything anybody has brought us.

But there were also real shortages, and sometimes the pleasant ironies of shortages: 'We have very pleasant neighbours and one of them has just had a baby girl and they had to name her Madeleine because the only safety pin gold of course that they had had the name Madeleine on it, you cannot these days buy a pin to suit the baby's name you name the baby to go with the gold safety pin.'

Above all, connected with all these discoveries, was the realisation of life in its simplest and best: 'A long war like this makes you realise the society you really prefer, the home, goats chickens and dogs and casual acquaintances. I find myself not caring at all for garden flowers or vegetables cats cows and rabbits, one gets tired of trees vines and hills, but houses, goats chickens dogs and casual acquaintances never pall.' Life came down to a few simple necessities, and the simplest and most necessary was, as Gertrude saw: '. . . that nowhere in the world should those who have not committed any crime should not live peacefully in their home, go peacefully about their business and not be afraid, not have uneasiness in their eyes, not.' 'Life dear life,' Gertrude repeats, again and again.

But the war was exhausting. Despite all the predictions of St Odile and all the cherished rumours of imminent victory, the war dragged on from one hard winter to the next. In October 1943, Gertrude wrote of a '. . . story they all told last fall. They were talking people in a position to know and one of them said it was going to be over now, and they all said eagerly how do you know and he said very easily, my wife has had enough of it.

'Yes everybody has had enough of it everybody's wife and everybody's husband and everybody's mother and everybody's father and everybody's daughter and everybody's son, they have all had enough of it.'

In January 1944, Gertrude wrote: 'Just now . . . nobody seems to think that the war will ever end. We all were hopeful in '43, but in '44 it is going much better but we have so much less hope of it ever being over so very much less hope.'

In the spring of 1944, the war was visibly deteriorating for the Germans, and the situation became more and more dangerous. Younger boys and girls were now being rounded up to join munitions factories in Germany, the maquis were blowing up the bridges, and both they and the villagers were frequently shot. The Allies themselves, furthermore, were destroying Savoy villages in their bombing campaigns. 'It is queer,' Gertrude wrote as tales of atrocities came to her, 'the world is so small and so knocked about.'

Nervous and vindictive, the Germans came and went through Belley. On one night a few were billeted with Gertrude and Alice. They did not notice the Picasso paintings in the house, nor the American accents of the women, and Gertrude and Alice safely avoided them, leaving the servants to deal with the intruders. The Italian soldiers, on the other hand, who followed the Germans, spent long evenings talking to Gertrude, united in their hatred of the German army.

Gertrude's escapes during the war were remarkable. Again and again she came through such adventures, until she and Alice were both almost tempting the Nazis to action, on one occasion denying them access to their cellars, on another openly autographing a copy of *The Autobiography* for a French guard on the German-occupied railway station at Aix-les-Bains.

By May 1944 Rome had been taken by the Allies. In the weeks that followed the maquis came down from the mountains and declared themselves the official French army. By the time of the D-Day landing, Gertrude's joy was without limit:

. . . to-day is the landing and we heard Eisenhower tell us he was here they were here and just yesterday a man sold us ten packages of Camel cigarettes, glory be, and we were singing glory hallelujah, and feeling very nicely, and everybody has been telephoning to us congratulatory messages upon my birthday which it isn't but we know what they mean. And I said in return I hoped their hair was curling nicely, and we all hope it is, and to-day is the day.

In the last section of *Wars I Have Seen*, she describes the return of freedom to France at the end of August 1944:

And now at half-past twelve to-day on the radio a voice said attention attention attention and the Frenchman's voice cracked with excitement and he said Paris is free. Glory hallelujah Paris is free, imagine it less than three months since the landing and Paris is free. All these days I did not dare to mention the prediction of Saint Odile, she said Paris would not be burned the devotion of her people would save Paris and it has vive la France. I can't tell you how excited we all are and now if I can only see the Americans come to Culoz I think all this about war will be finished yes I do.

Then on 1 September 1944 Gertrude Stein saw her first Americans: 'There have been six of them in the house, two of them stayed the night. . . . Oh happy day, that is all that I can say oh happy day.'

'. . . And I said you are going to sleep in a bed where German officers slept six weeks ago, wonderful my gracious perfectly wonderful.' And then, on the next day: 'How we talked and talked and where they were born was music to the ears Baltimore and Washington D.C. and Detroit and Chicago it is all music to the ears so long long long away from the names of the places where they were born. Well they have asked me to go with them to Voiron to broadcast with them to America next Sunday and I am going and the war is over and this certainly this is the last war to remember.'

That Sunday, after Gertrude had given lunch to her Americans, after Alice had baked her victory cake, after the villagers had come to greet the Americans in the English phrases Gertrude had taught them, Gertrude drove the forty miles from Culoz to Voiron to broadcast to America. Eric Sevareid, who was one of the war correspondents who sought her out in those first days of the Liberation, remembers some of what she said on the radio about her recent experiences and her gratitude to Americans:

It was a wonderful time, it was long and it was heartbreaking . . . and now thanks to the land of my birth and the land of my adoption we are free, long live France, long live America, long live the United Nations and above all long live liberty. I can tell you that liberty is the most important thing in the world more important than food and clothes more important than anything on this mortal earth, I who spent four years with the French under the German yoke tell you so. . . . I am so happy to be talking to America today so happy.

And so, Gertrude's life without the Germans began, a happy one. And Gertrude's life with the GIs. For the next few months in Culoz, Gertrude and Alice fed, broadcast for, and conversed with as much of the American army as they could find. Even Lieutenant General A. M. Patch fell within the range of their hospitality. Unable to visit while the war continued, he replied to Gertrude's invitation with correct solemnity: 'The opportunity of meeting the lady whose literary works and humanitarian achievements I have long admired, together with the tempting offer of a chicken dinner, have convinced me that I cannot long postpone a trip to your delightful countryside. I shall make every effort, as soon as the military situation permits, to accept and thank you in person for your thoughtful invitation.'

With other members of the American army, Gertrude's relations were less formal. From September 1944 until her death in July 1946 she surrounded herself with young GIs. As Virgil Thomson described her in Paris just after the war: 'Gertrude Stein was in love with the GIs. Every day, as she walked her dog, she picked up dozens, asked them questions, took them home, fed them cake and whiskey, observed their language.' They, in turn, called her Gerty and spoke freely to her, some as to a celebrity of whom they had known ten years ago, some as to an extraordinarily wise (and sometimes slightly dotty) old lady. For Gertrude, the sudden society of these young Americans was, after five long years of immobility and anxiety, and after what at times must have been a strangely lonely life as an expatriate for over forty years in Paris, like coming home again, like belonging, like a return to childhood and its companions. As she said of the GIs, 'People do not change no they don't . . . I could have gone to school with any of them they were just like the ones I went to school with. . . .'

She repeated out loud the names of their states, asked them again and again to recount where they had come from, and by incantation brought herself back to the reality of what she called American geography. The names of the states 'make music and they are poetry, you do not have to recite them all but you say any one two three four or five of them and you will see they make music and they make poetry'. She continues, in this last section of *Wars I Have Seen*:

> . . . I do not know why but Arkansas touched me particularly, anything touches me particularly now that is American. There is something in this native land business and you cannot get away from it, in peace time you do not seem to notice it much particularly when you live in foreign parts but when there is a war and you are all alone and completely cut off from knowing about your country well then there it is, your native land is your native land, it certainly is.

When the GIs in their turn asked Gertrude how the war had been, she told them how she had managed. Eric Sevareid wrote in his account of their meeting in 1944:

> . . . With all the difficulties, the isolation from lifelong friends, these had been the happiest years of her life, she said, and one could only believe her. She felt she had come very close to the ordinary French people and had learned more about them in this sharing of their tribulations than in all her previous thirty years in the country. The village people had learned to share, not only their sorrows, but their little pleasures and their material goods in a way one would not have believed of the parsimonious French.

Or of Gertrude Stein. Indeed, the powers of *Wars I Have Seen* lies not just in the moving personal record of the days of the war, but in the evidence of the changes in the writer that hardship, sharing, being one among many created.

Wartime life in Belley was an extraordinary experience for Gertrude, isolated for so many years by her writing and her abstract interest in people. In the late twenties and thirties, Bravig Imbs had seen through her love of meeting people:

Gertrude's principal diversion [he wrote in his memoir] was analyzing characters, taking people apart, as though they were so many clocks in order to find the secret springs which motivated their action. She had become uncannily skilful at this accomplishment through years of experience, and it was her greatest pleasure. I began to understand her insatiable appetite for people, especially complicated and abnormal people who presented problems of fascinating intricacy. She would have adored meeting criminals but, of course, Alice would never have stood for that. Alice was every inch a lady in the pleasant Victorian sense of the word, and she set limits to her curiosity.

Imbs's account of Gertrude's interest in people accords with what we know about people in her writing: her early interest in archetypes, her records of individuals and their similarities and differences from other individuals in *The Making of Americans*, her detached interest in the real 'rhythm of personality' in her Portraits, her cold descriptions of her family and her former friends in the autobiographies. Her loyalties and her passions were always for ideas or for ideas of people, and rarely for people themselves. She used acquaintances and she discarded them, she played with them until she got bored. During World War II in Culoz there was no one more amusing than the villagers she knew. They ceased to be entertainers and they became real for her, almost as real as she was herself to herself. The experience effected in Gertrude a profound change, and it showed in her openness after the war, and in her long talks with the GIs.

But there was another side of these long talks. The existence of the Nazis and their constant presence during the last years of the war had been for Gertrude 'like a fog – something that was always there but which you walked right through and hardly saw or thought about'. Now, as she exchanged war tales with the GIs, there came a gradual realisation of the real danger of death she had recently faced:

They used all of them to want to know how we managed to escape the Germans and gradually with their asking and with the news that in the month of August the Gestapo had been in my apartment in Paris to look at everything, naturally I began to have what you might call a posthumous fear. I was quite frightened. All the time the Germans were here we were so busy trying to live through each day that except once in a while when something happened you did not know about being frightened, but now somehow with the American soldiers questions and hearing what had been happening to others, of course one knew it but now one had time to feel it and so I was quite frightened, now that there was nothing dangerous and the whole American army between us and danger. One is like that.

The news of the Gestapo search of her apartment in Paris was indeed a shock. In November that year, Gertrude's friend Katherine Dudley, a neighbour for a time in

225

Paris, and an American who had been interned during the war, wrote to Gertrude about her near-miss:

> . . . it's a miracle that your collection is still there for about 2 weeks before the Boches left 4 men of the Gestapo came, demanded the key of the concierge who protested in vain that you were American. The young girl who is secretary in the Bureau Weil heard steps overhead, rushed up, banged on the door till they opened it, pushed in past them and asked by what right they were there – that the proprietor was American, that she had charge of the house. They tried to put her out but she stayed. They were lashing themselves into a fury over the Picassos saying they would cut them to pieces and burn them. 'De la saloperie juive, bon à bruler.' The big pink nude 'cette vache'. They recognised your Rose portrait – they had a photo of you with them – and the other Rose heads in the long gallery, 'Tous des juifs et bon à bruler'. The girl rushed downstairs to her office, telephoned the police and in 10 minutes there was the Commissaire & 30 agents before the door much to the excitement of the street. By this time they – the G.s – were trying on your Chinese coats in your bedroom. The Commissaire asked them for their order of perquisition which they had neglected to bring with them and they had to go but taking the key with them. So she waited before the door until a menuisier could be found to change the lock. They opened the coffre with the rugs & tore the papers but Svidko doesn't remember how many packages he did up in '39. Also they opened one or two other boxes of ornaments. But I doubt if much is missing – the only thing is the carpet cleaner but it is more likely the workman on the roof who took that. . . .

Gertrude's paintings had had a near escape, but so had she and Alice. Had it not been the month of August 1944, when the relative strength of the Nazis was less than that of the French police, the Gestapo invasion of the rue Christine might have had severe consequences for the refugees in the Ain. The news of the raid made Gertrude jumpy, and eager to get back to Paris. She had, she said, kept her Paris home safe all through the war by the simple device of never speaking about it to anyone. Now she would have to go. Besides, as she had written that winter in Culoz: '. . . landscape is all very well but you do long to see a street and streets.'

After a long night 'being driven in a charcoal-burning taxi and being sustained on K rations', Gertrude, Alice, Basket, and the Picassos were back in Paris. 'Yes it was the same,' she wrote ecstatically, 'so much more beautiful, but it was the same.' They arrived at the rue Christine after midnight: 'All the pictures were there,' she wrote, 'the apartment was all there, and it was all clean and beautiful. We just looked, and then everybody running in, the concierge, the husband of the laundress downstairs, the secretary of our landlord, the bookbinder, they all came rushing in to say how do you do and tell us about the visit of the Gestapo; their stamp was still on the door.'

In the days that followed her return to Paris, Gertrude was reunited with friends she had not seen for five years, chief among them Picasso, Francis Rose, and Bernard Faÿ. Faÿ was soon to be imprisoned as a collaborator, but there were many who thought he had been instrumental, as head of the Bibliothèque Nationale, not only in keeping the French treasures intact, and in France, but also in preserving Gertrude Stein and her paintings from what would ordinarily have been their fate under a Nazi regime. That she, Alice and the Picassos *had* survived was for many a miracle, and one in which they thought they could see Bernard Faÿ's hand. Others, oddly enough, underestimated Gertrude's good fortune during the war. According to Virgil Thomson, Picasso blamed Gertrude for having left Paris. 'Why do you suppose she ran away?' he asked Virgil. 'Sometimes old ladies are afraid.' 'Old men, too,' replied Picasso, with rather characteristic lack of feeling.

With Gertrude's return to Paris the miseries of the last few years quickly disappeared.

> I began to think that the whole thing was a nightmare [she wrote], it wasn't true we had just been away for a summer vacation and had come back. Every little shop was there with its same proprietor, the shops that had been dirty were still dirty, the shops that had been clean before the war were still clean, all the little antiquity shops were there each with the same kinds of things in it that there used to be, because each little antiquity shop runs to its own kind of antiquities; there they all were, with, I almost thought, the same stock of antiquities. It was a miracle, it was a miracle.

As Gertrude ended her account of her recent life in *Wars I Have Seen*, she wrote: 'Yes, I walk around Paris, we all walk around Paris all day long and night too. Everybody is walking around Paris, it is very nice. How many days are there in a week so nice? Very many, happily, very many.'

Gertrude's ability to take pleasure in the simplest sights and sounds of her life had always been one of her greatest gifts as a writer. It had been strengthened by her enforced stay in the Ain during the war, and it was now evident to thousands when *Wars I Have Seen* was published in America in the spring of 1945. For her closest friends it was an extraordinary revelation of the grace and gift she had for life. As Carl Van Vechten wrote to her from New York in February:

> . . . It is an amazing book in which you have imprisoned your feeling about all the world in the microcosm of a small French village. Never has your 'style' been so perfectly wedded to your subject-matter or to the effect you planned to make on your reader. The end of course sent me up in an airplane; it explodes like a rocket and fills the sky with showers of pink and blue and silver stars! Dear Baby Woojums your love for America, as expressed in these pages, is as alive as Nijinsky at top career. You DANCE your way out of this superb book and I wish Gershwin were alive to write music about these pages! . . .

During the year of 1945, while Gertrude received reports from Bennett Cerf of the enormous popularity and sale of this book, Gertrude worked on a project which she had recently begun: a book about the GIs called *Brewsie and Willie*. In 1945, at the age of seventy-one, Gertrude was clearly at the height of her powers as a writer, as this book shows. In it she creates a dialogue in American slang between a group of GIs who think aloud the problems that will face them when they return to America. They discuss fraternization, women, American sexual drive, 'lousy foreigners', industrialism in the United States, American blacks, the loss of the 'pioneer spirit' and the increase of 'job mentality' at home, and the impending future decline of America.

Brewsie and Willie successfully creates the characters of these GIs, for Gertrude 'more solid, more scared, more articulate' than the doughboys of the previous war, while managing to make Gertrude's theories of politics and economics mostly plausible. But there are certain patches of resistance. For example, her view of Roosevelt, which had hardly altered since the late thirties: 'Roosevelt . . . was a benevolent despot and I hate all despots, the benevolent ones are worse than the others because nobody wants to hurt their feelings by telling them so.' And her proposed solution to the economic problems that faced America (she felt that over-industrialisation would destroy America as it had destroyed England, since both had lost their world markets, and that the only hope for America was that it return to a simple economy, as she had seen happen in Culoz during the war):

> Listen, said Ed, listen. I know I just do know. Listen. That sister aint so phony as she sounds, listen. You see like this, when factories work hard and lots of money moves around, then there are chain stores and mail-order houses and little businesses cant live, cause they cant make enough money to compete, but when the factories they don't work, and everybody just walks around like sister says, why then chain stores and mail-order places go bust, there is too much overhead if there aint a big volume of business, and that's the time for a new start of little business, so that's it boys that's it, if we can stall going home till there is a depression, then we can start our little businesses like we all want to do. How about it everybody, dont that listen good.

Gertrude Stein was worried most about what she called American softness: 'We love sweets like babies,' says one of her GIs, 'we dont love no lumps of cheese, and tough bread, no we just like to eat soft stuff, soft bread, soft ice-cream, soft chocolate, soft mush, soft potatoes, soft jam, and peanut butter, we don't except at a little meat we dont really chew. Well, and if we dont, said Jo. Soft eats make soft men, said Peter.'

Gertrude Stein genuinely feared for the future of Americans. In a unique passage of patriotic near-hysteria, she pleads for the simplification of America, for the return of eighteenth-century individualism in the face of the twentieth-century corporate mentality, for the return of the independent, pioneering spirit to America, and for the understanding of the lessons of the Depression. Turning away from the characters in the book, Gertrude Stein addresses her readers:

> G.I.s and G.I.s and G.I.s and they have made me come all over patriotic. I was always patriotic, I was always in my way a Civil War veteran, but in between there were other things, but now there are no other things. And I am sure that this particular moment in our history is more important than anything since the Civil War. . . .

228

You have to learn to be individual and not just mass job workers, you have to get courage enough to know what you feel and not just all be yes or no men. . . .

. . . Look facts in the face, not just what they all say, the leaders, but every darn one of you so that a government by the people, for the people shall not perish from the face of the earth, it wont, somebody else will do it if we lie down on the job, but of all things dont stop, find out the reason why of the depression, find it out each and every one of you and then look the facts in the face. We are Americans.

With this message, Gertrude Stein continued to campaign for the future of Americans. She broadcast to the troops in France, she toured the US army bases in Germany, in Austria, in Belgium. She wrote articles about the GIs and about America for *Life*, for the *New York Times*, and for the army paper *Yank*.

In the last months of her life, between the first attack of intestinal pain which struck during her journey to lecture to the US army in Brussels in November 1945, and her death from stomach cancer the following July, Gertrude was perhaps more active than she had ever been before. She, together with Alice, who wrote the introductory catalogue, helped to arrange the opening of the first fashion show of a young friend from Savoy, Pierre Balmain. She wrote articles for American magazines, continued with half-finished novels and meditations, corresponded about the performance of her play 'In Savoy . . . or Yes is For A Very Young Man' in California, campaigned for the freedom of Bernard Faÿ in prison, and worked on an opera with Virgil Thomson based on the life of Susan B. Anthony, the American suffragette. The title of this opera, the last complete work she was to write was 'The Mother of Us All', and it has had significance for her followers ever since.

Gertrude was by no means interested in bidding adieu, nor in death. In her very last article: 'Reflection on the Atomic Bomb', she dismissed the ultimate weapon as 'not interesting', just as Saint Theresa had dismissed the concept of the death of five million chinamen in 'Four Saints in Three Acts'.

What is the use [she wrote about the bomb], if they are really as destructive as all that there is nothing left and if there is nothing there nobody to be interested and nothing to be interested about. If they are not as destructive as all that then they are just a little more or less destructive than other things and that means that in spite of all destruction there are always lots left on this earth to be interested or to be willing and the thing that destroys is just one of the things that concerns the people inventing it or the people starting it off, but really nobody else can do anything about it so you have to just live along like always, so you see the atomic [bomb] is not at all interesting. . . . Sure it will destroy a lot and kill a lot but it's the living that are interesting not the way of killing them, because if there were not a lot left living how could there be any interest in destruction. Alright, that is the way I feel about it. And really way down that is the way everybody feels about it.

Gertrude Stein's business was with life and with living in the present: 'How many days are there in a week so nice? Very many, happily, very many.' When, on 19 July 1946, on her way to stay at the country house Bernard Faÿ had lent her, she suffered another attack of stomach pain, she was rushed to the American Hospital at Neuilly. There, as she lay in bed for the first few days of her collapse the room and its corridors outside gradually filled with hundreds of gifts of flowers from worried friends. Though the doctors refused to operate because the risks were too great, Gertrude insisted. Just before she was taken away to the operating theatre, she turned to Alice Toklas: 'What is the answer?' she said. Alice was silent. 'In that case What is the question?' Alice never saw her again. Gertrude died under anaesthetic at 6.30 that evening.

In her last, now legendary words, Gertrude had quoted from her own work. In so doing she directed her hearer back to the source and end of her living. For Gertrude, death, even her own, was not interesting. As she wrote in one of her American lectures what was important was something else, and something else than the mere events of a life:

> But now to make you understand, that although I was as usual looking listening and talking perhaps more than ever at that time and leading a very complicated and perhaps too exciting every day living, never the less it really did not matter what I saw or said or heard, or if you like felt, because now there was at last something more vibrant than any of all that and somehow some way I had isolated it and in a way had gotten it written.

The work was there, the life was simply over.

Autobiography number II
I tried in Making of Americans to make any one one. How.
By having a beginning and middle and ending.
But is there any such thing as a beginning. Be natural is there.
And a middle.
And an ending.

Notes

For details of publications see bibliography
Gertrude Stein's works are referred to by title only

1 *Being The Youngest*

1	There is something . . . *Wars I have Seen* p. 170	8	My sister four years older . . . *Ibid* p. 115
1	America was . . . *Idem*	8	It is natural . . . *Idem*
2	in a kind of way . . . *Ibid* p. 2	8	I was a very . . . *Wars I Have Seen* p. 3
2	picture books . . . *Idem*	8–9	very loving . . . *The Making of Americans* p. 51
3	Our little Gertie . . . John Malcolm Brinnin, *The Third Rose: Gertrude Stein and Her World* p. 6	8–9	The little mother . . . *Idem*
3	You are privileged . . . *Wars I Have Seen* p. 1	9	the little stubborn . . . *Ibid* p. 56
3–4	This child . . . Wyndham Lewis, 'The Prose-Song of Gertrude Stein' in *Time and Western Man* p. 62	9–10	My father was . . . Leo Stein, *Journey Into the Self* p. 188
4	these always . . . *The Making of Americans* p. 122	10	Medieval means that life . . . *Wars I Have Seen* pp. 16–17
4	these have not . . . *Idem*	10	It was frightening when . . . *Everybody's Autobiography* p. 97
4	my mother had . . . *Wars I Have Seen* p. 2	10	Funny things . . . *Wars I Have Seen* p. 17
4–5	bought everything . . . *The Autobiography of Alice B. Toklas* p. 68	10	Fifteen the time . . . *Ibid* p. 18
5	of course we . . . *Wars I Have Seen* p. 1	10	She once told me . . . *The Autobiography of Alice B. Toklas* p. 52
5	with no book learning . . . Leo Stein, *Journey Into the Self: Being the Letters, Papers and Journals of Leo Stein* p. 187	10–11	Gertrude and I . . . Leo Stein, *Journey Into the Self* p. 185
5–6	I naturally did remember . . . *Wars I Have Seen* p. 3	11	Then one morning we . . . *Everybody's Autobiography* p. 120
6	There was . . . *The Making of Americans* pp. 39–40	11	Then our life without . . . *Ibid* p. 121
6–7	In the summer . . . *Ibid* p. 40	11	Then I found out . . . *Ibid* p. 122
8	It is better . . . *Everybody's Autobiography* p. 55	11	Mike's own statement . . . *Ibid* p. 128
		11	really suited him . . . *Ibid* p. 116
		11	It was then . . . *Ibid* pp. 125–6
		12	He used . . . *Ibid* p. 122
		12	Mike would always . . . *Ibid* p. 210
		12	When we left . . . *Ibid* p. 127

2 *Knowledge Is What You Know*

13	the rather desperate . . . *The Autobiography of Alice B. Toklas* p. 71	14	Whose record . . . *The Autobiography of Alice B. Toklas* p. 74
13	Baltimore, sunny Baltimore . . . Rosalind Miller, 'The Radcliffe Themes' in *Gertrude Stein: Form and Intelligibility* p. 139	14	I am so sorry . . . *Ibid* pp. 74–5
		14	Dear Miss Stein . . . *Idem*
		14	gave her . . . *Idem*
14	The landlord . . . *Everybody's Autobiography* p. 132	15	I like a thing simple . . . Robert B. Haas, 'Afterword' in *What Are Masterpieces* p. 104

16 I was tremendously . . . 'The Gradual
Making of *The Making of* Americans'
in *Look At Me Now and Here I Am:
Writings and Lectures 1909–45* p. 85

16 I am having . . . 'Fernhurst' in
*Fernhurst, Q.E.D., and Other Early
Writings of Gertrude Stein* p. 4

17 She always says . . . *The Autobiography
of Alice B. Toklas* p. 78

18 It would be . . . Leo Stein, *Journey Into
the Self* p. 7

18 moved about . . . 'Fernhurst' p. 12

19 heavy about the mouth . . . 'Q.E.D.'
p. 55

19 That is what makes . . . *Ibid* pp. 59–60

19 I am afraid . . . *Ibid* p. 63

19 her deepest . . . 'Fernhurst' pp. 19–20

20 You have a . . . 'Q.E.D.' p. 56

20 agreeing and . . . *Ibid* p. 67

20 We spent one summer . . . *Wars I Have
Seen* p. 134

29 I knew the . . . Leo Stein, *Journey Into
the Self*, p. 3

29 His house . . . *Idem*

29 I saw Berenson . . . *Ibid* p. 4

30 By the way . . . *Ibid* pp. 12–13

30 so absolutely lovely . . . *Ibid* p. 10

30 set among . . . *Idem*

30 absorbed in Elizabethan . . . *The
Autobiography of Alice B. Toklas* p. 78

31 she wandered about . . . *Idem*

31 just like Dickens . . . *Ibid* p. 79

31 There is no passion . . . 'Q.E.D.'
pp. 99–100

32 Honorable and manly . . . 'Fernhurst'
p. 6

32 I never claimed to be . . . 'Q.E.D.' p. 59

32 I simply rejoiced . . . *Ibid* p. 101

32 The funny thing . . . *The Autobiography
of Alice B. Toklas* pp. 79–80

3 *What Are Masterpieces?*

35 It happens often . . . 'Fernhurst'
pp. 29–30

36 One night when . . . Leo Stein,
*Appreciation: Painting, Poetry and
Prose* p. 151

36 Art is having its revenge . . . Leo Stein,
Journey Into the Self p. 13

36 my brother needed . . . *Everybody's
Autobiography* p. 59

45 Do you know Cézanne . . . Leo Stein,
Appreciation p. 154

45 one saw there . . . *Ibid* p. 152

45 the obligation . . . Leo Stein, *Journey
Into the Self* p. 15

46 Life was then . . . Leo Stein,
Appreciation pp. 196–7

46 Vollard liked . . . *Ibid* p. 194

46–7 Matisse came out . . . *Ibid* p. 158

47 I still can see . . . Louise M. Golson,
'The Michael Steins of San Francisco:
Art Patrons and Collectors' in *Four
Americans in Paris* p. 42

48 In those early days . . . Mabel Dodge
Luhan, *European Experiences*, Volume
II of *Intimate Memories*, p. 322

48 Buying those . . . *Idem*

48 One man who . . . Leo Stein,
Appreciation p. 84

49 He was not . . . Mabel Weeks's
Foreword to Leo Stein, *Journey Into
the Self* p. vii

49 Although he wanted . . . *Ibid* p. ix

49 he would interrupt . . . Leo Stein,
Appreciation pp. 168–9

50 his extraordinary seeing . . . *Ibid* p. 170

50 He felt himself . . . *Ibid* p. 172

50 This is not . . . *Idem*

50 This said Picasso . . . *The Autobiography
of Alice B. Toklas* p. 43

50 She laughed . . . *Idem*

50 The world is . . . *Ibid* p. 14

51 Oh how badly . . . Fernande Olivier,
Picasso and his Friends p. 37

51 He would deliberately . . . *Ibid* p. 36

51 She had the face . . . *Ibid* p. 85

52 Their collection . . . *Ibid* pp. 83–4

52 What is a Genius? . . . *Everybody's
Autobiography* p. 67

69 Picasso and I . . . *Ibid* p. 72

69 One of the things . . . *The Autobiography
of Alice B. Toklas* p. 66

70 I was much interested . . . *Everybody's
Autobiography* p. 231

71 Don't you ever think . . . *Three Lives*
p. 176

72 Gertrude used to sit . . . *Luhan, op. cit.*
p. 324

72 Jeff never . . . *Three Lives* p. 156

73 He was convincing . . . *The Making of
Americans* p. 384

74 You see Mikey . . . letter from Sarah
Stein in *The Flowers of Friendship:
Letters Written to Gertrude Stein*, ed.
Donald Gallup, p. 37

74–5 I was and . . . *Picasso* p. 8

75 [Picasso and Matisse] . . . *The
Autobiography of Alice B. Toklas* p. 60

75 Picasso was pleasantly . . . Leo Stein,
Appreciation p. 175

76 In the effort . . . *Picasso* p. 9

76 For two brief years . . . Aline Saarinen,
The Proud Possessors p. 197

76 I was the only . . . Leo Stein, *Appreciation* p. 188

76 in the six years . . . *Ibid* p. 166

76 There was a friend . . . *Ibid* pp. 175–6

77 When analysis . . . *Ibid* p. 184

77 a disguised . . . 'Pictures for a Picture of Gertrude Stein as a Collector and Writer on Art and Artists' p. 26

77 Once an oil painting . . . 'Pictures' in *Lectures in America* p. 61

77 to the cubism of Picasso . . . *Ibid* pp. 84–5

78 daring in a snobbish . . . Luhan, *op. cit.* p. 325

78 By the way . . . Leo Stein, *Appreciation* p. 190

78 That sounds . . . *Idem*

4 *Grammar Is As Disappointed*

79 I was impressed . . . *The Autobiography of Alice B. Toklas* p. 5

79–80 She was slight and dark . . . Luhan, *op. cit.* p. 324

80 Alice Toklas . . . *Ibid* p. 325

80 Two knowing each other . . . *The Making of Americans* p. 360

80 Disillusionment in living . . . *Ibid* p. 282

81 You write a book . . . *Ibid* pp. 282–3

81 I think Cubism . . . Leo Stein, *Journey Into the Self* pp. 48–9

81 It is funny . . . *Everybody's Autobiography* p. 60

81 I recognized a talent . . . Leo Stein, *Appreciation* p. 182

81–2 a week from Saturday . . . *Ibid* p. 191

82 poor Marie Laurencin . . . Olivier, *op. cit.* p. 69

82 There were the Pichots . . . *Ibid* p. 70

82 Indeed . . . *Ibid* p. 69

83 My proof-readers . . . Gallup, *op. cit.* p. 42

83 I want to say . . . *Ibid* p. 44

83 I have just read . . . *Ibid* pp. 69–70

83 I have had . . . *Ibid* p. 50

84 Quite lately . . . Leo Stein, *Journey Into the Self* p. 22

83 See that man . . . *Ibid* p. 25

84 Darling . . . *Ibid* p. 29

93 grieving over . . . Luhan, *op. cit.* pp. 326–7

94 One whom . . . 'Picasso' in *Look At Me Now and Here I Am* p. 333

94 Letter from A. C. Fifield . . . Gallup, *op. cit.* p. 58

95 All the attention is when . . . *Portrait of Mabel Dodge at the Villa Curonia* p. 528

95 As for your prose . . . Gallup, *op. cit.* p. 66

95 I start reading . . . *Ibid* p. 56

95 what is known . . . *Everybody's Autobiography* p. 276

96 Gertrude always . . . Luhan, *op. cit.* p. 328

96 One whom . . . 'Picasso' in *Look At Me Now and Here I Am* pp. 333–4

97 I can't . . . Luhan, *op. cit.* p. 332

97 Gertrude Stein was prodigious . . . *Ibid* p. 324

97 arrive just sweating . . . *Ibid* p. 327

97 She was forever . . . *Ibid* p. 324

97 She loved beef . . . *Idem*

98 One day at lunch . . . *Ibid* pp. 332–3

98 Don't be surprised . . . Mabel Dodge Luhan, *Movers and Shakers*, Volume III of *Intimate Memories* p. 29

98–9 We are having . . . *Ibid* pp. 33–4

99 Zangwill got angry . . . *Ibid* p. 34

99 Roger Fry . . . *Idem*

99 the table . . . *Ibid* p. 33

99 Also the futurists . . . *Idem*

99 Did I tell you . . . *Ibid* p. 31

100–1 The Sound . . . *Tender Buttons* in *Selected Writings of Gertrude Stein* p. 474, p. 471, p. 487, p. 491, p. 509

101 Gertrude and Alice . . . Leo Stein, *Journey Into the Self* p. 49

101 One of the greatest changes . . . *Ibid* pp. 52–3

102 and that was one . . . Leo Stein, *Appreciation* p. 186

102 You can tell Pablo . . . Leo Stein, *Journey Into the Self* p. 51

102 I very much . . . *Ibid* p. 57

102 We had always been . . . *Everybody's Autobiography* p. 61

5 *The Last Nineteenth-Century War*

103 We hag to . . . *The Autobiography of Alice B. Toklas* p. 137

103 I can still hear . . . *Ibid* pp. 138–9

103–4 But, said Lytton . . . *Ibid* p. 143

104 said solemnly to Gertrude Stein . . . *Ibid* p. 144

104 The germans were getting . . . *Ibid* p. 141

104–5 I was sitting . . . *Ibid* p. 142

105 The first year of the war . . . *Ibid* pp. 84–5

106 Matisse also writes . . . Juan Gris, *Letters of Juan Gris* pp. 14–15
106 Marcous . . . *Ibid* p. 25
106 As for news . . . *Ibid* p. 28
106 Max who gets sillier . . . *Ibid* pp. 28–9
106 There are times . . . *Ibid* p. 30
107–8 We went outside . . . *The Autobiography of Alice B. Toklas* p. 163
108 One had to remember . . . *Ibid* p. 165
108 It was quite a . . . *Ibid* p. 170
109 A young french soldier . . . *Everybody's Autobiography* p. 169
109 One of them . . . *The Autobiography of Alice B. Toklas* p. 174

109 I like *Parade* . . . Gris, *op. cit.* p. 49
110 To anyone who . . . *The Autobiography of Alice B. Toklas* p. 176
110 The french . . . *Ibid* p. 178
110 We saw a tremendous . . . *Ibid* p. 180
110 All the pictures . . . *Ibid* p. 103
111 Matisse said . . . *Idem*
111 My life had been . . . Leo Stein, *Journey Into the Self* p. 87
111 Everybody was on the streets . . . *The Autobiography of Alice B. Toklas* pp. 180–1

6 *Such Nice Young Men*

113 Guillaume would have been . . . *Ibid* p. 56
114 Where, she asked . . . Sylvia Beach, *Shakespeare and Company* p. 28
114 Gertrude Stein's admirers . . . *Ibid* p. 29
114 He is so anxious . . . Gallup, *op. cit.* p. 138
115 I knew the rules . . . Beach, *op. cit.* p. 31
115 It was like . . . Ernest Hemingway, *A Moveable Feast* p. 16
115 Imitate a cheese . . . Richard Bridgman, *Gertrude Stein In Pieces* p. 166
116 *Melanctha* . . . Hemingway, *op. cit.* pp. 19–20
121 If you brought up . . . *Ibid* p. 26
121 She once said . . . Alice B. Toklas, *Staying On Alone: Letters of Alice B. Toklas* p. 91
121 Picasso once said . . . *The Autobiography of Alice B. Toklas* p. 200
121 Sweet sweet sweet . . . 'Susie Asado' in *Geography and Plays* p. 13
121–2 Pillow . . . 'Pink Melon Joy' in *Ibid* p. 349
122 Act II . . . 'Ladies Voice' in *Ibid* p. 203
122 I assure you . . . Gallup, *op. cit.* p. 144
122 Would it not . . . Sherwood Anderson, Introduction to *Geography and Plays* p. 8
122 It was during . . . *The Autobiography of Alice B. Toklas* p. 197
123 Halve Rivers and Harbours . . . 'An Elucidation' in *Portraits and Prayers* p. 246
123 Can you tell me . . . Alice B. Toklas, *What Is Remembered* p. 124
124 I had always . . . Hemingway, *op. cit.* p. 63
124 I made it clear . . . Gallup, *op. cit.* p. 159
124 and I thought . . . Hemingway, *op. cit.* p. 29
125 I should be very . . . Gallup, *op. cit.* p. 166
125 It doesn't mean . . . *Ibid* p. 141

126 He came home . . . *The Autobiography of Alice B. Toklas* p. 189
126 It is in a thick . . . Wyndham Lewis, *op. cit.* p. 61
126 Poor Scott . . . Beach, *op. cit.* p. 116
126 on a plate . . . *Ibid* p. 117
126 spent an entire . . . *Ibid* pp. 116–17
126 their famous . . . Janet Flanner, *Paris Was Yesterday* pp. xviii–xix
127 My wife and I . . . Gallup, *op. cit.* p. 174
127 One afternoon . . . Alice B. Toklas, *What Is Remembered* p. 26
127 She thinks . . . *The Autobiography of Alice B. Toklas* p. 206
128 I find . . . Gallup, *op. cit.* p. 178
128 I'm trying to do . . . *Ibid* pp. 164–5
129 REJECTING . . . Carlos Baker, *Ernest Hemingway* p. 246
129 my feeling . . . Gallup, *op. cit.* p. 154
130 I find the same . . . *Ibid* p. 192
130 The intellectual success . . . Flanner, *op. cit.* p. 185
130 Very tall . . . *The Autobiography of Alice B. Toklas* pp. 218–19
130 I am still working . . . Gallup, *op. cit.* p. 185
131 She stayed there . . . *The Autobiography of Alice B. Toklas* p. 219
131 He so thoroughly . . . *Ibid* p. 220
131 like an uncle . . . *Idem*
132 Owing to the critics . . . Harold Acton, *Memoirs of an Aesthete* p. 161
132 the litany . . . *Idem*
132 Everything is the same . . . 'Composition as Explanation' in *Look At Me Now and Here I Am* p. 24
132 it was hard . . . Acton, *op. cit.* p. 161
132 Introduces have and heard . . . 'Sitwell Edith Sitwell' in *What Are Masterpieces* p. 51
133 While she read . . . Acton, *op. cit.* pp. 161–2
133 Gertrude Stein's deep . . . *Ibid* pp. 162–3
134 I doubt if . . . Katherine Anne Porter,

'Everyone is a Real One' in *The Days Before* p. 36   134   Your reputation . . . Gallup, *op. cit.* a. 205

7 Saints And Landscapes

135   She became an official . . . Bravig Imbs, *Confessions of Another Young Man* p. 126

135   selling exceedingly well . . . Gallup, *op. cit.* p. 178

136   He understood . . . Alice B. Toklas, *Staying on Alone* p. 154

136   Juan Gris was . . . 'The Life and Death of Juan Gris' in *Portraits and Prayers* p. 48

136   the only real cubism . . . *The Autobiography of Alice B. Toklas* p. 85

136–7   Gertrude Stein . . . *Ibid* pp. 198–9

137   The surrealists still . . . *Picasso* p. 43

137   the surrealistes . . . *The Autobiography of Alice B. Toklas* p. 198

138   most people that . . . *Everybody's Autobiography* p. 7

138   absolutely cannibal . . . Alice B. Toklas, *Staying on Alone* p. 154

138   He was painting . . . *The Autobiography of Alice B. Toklas* pp. 212–13

138   And then it came . . . *Everybody's Autobiography* p. 12

139   Then one day . . . Alice B. Toklas, *Staying on Alone* pp. 223–4

139   To her reply . . . Virgil Thomson, *Virgil Thomson* p. 93

139   money, caviar . . . *Ibid* p. 152

140   There was never . . . Imbs, *op. cit.* p. 166

141   Alice Toklas . . . Thomson, *op. cit.* p. 89

141   After all . . . *Paris France* p. 38

141   With meanings . . . Thomson *op. cit.* p. 90

141   lies closer . . . *Ibid* p. 105

141   Spaniards know . . . *Picasso* p. 24

142   A saint . . . *Everybody's Autobiography* p. 91

142–3   In Four Saints . . . 'Plays' in *Look At Me Now and Here I Am* p. 81

143   Very little daisies . . . *Lucy Church Amiably* p. 197

143   The scene took place . . . Thomson, *op. cit.* p. 171

143–4   Capitals swell success . . . Gallup, *op. cit.* p. 229

144   perhaps we will . . . Thomson, *op. cit.* p. 141

144   She says . . . *The Autobiography of Alice B. Toklas* p. 233

158   I knew it was . . . *Ibid* p. 236

158   You must know . . . Gallup, *op. cit.* p. 242

8 Remarks Are Not Literature

162   There has been . . . *Ibid* pp. 260–1

162   she realises . . . *The Autobiography of Alice B. Toklas* p. 72

163   I read the first . . . Gallup, *op. cit.* p. 262

163   it is a joy . . . *Ibid* p. 267

163   First I bought . . . *Everybody's Autobiography* p. 28

163   there is no doubt . . . *Ibid* p. 34

163   Everybody invited . . . *Ibid* p. 73

164   These documents . . . Eugene Jolas, Foreword to 'Testimony Against Gertrude Stein' p. 2

164   And identity is funny . . . *Everybody's Autobiography* p. 53

164   And so autobiography . . . *Idem*

165   The *Autobiography* . . . Jolas, *op. cit.* p. 2

165   What we should have . . . Maria Jolas in 'Testimony Against Gertrude Stein' pp. 11–12

165   a considerable display . . . Tristan Tzara in *Ibid* p. 13

166   For one who poses . . . Georges Braque in *Ibid* p. 14

166   We in Paris . . . *Idem*

166   Miss Stein often . . . André Salmon in *Ibid* p. 15

166   I am all the more . . . *Ibid* p. 14

167   if one had a son . . . *Everybody's Autobiography* p. 23

167   A Bitch Is A Bitch . . . reported in 'Steiniana', a review of the New York Grolier Club's centennial exhibition, 'A Tribute to Gertrude Stein', in *The New Yorker* magazine, March 11, 1974, p. 28

167   God what a liar . . . Leo Stein, *Journey Into the Self* p. 134

168   I wonder how near . . . *Ibid* p. 135

168   Imagine the stupidity . . . *Ibid* p. 142

168   Gertrude and I . . . *Ibid* p. 149

168   a real celebrity . . . *Everybody's Autobiography* p. ix

168   The moment you . . . *Ibid* p. 74

168   Inside and outside . . . *Ibid* p. 50

169   Before one is successful . . . *Ibid* p. 27

169   somehow if my writing . . . *Ibid* p. 67

170–1   I am not I . . . *Four in America* p. 119

170 It is always astonishing . . . *Picasso* pp. 45–6
171 I was sure . . . Thomson, *op. cit.* p. 217
171 If a magpie . . . 'Four Saints in Three Acts' p. 605
171–2 The cast . . . Thomson, *op. cit.* p. 241
172 not only for . . . *Idem*
172–3 Four Saints . . . Gallup, *op. cit.* p. 275
173 we were totally . . . *Ibid* p. 278
173 For six months . . . Thomson, *op. cit.* p. 243
173 People walking on . . . Gallup, *op. cit.* p. 276
174 It was really . . . *Everybody's Autobiography* p. 135
174 As I say . . . *Ibid* p. 94
174 After all . . . *Idem*
174 if any of . . . *The Autobiography of Alice B. Toklas* p. 174

175 I get quite a . . . William Rogers, *When This You See Remember Me: Gertrude Stein in Person* p. 116
175 The lectures are . . . *Ibid* pp. 118–19
175 Poetry is I say . . . 'Poetry and Grammar' in *Look At Me Now and Here I Am* p. 138
175 Poetry is doing . . . *Idem*
175 You can love . . . *Ibid* p. 193
175 When I said . . . *Ibid* p. 138
175 As I say . . . *Ibid* p. 126
175 I do see . . . *Ibid* p. 129
176 A comma . . . *Ibid* pp. 131–2
176 everything was . . . *Everybody's Autobiography* p. 140
176 I used to say . . . *Ibid* p. 143

9 *La Gloire*

177 People had always . . . *Idem*
177 Reporters' questions, Gertrude Stein's answers, and New York headlines cited in Rogers, *op. cit.* pp. 121–5
178 I always knew . . . *Everybody's Autobiography* p. 188
178 In France . . . *Ibid* p. 147
178 most of the time . . . *Ibid* p. 149
179 she said my knees . . . *Idem*
179 Besides it was silly . . . *Ibid* p. 172
179 his voice was . . . *Ibid* p. 144
180 its name is Negro . . . *Ibid* p. 172
180 I was the first . . . *Ibid* pp. xiii–xiv
180 Remember . . . *Ibid* p. xiii
180 I was always . . . *Ibid* p. 161
180 it is not the way . . . *Ibid* p. 174
180 It was nice . . . *Ibid* p. 163
181 whenever we could . . . *Ibid* p. 164
181 It was then . . . *Idem*
181 recognised nothing . . . *Ibid* p. 160
182–3 The short quotations from Gertrude Stein's lectures are from the lectures published in *Look At Me Now and Here I Am*: 'What Is English Literature' p. 45, 'Poetry and Grammar' p. 130, 'Portraits and Repetitions' p. 105, p. 106, 'The Gradual Making of *The Making of Americans*' p. 98, p. 96, 'Portraits and Repetitions' p. 103 p. 108, p. 108, p. 124, 'What is English Literature' p. 44
183 When I was up . . . 'The Gradual Making of *The Making of Americans*' pp. 90–1
183 In the portraits . . . 'Portraits and Repetitions' in *Look at Me Now and Here I Am* pp. 117–18
183–4 This melody . . . *Ibid* p. 118
184 I began again . . . *Ibid* p. 119

184 And the thing . . . *Ibid* p. 115
184 When it gets . . . 'Poetry and Grammar' *Ibid* p. 132
184 The business of Art . . . 'Plays' *Ibid* p. 66
184 I have of course . . . *Ibid* p. 76
184 if you have vitality . . . *Four in America* pp. 127–8
185 I feel that . . . Gallup, *op. cit.* p. 292
185 it seemed . . . *Everybody's Autobiography* p. 183
185 she was *the* . . . interview with Thornton Wilder in *The Guardian*, London, June 29, 1974, p. 6
185 Thornton has . . . Alice B. Toklas, *Staying on Alone* p. 103
185–6 just worn out literary words . . . Thornton Wilder in Introduction to *Four in America* p. vi
186 Government is the least . . . *Everybody's Autobiography* pp. 177–8
186 Fanny Butcher . . . *Ibid* p. 178
186–7 you see why . . . *Ibid* p. 184
187 when it rained . . . *Ibid* p. 178
187 not being entertained . . . *Ibid* p. 187
187 there is something of . . . *Ibid* p. 91
188 Americans . . . *The Autobiography of Alice B. Toklas* p. 86
188 In America . . . *Everybody's Autobiography* p. 168
188 a space of time . . . 'The Gradual Making of *The Making of Americans*' p. 98
188 Think of anything . . . *Idem*
188–9 I hate the . . . Saarinen, *op. cit.* p. 233
189 You were the same . . . Gallup, *op. cit.* p. 294
189 everyone . . . *Idem*

189 I did not know . . . *Everybody's Autobiography* p. 205

189 I don't care to say . . . Rogers, *op. cit.* pp. 140–1

190 she regarded . . . *Ibid* p. 111

190 the American . . . *Narration: Four Lectures by Gertrude Stein* p. 13

191 I have asked . . . Gallup, *op. cit.* p. 296

191 Of course I liked . . . *Everybody's Autobiography* p. 245

191 It is very curious . . . 'What Are Masterpieces' in *What Are Masterpieces* p. 87

192 There is nothing . . . from an interview with the *New York Times*, April 6, 1935

10 *Altogether Too Much Fathering Going On*

193 Yes I am married . . . Rogers, *op. cit.* p. 152

194 A play . . . *The Geographical History of America or The Relation of Human Nature to the Human Mind* pp. 99–100

194 Whether or whether not . . . *Ibid* pp. 76–7

194 Short excerpts from *The Geographical History*: p. 105, p. 194, p. 87, p. 228, p. 229, p. 83, p. 91, p. 82

194 Become . . . *Ibid* p. 192

194 Detective story . . . *Ibid* p. 123

194 Now is just the time . . . *Ibid* p. 176

194–5 I do not know . . . *Ibid* p. 92

195 That is what I mean . . . *Ibid* p. 57

195 You don't understand . . . *Everybody's Autobiography* p. 5

196 When I first heard . . . *Ibid* pp. 6–7

196 You know perfectly . . . *Ibid* p. 7

196 And then I said . . . *Ibid* pp. 8–9

196 I will never paint . . . *Ibid* p. 9

196 I was bored . . . *Ibid* p. 20

205 Why I said . . . *Ibid* p. 25

205 What he said . . . *Idem*

205 Well he said . . . *Ibid* p. 26

205 Rosenberg went out . . . *Idem*

206 Of course . . . *Ibid* p. 265

206 I said to him . . . *Ibid* p. 266

206–7 Everybody just now . . . 'Money' in *Look At Me Now and Here I Am* p. 331

207 Short excerpts from *Everybody's Autobiography*: p. 52, p. 55, p. 65, p. 18, p. 89, p. 96

207 London and Paris . . . Rogers, *op. cit.* p. 45

208 In the country . . . *Everybody's Autobiography* p. 276

208 As yet . . . *Ibid* p. 167

208 And then we . . . *Ibid* p. 277

208 After every great war . . . *Ibid* p. 39

208–9 Nobody in France . . . *Ibid* p. 33

209 It is curious . . . *Ibid* p. 2

209 But that is natural . . . *Ibid* p. 41

209 There is too much . . . *Ibid* p. 113

209 The periods of . . . *Idem*

209–10 The beginning of . . . 'My Last About Money' in *Look At Me Now and Here I Am*, pp. 336–7

210 They kind of read . . . *Everybody's Autobiography* p. 193

210 the men in politics . . . *Ibid* p. 101

210 Frenchmen do not . . . *Ibid* p. 83

210 one of the curious things . . . *Ibid* p. 77

210 As to their not . . . Rogers, *op. cit.* p. 219

210 I cannot write . . . *Paris France* p. 38

211 All the time . . . *Everybody's Autobiography* p. 71

211 anybody can know . . . *Ibid* p. 100

211 If it were possible . . . 'Four Saints in Three Acts' p. 586

211 I could not see . . . *Everybody's Autobiography* p. 100

211 You see what in Europe . . . Rogers, *op. cit.* pp. 210–20

212 We were tired . . . *Ibid* p. 199

212 [Picasso] understands . . . *Picasso* p. 50

11 *A Small Hard Reality*

213 I do not believe . . . Rogers, *op. cit.* pp. 185–6

213 Paris was the place . . . *Paris France* p. 39

213 french people . . . *Ibid* p. 9

213 I remember so well . . . *Idem*

213 Tradition . . . *Ibid* p. 10

213–14 But after all . . . *Ibid* p. 31

214 The characteristic art product . . . *Ibid* p. 36

214 They all were upset . . . 'The Winner Loses, A Picture of Occupied France' p. 615

214 we had . . . *Ibid* p. 616

214 We were in the . . . *Ibid* pp. 627–8

215 The hoot-owl . . . *Mrs Reynolds and Five Earlier Novelettes* p. 25

215 Mrs Reynolds stayed at home . . . *Ibid* p. 22

215 Hope dreamed . . . *Ibid* p. 17

215 Angel Harper looked . . . *Ibid* p. 25

215 Mrs Reynolds the wife . . . *Ibid* p. 22

215 Not easily . . . *Ibid* p. 29

215 Mr Reynolds turned . . . *Ibid* p. 27

215 a perfectly ordinary . . . *Ibid* p. 267

216	Hitler will never . . . Eric Sevareid, *Not So Wild A Dream* p. 90	224	People do not . . . *Wars I Have Seen* p. 164
216	They all said . . . 'The Winner Loses' p. 623	224	make music . . . *Idem*
216	Everybody knows you . . . *Ibid* p. 624	224	I do not know why . . . *Ibid* p. 165
216	we go along . . . Rogers, *op. cit.* p. 191	224	With all the difficulties . . . Sevareid, *op. cit.* p. 459
216–7	there is a deplorable . . . *Ibid* p. 188	225	Gertrude's principal diversion . . . Imbs, *op. cit.* p. 181
217	Everybody is very busy . . . 'The Winner Loses' p. 639	225	They used all of them . . . *Wars I Have Seen* p. 168
217	I have been talking to . . . *Ibid* pp. 636–7	226	it's a miracle . . . Gallup, *op. cit.* 370–1
217	You just go on talking . . . *Paris France* p. 85	226	Yes it was the same . . . *Wars I Have Seen* pp. 173–4
217–18	The first days of the attack . . . Rogers, *op. cit.* p. 46 and p. 209	227	Thomson/Picasso exchange in Thomson, *op. cit.* p. 310
218	we were all glad . . . *Wars I Have Seen* p. 56	227	I began to think . . . *Wars I Have Seen* p. 175
218–19	Everybody knows . . . *Ibid* p. 62	227	Yes, I walk around . . . *Idem*
219	Just at present . . . Rogers, *op. cit.* p. 197	227	it is an amazing . . . Gallup, *op. cit.* p. 374
219–20	Alice Toklas and I . . . *Wars I Have Seen* p. 32	228	Roosevelt . . . *Brewsie and Willie* p. 68
220	now in June 1943 . . . *Ibid* p. 26	228	Listen, said Ed . . . *Ibid* p. 74
220–1	And every neighbour . . . *Ibid* pp. 23–4	228	We love sweets . . . *Ibid* p. 78
221	and now there . . . *Ibid* p. 42	228–9	GIS and GIS . . . *Ibid* pp. 113–14
221	There are so many things . . . *Ibid* p. 80	229	What is the use . . . 'Reflection on the Atomic Bomb' in *Reflection on The Atomic Bomb*, Volume I of the *Previously Uncollected Writings of Gertrude Stein*, ed. Robert B. Haas, Black Sparrow Press, Los Angeles, 1973, p. 161
221	We have very pleasant . . . *Ibid* pp. 117–18		
221	A long war . . . *Ibid* pp. 105–6		
221–2	that nowhere . . . *Ibid* p. 102		
222	a story told . . . *Ibid* p. 50		
222	Just now . . . *Ibid* p. 86		
222	to-day is the landing . . . *Ibid* p. 127		
223	And now at . . . *Ibid* p. 156	230	But now to make you . . . 'Portraits and Repetitions' in *Look At Me Now and Here I Am* p. 122
223	There have been six . . . *Ibid* pp. 161–2		
223	It was a wonderful time . . . Sevareid, *op. cit.* p. 462		
223–4	The opportunity . . . Gallup, *op. cit.* p. 367	230	Autobiography number II . . . *The Geographical History of America* pp. 181–2
224	Gertrude Stein . . . Thomson, *op. cit.* p. 310		

Select Bibliography

Acton, Harold, *Memoirs of an Aesthete*, Methuen, London, 1948.

Allen, Gay Wilson, *William James*, Viking Press, New York, 1967.

Baker, Carlos, *Ernest Hemingway*, Penguin Books, Harmondsworth, 1969.

Barr, Alfred H., Jr., *Matisse: His Art and His Public*, Museum of Modern Art, New York, 1951.

Beach, Sylvia, *Shakespeare and Company*, Harcourt, Brace, New York, 1959.

Beaton, Cecil, *Photobiography*, Doubleday, Garden City, New York, 1951.

Bridgman, Richard, *Gertrude Stein in Pieces*, Oxford University Press, New York, 1970.

Brinnin, John Malcolm, *The Third Rose: Gertrude Stein and Her World*, Little, Brown & Co., Boston, 1959.

Eastman, Max, *Great Companions*, Farrar, Straus & Cudahy, New York, 1959.

Flanner, Janet, *Paris Was Yesterday*, Angus & Robertson, London, 1973.

Gallup, Donald, ed. *The Flowers of Friendship: Letters Written to Gertrude Stein*, A. Knopf, New York, 1953.

Gilot, Françoise and Carlton Lake, *Life With Picasso*, McGraw-Hill, New York, 1964.

Glassco, John, *Memoirs of Montparnasse*,

Oxford University Press, New York, 1970.

Golding, John, *Cubism: a History and an Analysis 1907–1914*, Faber & Faber, London, 1959.

Gris, Juan, *Letters of Juan Gris*, trans. by Douglas Cooper, privately printed, London, 1956.

Haas, Robert B., Interview with Gertrude Stein, 1946, in *What Are Masterpieces*, ed. and with Foreword by Robert B. Haas, Pitman Publishing Company, New York, 1970.

Hapgood, Hutchins, *A Victorian in the Modern World*, Harcourt, Brace, New York, 1939.

Hemingway, Ernest, *The Sun Also Rises* (various editions).
A Moveable Feast, Penguin Books, Harmondsworth, 1964.

Imbs, Bravig, *Confessions of Another Young Man*, Henkle-Yewdale, New York, 1936.

James, William, *Pragmatism*, New American Library, New York, 1955.
Psychology: The Briefer Course, Harper Torchbooks, New York, 1961.
Varieties of Religious Experience, Collier Books, New York, 1973.

Jolas, Eugene, ed. 'Testimony Against Gertrude Stein', Transition Pamphlet no. 1, Supplement to *Transition* 1934–35 (no. 23), Servire Press, The Hague, February 1935.

Kahnweiler, Daniel-Henry, *My Galleries and Painters*, trans. by Helen Weaver, Viking Press, New York, 1971.

Kazin, Alfred, *Contemporaries*, Little, Brown, & Co., Boston, 1962.

Lewis, Wyndham, *Time and Western Man*, Beacon Press, Boston, 1957.

Luhan, Mabel Dodge, *European Experiences*, Vol. 2 of *Intimate Memories*, Harcourt, Brace, New York, 1935.
Movers and Shakers, Vol. 3 of *Intimate Memories*, Harcourt, Brace, New York, 1936.

Miller, Rosalind, *Gertrude Stein: Form and Intelligibility*, Exposition Press, New York, 1949.

Moore, Marianne, 'The Spare American Emotion', *Dial*, LXXX (February 1926), pp. 153–6.

Museum of Modern Art, *Four Americans in Paris*, Museum of Modern Art, New York, 1970.

Olivier, Fernande, *Picasso and His Friends*, trans. by Jane Miller, Appleton-Century, New York, 1965.

Paul, Elliot, *Understanding the French*, Random House, New York, 1955.

Penrose, Roland, *Picasso: His Life and Work*, Pelican Books, Harmondsworth, 1971.

Pollack, Barbara, *The Collectors: Dr. Claribel and Miss Etta Cone*, Bobbs-Merrill, New York, 1962.

Porter, Katherine Anne, *The Days Before*, Harcourt, Brace, New York, 1952.

Rogers, W. G., *When This You See Remember Me: Gertrude Stein in Person*, Rinehart, New York, 1948.

Rose, Francis, *Saying Life*, Cassell, London, 1961.

Saarinen, Aline B., *The Proud Possessors*, Vintage Books, Random House, New York, 1968.

Sevareid, Eric, *Not So Wild a Dream*, A. Knopf, New York, 1946.

Shattuck, Roger, *The Banquet Years*, Vintage Books, Random House, New York, 1968.

Sprigge, Elizabeth, *Gertrude Stein: Her Life and Work*, Harper Bros., New York, 1957.

Steegmuller, Francis, *Apollinaire: Poet Among the Painters*, Farrar, Straus, New York, 1963.

Stein, Gertrude (see p. vi) for list of most important individual titles and collections.

Stein, Leo, *ABC of Aesthetics, The*, Boni & Liveright, New York, 1927.
Appreciation: Painting, Poetry and Prose, Crown Publishers, New York, 1947.
Journey Into the Self: Being the Letters, Papers and Journals of Leo Stein, ed. by Edmund Fuller, with Intro. by Van Wyck Brooks and Foreword by Mabel Weeks, Crown Publishers, New York, 1950.

Sutherland, Donald, *Gertrude Stein: A Biography of her Work*, Yale University Press, 1951.

Thomson, Virgil, *Virgil Thomson*, Weidenfeld & Nicolson, London, 1967.

Toklas, Alice, *Alice B. Toklas Cookbook, The*, Anchor Books, New York, 1960.
Staying On Alone: Letters of Alice B. Toklas, ed. by Edward Burns, Angus & Robertson, London, 1973.
What Is Remembered, Holt, Rinehart & Winston, New York, 1963.

Vollard, Ambroise, *Recollections of a Picture Dealer*, Little, Brown & Co., Boston, 1936.

Williams, William Carlos, 'The Work of Gertrude Stein', *Pagany*, I (Winter 1930), 41–46.

Wilson, Edmund, *Axel's Castle*, Charles Scribner's Sons, New York, 1959.
Shores of Light, The, Farrar, Straus & Young, 1952.

Yale University Art Gallery, 'Pictures For a Picture of Gertrude Stein as a Collector and Writer on Art and Artists', catalogue of an exhibition held at Yale University Art Gallery February 11–March 11, 1951.

Index